Praise for
Weak Verb Morphology

Morphology is all important. I used to tell my students, "If you have no morphology, you have no theology." Apparently 68,000 of 72,000 verbs in the Hebrew Bible are weak verbs. In addition, 70 percent of all verbs are *qal* stem, so mastering the weak verb is essential to reading biblical Hebrew. Here Adam Howell has done a remarkable job of assisting students in building a foundation that is solid for a lifetime of exegesis in the Old Testament. Based upon solid, up-to-date scholarship, I heartily recommend this work.

Peter J. Gentry, Senior Professor,
The Southern Baptist Theological Seminary

Adam Howell continues to solidify himself as one of the most helpful voices in Hebrew language pedagogy today. This book fills a strategic gap in many introductory grammars, outlining a reliable process for approaching weak verbs. Rather than expecting students to memorize endless pages of paradigms, the methodology presented in this book gives students a systematic framework to parse and recognize weak verbs in context. Beyond this, Howell's aptitude as a teacher comes through in his accessible writing style and clear explanations. The abundant examples and exercises provide ample opportunity to practice applying the method. For anyone who has struggled to grasp the formation of weak verbs, this is the book for you!

Andrew M. King, Associate Professor of Biblical Studies,
Midwestern Baptist Theological Seminary & Spurgeon College

Emphasizing consistencies and regularities in the patterns of biblical Hebrew verbs, Howell's book helpfully breaks down for students how to identify weak verbal forms. The presentation is accessible, employing easy-to-read charts and diagrams, while at the same time not neglecting some of the more complex aspects of verb morphology. The book will be an asset to students wishing to bridge the gap between elementary grammars and more technical reference grammars.

Eric D. Reymond, Senior Lector II in Biblical Hebrew,
Yale Divinity School

For the intermediate student of biblical Hebrew, weak verbs can feel chaotic and unpredictable and so pose a major obstacle to developing proficiency in reading. What if Adam Howell convinced you that weak verb spelling changes are not random or haphazard? What if he helped you to understand the consistent and predictable patterns they follow that make identification manageable? In this book—that is accessible to second-year students and useful for seasoned readers of biblical Hebrew—Adam Howell serves as a gifted, wise guide who will not only lead readers to greater proficiency in reading Hebrew but also greater delight in encountering God in his precious word.

    Ian J. Vaillancourt, Professor of Old Testament and Hebrew, Heritage Theological Seminary

Adam Howell's *Weak Verb Morphology* is poised to become one of the most significant contributions to Hebrew pedagogy in the 21st century. Weak verbs are notoriously challenging for students, but Howell's method to demystify verbs will bring order out of chaos for those learning Hebrew. Drawing on both modern insight and rabbinic tradition, Howell enables students not merely to memorize paradigms but to truly understand the structure and beauty of the Hebrew verb. This volume will benefit beginners and advanced students alike—and promises to reshape how Hebrew is taught and learned.

    Michael C. Lyons, Associate Professor of Old Testament & Hebrew, Columbia International University

Weak Verb Morphology

ADVANCING BIBLICAL HEBREW

Weak Verb Morphology

Adam J. Howell
MILES V. VAN PELT, SERIES EDITOR

ZONDERVAN ACADEMIC

Weak Verb Morphology
Copyright © 2025 by Adam J. Howell

Published by Zondervan, 3950 Sparks Drive SE, Suite 101, Grand Rapids, MI 49546, USA. Zondervan is a registered trademark of The Zondervan Corporation, L.L.C., a wholly owned subsidiary of HarperCollins Christian Publishing, Inc.

Requests for information should be addressed to customercare@harpercollins.com.

Zondervan titles may be purchased in bulk for educational, business, fundraising, or sales promotional use. For information, please email SpecialMarkets@Zondervan.com.

Library of Congress Cataloging-in-Publication Data

Names: Howell, Adam J., 1980- author
Title: Weak verb morphology / Adam J. Howell.
Description: Grand Rapids, Michigan : Zondervan Academic, 2025. | Series: Advancing biblical Hebrew | Includes bibliographical references and index.
Identifiers: LCCN 2025025153 (print) | ISBN 9780310165514 paperback
Subjects: LCSH: Hebrew language--Verb | Hebrew language--Morphology
Classification: LCC PJ4645 .H69 2025 (print)
LC record available at https://lccn.loc.gov/2025025153
LC ebook record available at https://lccn.loc.gov/2025025154

All Scripture quotations unless otherwise noted are the author's own translation.

Any internet addresses (websites, blogs, etc.) and telephone numbers in this book are offered as a resource. They are not intended in any way to be or imply an endorsement by Zondervan, nor does Zondervan vouch for the content of these sites and numbers for the life of this book.

All rights reserved. No part of this publication may be reproduced, stored in a retrieval system, or transmitted in any form or by any means—electronic, mechanical, photocopy, recording, or any other—except for brief quotations in printed reviews, without the prior permission of the publisher.

Without limiting the exclusive rights of any author, contributor, or the publisher of this publication, any unauthorized use of this publication to train generative artificial intelligence (AI) technologies is expressly prohibited. HarperCollins also exercise their rights under Article 4(3) of the Digital Single Market Directive 2019/790 and expressly reserve this publication from the text and data mining exception.

HarperCollins Publishers, Macken House, 39/40 Mayor Street Upper, Dublin 1, D01 C9W8, Ireland (https://www.harpercollins.com).

Cover design: Studio Gearbox
Cover photo: © Yatsun Lee / Shutterstock
Interior design: Kait Lamphere

Printed in the United States of America

26 27 28 29 30 31 32 33 34 35 /TRM/ 15 14 13 12 11 10 9 8 7 6 5 4 3 2

Contents

Acknowledgments xiii
Abbreviations xv
    General Abbreviations xv
    Grammatical Abbreviations xv
Select Bibliography xvii

Introduction xix
    Some Historical Background xxi
    A Note on Resources xxiv
    The Methodology xxvii
    Terminology xxviii
        Roots and Root Consonants xxviii
        Stems xxix
        Conjugations xxix
        Preformatives and Sufformatives xxx
            Vocalic Sufformative/Ending xxx
            Syllabic Sufformative/Ending xxxi
        Prefixes and Suffixes xxxi
        Weak Verb Types xxxii

Part 1: A Strong Verb Methodology

1. A Strong Verb Methodology 3
    1.1 Introduction 3
    1.2 The *Qal* Paradigms 4
    1.3 The Derived Stems Chart 5
    1.4 The Meaning of the Thematic Vowel Symbols 7
    1.5 A Method for Building Hebrew Verbs 10
    1.6 Examples 11
    1.7 Parsing—Working Backwards 12
    1.8 Vowel Adjustment Rules 13
    1.9 Conclusion 15

Part 2: Weak Verb Morphology

2. Introduction to Weak Verbs................................... 19
   2.1   Introduction 19
   2.2   Types of Weak Verbs 19
   2.3   General Characteristics of Weak Verbs..................... 21
       2.3.1   Characteristics of Gutturals...................... 21
            2.3.1.1   Gutturals Reject *Dagesh Forte*.......... 22
            2.3.1.2   Gutturals Take Composite *Shewas*...... 23
            2.3.1.3   Gutturals Prefer /a/ Sounds Around
                          Them.................................... 24
            2.3.1.4   The Gutturals ה, ח, ע at the End of a
                          Word May Take a Furtive *Pataḥ*........ 25
            2.3.1.5   Guttural א Quiesces with a
                          Silent *Shewa* 25
       2.3.2   *Nun* (נ) with Silent *Shewa* May Assimilate 26
       2.3.3   *Vavs* and *Yods* in Weak Verbs.................... 27
            2.3.3.1   *Vavs* and *Yods* May Drop Out 27
            2.3.3.2   *Vavs* and *Yods* May Contract
                          into Vowels............................. 28
       2.3.4   Hebrew Tends to Avoid the Writing of Two
                 Identical Consecutive Consonants................. 29
       2.3.5   Many Preformative Vowels Shift to A-Class
                 Vowels 29
   2.4   The Strong Verb Equation 30

3. I-Guttural Verbs... 32
   3.1   Introduction 32
   3.2   Strong Forms of I-Guttural Verbs 32
   3.3   Gutturals (including ר) Reject *Dagesh Forte* 33
   3.4   Gutturals Take Composite Vocal *Shewas*.................. 34
       3.4.1   I-Gutturals Take Composite *Shewas* Rather Than
                 a Simple Vocal *Shewa* 34
       3.4.2   I-Gutturals Take a Composite *Shewa* Instead of a
                 Silent *Shewa* 35
            3.4.2.1   Why Is There Not a Composite *Shewa*? .. 36
       3.4.3   I-Gutturals May Retain a Silent *Shewa* 37
   3.5   I-א ōPV Verbs... 38
       3.5.1   The "Canaanite Shift" 39

		3.5.2	Dissimilation of Thematic Vowels	40

- 3.6 Conclusion 41

4. I-ו/י Verbs 42
- 4.1 Introduction 42
  - 4.1.1 Contractions 43
  - 4.1.2 I-ו/י General Principles 43
- 4.2 Original I-ו Verbs 44
  - 4.2.1 Original I-ו Contracts 44
    - 4.2.1.1 *Niphal* 44
    - 4.2.1.2 *Hiphil* 45
    - 4.2.1.3 *Hophal* 46
  - 4.2.2 Parsing: Working "Backwards" 46
  - 4.2.3 Original I-ו May Drop Out 47
    - 4.2.3.1 *Qal* Imperfect 47
    - 4.2.3.2 *Qal* Imperative 48
    - 4.2.3.3 *Qal* Infinitive Construct 49
  - 4.2.4 *Vav*-Consecutives and Jussives of I-ו Verbs 50
- 4.3 Original I-ו and II-צ Verbs (I-וצ Verbs) 51
- 4.4 הלך 52
- 4.5 יכל 53
- 4.6 I-י Verbs 54
  - 4.6.1 *Qal* Imperfect 55
  - 4.6.2 *Hiphil* 55
- 4.7 Mixed Forms: ירא and ירש 56
- 4.8 Conclusion 57

5. I-נ Verbs 58
- 5.1 Introduction 58
- 5.2 I-נ Assimilates 59
  - 5.2.1 *Qal* 59
  - 5.2.2 *Niphal* 60
  - 5.2.3 *Hiphil* 61
    - 5.2.3.1 Doubly Weak I-נ/III-ה Verbs 62
  - 5.2.4 *Hophal* 63
- 5.3 I-נ Drops Out 64
- 5.4 לקח 65
- 5.5 נתן 67
- 5.6 Conclusion 69

6. II-Guttural Verbs 70
    6.1   Introduction 70
    6.2   II-Guttural Verbs Reject *Dagesh Forte* 71
    6.3   II-Guttural Verbs Take Composite *Shewa* 72
    6.4   Minor Implications of II-Gutturals 73
        6.4.1   Thematic Vowels Often Become /A in the *Qal*
                Imperfect and Imperative 73
        6.4.2   *Qal* Imperative 2ms and Infinitive Construct
                Are Distinguishable 73
    6.5   Conclusion 74

7. II-ו/י (Biconsonantal) Verbs 75
    7.1   Introduction 75
    7.2   II-ו/י Verbs: *Qal* 76
        7.2.1   *Qal* Perfect and Participle [Compressed Forms] 77
            7.2.1.1   *Qal* Perfect 77
            7.2.1.2   *Qal* Participle 78
            7.2.1.3   *Qal Vav*-Consecutives (*Vayyiqtol*)
                        and Jussive 79
        7.2.2   *Qal* Imperfect, Imperative, and Infinitives 80
            7.2.2.1   *Qal* Imperfect 81
            7.2.2.2   *Qal* Imperative 82
            7.2.2.3   *Qal* Infinitive 83
                  7.2.2.3.1   *Qal* Infinitive Construct ... 83
                  7.2.2.3.2   *Qal* Infinitive Absolute 83
    7.3   II-ו/י Verbs: *Niphal* 84
        7.3.1   *Niphal* Perfect and Participle 85
        7.3.2   *Niphal* Imperfect, Imperative, and Infinitive 85
    7.4   II-ו/י Verbs: *Hiphil* 86
    7.5   II-ו/י Verbs: *Hophal* 88
    7.6   II-ו/י Verbs: *Polel, Polal, Hithpolel* (*Piel, Pual*, and *Hithpael*)... 88
    7.7   Conclusion 90

8. Geminate Verbs 91
    8.1   Introduction 91
    8.2   Strong Forms of Geminate Verbs 91
    8.3   General Characteristics of Geminate Verbs 92
        8.3.1   Collapsed Forms with Sufformatives Often Get
                a *Dagesh Forte* 92

		8.3.1.1	Doubling Usually Happens with R_2/R_3 . . 92
		8.3.1.2	Doubling May Happen with R_1: Transposition of Gemination 93
		8.3.1.3	Doubling May Happen in R_1 and R_2/R_3. 93
	8.3.2	Hebrew Does Not Double Final Consonants 94
	8.3.3	Thematic Vowel Shifts Between R_1 and R_2 94
	8.3.4	Gutturals Do Not Double 94
	8.3.5	Syllabic Sufformatives Use Helping Vowels 95
8.4	Specific Characteristics of Geminate Verbs. 95
	8.4.1	*Qal* 96
	8.4.2	*Niphal* 99
	8.4.3	*Poel, Poal, Hithpoel* (*Piel, Pual, Hithpael*) 100
	8.4.4	*Hiphil*. 101
	8.4.5	*Hophal* 102
8.5	Conclusion 102

9. III-ה Verbs (III-י Verbs). 103
   9.1   Introduction 103
   9.2   General Principles 103
   9.3   Basic Endings 105
   9.4   Specific Principles 105
         9.4.1 Perfect 105
         9.4.2 Imperfect. 107
         9.4.3 Imperative 109
         9.4.4 Infinitive 110
                9.4.4.1 Infinitive Absolute 110
                9.4.4.2 Infinitive Construct 111
         9.4.5 Participles 111
   9.5   Conclusion 113

10. III-ח, III-ע, and III-ה Verbs. 114
    10.1 Introduction 114
    10.2 III-Gutturals Prefer A-Class Vowels Under and
          Before Them 115
          10.2.1 Perfect, Imperfect, Imperative (Finite Verbs) 115
                 10.2.1.1 *Tsere* becomes *Pataḥ* 115
                 10.2.1.2 III-Gutturals Retain Thematic Vowel
                          but with Furtive *Pataḥ* 115

       10.2.2 Infinitive and Participle (Nonfinite Verbs) 116
  10.3 Miscellaneous Issues 117
       10.3.1 III-Gutturals in the *Qal* Imperfect and
              Imperative. 117
       10.3.2 Segolate Patterns with Gutturals 118
       10.3.3 III-Gutturals and *Shewas* 118
              10.3.3.1 III-Gutturals Often Retain Silent
                     Shewas 118
              10.3.3.2 Perfect 2fs Forms. 119
              10.3.3.3 Addition of "Heavy" Pronominal
                     Suffixes 120
  10.4 Conclusion 120

11. III-א Verbs 121
  11.1 Introduction 121
  11.2 III-א Often Quiesces with a Silent *Shewa* 122
  11.3 III-א Verbs Display a Tendency Toward *Tsere* Thematic
       Vowels in the Perfect Conjugation 123
  11.4 Miscellaneous Issues 124
       11.4.1 *Qal* Imperfect and Imperative Take *Pataḥ*
              Thematic Vowel. 125
       11.4.2 Imperfect and Imperative 2/3fp Forms Take *Segol*
              Thematic Vowel. 125
       11.4.3 T-Form Participles Have a Quiescent א and *Tsere*
              Thematic Vowel. 126
  11.5 Conclusion 127

Part 3: Weak Verbs in Context

12. Weak Verbs in Context 131
  12.1 Introduction 131
  12.2 Exercises. 133

Scripture Index 149
Subject Index 155
Author Index 165

Acknowledgments

As with any project like this, the author never works alone, but is supported and encouraged by many people. First, I would like to thank the Board of Trustees of The Southern Baptist Theological Seminary for approving a sabbatical leave during the spring of 2024 to focus attention on this manuscript. I would also like to thank the Dean of Boyce College, Dustin Bruce, Southern Seminary Provost, Paul Akin, and President R. Albert Mohler, Jr. for their approval of the sabbatical request and encouragement through it. Without the generosity of the Board of Trustees and the academic administration this book would not have been completed.

I would also like to thank my colleague Joe Harrod for his help in analyzing all the weak verb spreadsheets I extracted from the Hebrew Bible. Joe helped me narrow down the exercises to 48 verses in the Hebrew Bible that contain at least one example of every weak verb type. You will see 70 verses as exercises in Part 3 of this book because I needed to find at least one example of each type of weakness in each type of weak verb. Joe's investment on the front end of this project provided some clarity on the vision of whether a volume like this could even work.

As I think about the beginning of my Hebrew training, I want to thank Dr. T. J. Betts at The Southern Baptist Theological Seminary, who taught me most of the nuts and bolts presented in this book. It is God's kindness to me that Dr. Betts is now a colleague and treasured friend in this endeavor to help students love the Lord more through loving his Word in the original Hebrew. I also want to thank Russell Fuller for his investment in my Hebrew training as my doctoral supervisor. Dr. Fuller's influence on my understanding of these concepts will be seen in the many footnotes to his work throughout the book.

I am also thankful for a small army of students and friends who helped read portions of the manuscript, compile research materials, double-check verb parsing and verse references, contribute translations, compile the answer key, and improve the overall quality of this book. Among this small army I must mention specifically Blaine Taylor, Isaac Reff, Wenya Yang, Justin Anderson,

Joshua Pittman, Carlo Cicero, Michael Portwood, Hannah Portwood, Esther Cann, Jayse Anspach, Kyung Tae Park, Bruce Steventon, and Phil Hohulin. Without their help, this project would not have been completed on time.

I would like to thank Miles Van Pelt for his trust in me to include this volume in the series. His encouragement over the years and while working on this project have been key in keeping a young "scholar" moving forward. As the series editor, Miles also offered a helpful list of edits in the first reading that has undoubtedly made this a better volume. I am also grateful to Nancy Erickson and the editorial team at Zondervan who have worked diligently to prepare this book for publication. I am especially thankful to the typesetting team for the painstaking work to typeset this volume. If you have never worked with left-to-right and right-to-left text in the same manuscript, you may not be aware of the countless hours it takes to ensure that every jot and tittle appears correctly. I am thankful to the Zondervan editing and typesetting team for their diligent work, but I will take the full responsibility for any errors you may see while reading.

Finally, and most importantly, I want to thank my family. It is impossible to adequately express my gratitude to my wife and children for the freedom they offer to pursue projects like this. We discovered during this project that it is not the workload of writing a book that is cumbersome to them, but it is the emotional weight of the work that must be completed prior to a deadline that weighs most heavily on them. And yet, my wife and children graciously support these projects and encourage me through the entire journey. Liz, you are a steady source of encouragement to me. I do not take that for granted. Noah, Tovah, Judah, and Norah, thank you for your patience and grace through another project.

Abbreviations

General Abbreviations

EHLL	Khan, Geoffrey, ed. *Encyclopedia of Hebrew Language and Linguistics*. 4 vols. Leiden: Brill, 2013.
ETCBC	Eep Talstra Centre for Bible and Computer
GKC	Gesenius, Wilhelm. *Gesenius' Hebrew Grammar*. Edited by Emil Kautzsch. Translated by Arthur E. Cowley. 2nd ed. Oxford: Clarendon Press, 1910.
HB	Hebrew Bible
IBHS	Waltke, Bruce K., and Michael Patrick O'Connor. *An Introduction to Biblical Hebrew Syntax*. Winona Lake, IN: Eisenbrauns, 1990.
JM	Joüon, Paul, and T. Muraoka. *A Grammar of Biblical Hebrew*. Rome: Pontifical Biblical Institute, 2006.
LSAWS	Linguistic Studies in Ancient West Semitic
Qimḥi	Chomsky, William, ed. *David Kimhi's Hebrew Grammar (Mikhlol) Systematically Presented and Critically Annotated*. New York: Bloch, 1952.
RBS	Resources for Biblical Study
SP	Samaritan Pentateuch
SESE	Stuttgart Electronic Study Edition (morphology database)
WIVU	Werkgroep Informatica, Vrije Universiteit (morphology database)

Grammatical Abbreviations

1	first person
2	second person
3	third person
a	*pataḥ*
c	common
CAPL	Closed Accented Prefers Long

cons	consecutive
CURS	Closed Unaccented Requires Short
CV	Consonant-Vowel
CVC	Consonant-Vowel-Consonant
ê	*tsere yod*
fs	feminine singular
fp	feminine plural
i	*hireq*
î	*hireq yod*
inf abs	infinitive absolute
inf cstr	infinitive construct
I-א ōPV verb	I-א verb that in the imperfect conjugation quiesces the א and takes a *holem* (ō) as the Preformative Vowel
impf	imperfect
impv	imperative
J.I.I.V.E.	Jussive; Imperative 2ms; Infinitive absolute; *Vav-*Consecutive all get an E (*tsere*) thematic vowel
ms	masculine singular
mp	masculine plural
ō	*holem*
ô	*holem vav*
OAPS	Open Accented Prefers Short
OOPPS	Originally Open ProPretonic reduces short vowel to a vocal *Shewa*
OPRL	Open Pretonic Requires Long
pass	passive
pf	perfect
PGN	person, gender, number
ptc	participle
SQNMLVY	The mnemonic to remember the consonants that may omit a dagesh forte with a vocal *shewa* (sibilants, ק, ג, מ, ל, ו, י).
R_1	first root radical
R_2	second root radical
R_3	third root radical
TAM	tense, aspect, mood
u	*qibbuts*
û	*shureq*
w	*waw/vav*
y	*yod*

Select Bibliography

Blau, Joshua. *Phonology and Morphology of Biblical Hebrew: An Introduction.* LSAWS 2. Winona Lake, IN: Eisenbrauns, 2010.

Fuller, Russell T., and Kyoungwon Choi. *Invitation to Biblical Hebrew: A Beginning Grammar.* Grand Rapids: Kregel, 2006.

Kutz, Karl V., and Rebekah L. Josberger. *Learning Biblical Hebrew: Reading for Comprehension: An Introductory Grammar.* Bellingham, WA: Lexham, 2018.

Reymond, Eric, D. *Intermediate Hebrew Grammar: A Student's Guide to Phonology and Morphology.* RBS 89. Atlanta, GA: SBL Press, 2018.

Suchard, Benjamin D. *The Development of the Biblical Hebrew Vowels: Including a Concise Historical Morphology.* Studies in Semitic Language and Linguistics 99. Leiden: Brill, 2020.

Introduction

According to the Groves-Wheeler Westminster Hebrew Morphology database, there are 72,396 verbs in the Hebrew Bible (excluding Aramaic). Statistics may vary on the total number of weak verbs depending on whether one includes verbal roots with guttural consonants as "weak" or how one counts verbal roots with two (or more) weak letters. However, if we tally all of the verbal roots that have at least one "weak" consonant and include geminate verbal roots, the number of weak verbs in the Hebrew Bible begins to push 85–90 percent of the total verbs. If we state the point a little differently: It is vital that Hebrew students master weak verbs because they will see them everywhere in the Hebrew Bible!

Often, when Hebrew students begin to learn verb morphology, they learn a set of paradigms or patterns for what they presume verbs *should* look like when they see them in the Hebrew Bible. But then, nearly 90 percent of the verbs they encounter have what seem to be morphological "exceptions" because of some sort of weakness. These changes to what the students have learned can lead to discouragement and frustration as Hebrew professors may say, "Yeah, we'll cover that in more detail with a different paradigm later," or "Yeah, that's just the way Hebrew works." Students genuinely sense that they are learning Hebrew because they can reproduce a *qal* or *niphal* strong verb paradigm on a quiz, but the majority of the verbs they see when reading the text do not appear with the same paradigm patterns they worked so hard to memorize.

In this book, I want to offer some morphological principles for the various types of weak verbs to minimize—and perhaps even alleviate—that discouraging experience for students. What I have found is that weak verbs are *not* all the exceptions to strong verb morphology. Rather, weak verbs differ from the strong verb based on consistent patterns specific to the particular weakness of the verb. While it certainly takes more time and effort to learn these "consistent patterns," once those are in the student's tool belt, weak verbs are no longer the exceptions, but are, in fact, "normal" as it pertains to what is phonologically and morphologically expected with specific weak verbal roots.

I regularly tell my first-year students that with Hebrew, we are trying *to describe* the morphology we observe in the Hebrew Bible. We are not trying to tell the Hebrew language what it ought to do morphologically. When we discuss morphology in English, we often say things like, "to make a word plural, add 's.'" Or, "If the word already ends with a sibilant (an "s" sound as with s, c, or z), then add 'es.'" We all realize there are exceptions, but take the illustrative journey with me. When we speak about rules like this, we are telling students what English ought to do to make a word plural. With the Hebrew Bible, morphology is the inverse of that. We look at all the morphological patterns, and then try to describe what we see across the pages of the Hebrew Bible. We can combine these observed patterns with what we know from diachronic linguistics and comparative Semitics to get a clearer picture of the morphological expectations, but we never reach a point where we are telling the Hebrew language what it ought to do. We are always describing what we see.

With weak verbs, there are certainly some exceptional forms that do not follow the consistent patterns presented in this book. But there is also a considerable amount of consistency within the various categories of weak verbs. That consistency can be observed and described by looking at all of the forms of a specific weak verb type, and then we can begin to anticipate how a weak verb might appear in the Hebrew Bible. What I hope to present here is a description of those patterns and some of the morphological principles behind them so that lifelong learners can revisit those pesky weak verbs that caused so much trouble in class and find that they are quite "normal" within their own categories.

In addition to the discussions about weak verb morphology, this volume also provides exercises to practice parsing weak verbs. Similarly to Van Pelt and Pratico's *Biblical Hebrew Vocabulary in Context: Building Competency with Words Occurring 50 Times or More* (Grand Rapids: Zondervan, 2019), the verses in Part 3 of this book will give you plenty of practice parsing all types of weak verbs. One of my colleagues at Southern Seminary helped me find the fewest number of verses from the Hebrew Bible that contain at least one example of every type of weak verb.[1] The initial list contained forty-eight verses from the Hebrew Bible. By my count, II-guttural verbs had the lowest representation at fifteen occurrences in those forty-eight verses. The highest representation was II-ו/י verbs at seventy-six occurrences. If you were

---

[1]. I am very thankful to Joe Harrod for his help to analyze several spreadsheets to produce our initial list of verses.

to translate those forty-eight verses, you would encounter several examples of each weak verb category *in context*. In my opinion, this type of practice is more beneficial than parsing lists of weak verbs without any context.

In Part 3 of this resource, you will notice that there are seventy verses for the "Weak Verbs in Context" exercises. While the original list provided at least fifteen examples of each type of weak verb, those verbs did not represent each type of morphological change for each type of weak verb. For example, verbal roots with a ו as the first root consonant (I-ו/י verbs) sometimes contract the I-ו and sometimes the ו will drop out. The initial list may have had one of these morphological changes, but not both. After analyzing all the verbs in the original forty-eight verses, I added enough verses to provide at least one example of each type of morphological change for each type of weak verb. All in all, these examples should give readers an opportunity to encounter weak verbs "in the wild," rather than staring at a paradigm or working exercises from a list of verbs with no context.

Some Historical Background

In the medieval period, mainly the tenth–eleventh centuries AD, Karaite and Rabbanite grammarians produced several grammars of the Hebrew language.[2] The first major Karaite grammarian was ʾAbū Yaʿqūb Yūsuf ibn Nūḥ, who produced דקדוק ("fine grammatical investigation") in the second half of the tenth century.[3] His work was more a compilation of grammatical notes than an organized "Hebrew grammar." In his notes, ibn Nūḥ "attempted to discover consistent rules governing the formation of words."[4] His goal was to show that odd word formations were not the product of random and haphazard vowel pointing. Rather, they followed consistent patterns from historical word bases.[5] This book does not follow the Karaite tradition in full, but it certainly approaches the morphology of weak verbs from a similar perspective.

---

2. The Karaites were a group of medieval Jews who believed that the Scriptures (the written *torah*) were the only source of divine authority. They often found themselves at odds with the Rabbanites who favored oral tradition and Talmudic authority in the tenth and eleventh centuries AD. For our purposes, these groups represent two traditions from which we can discern longstanding, deep study of Hebrew morphology.

3. Geoffrey Khan, "Grammarians: Karaite," *EHLL*, 2:76. Geoffrey Khan, *The Early Karaite Tradition of Hebrew Grammatical Thought: Including a Critical Edition, Translation and Analysis of the Diqduq of ʾAbū Yaʿqūb Yūsuf ibn Nūḥ on the Hagiographa*, Studies in Semitic Languages and Linguistics 32 (Leiden: Brill, 2000).

4. Khan, "Grammarians: Karaite," *EHLL*, 2:77.

5. Ibn Nūḥ did not affirm the concept of Hebrew verbal roots, but rather built his morphological arguments on historical "bases."

Weak verbs are not the exceptions and anomalies. Rather, they show consistent patterns based on phonological and morphological principles that are analogous to other forms in the Hebrew Bible. Geoffrey Khan states, "In the early Karaite tradition, therefore, *diqduq* was a method of investigating Scripture by the study of the subtle details of its language. The purpose of this investigation was both to establish the fine details of its meaning and also to demonstrate that the language conformed to a logical system."[6]

Another Karaite grammarian was 'Abū al-Faraj Hārūn ibn Faraj, a resident of Jerusalem in the first half of the eleventh century.[7] 'Abū al-Faraj's longest grammatical work, *The Comprehensive Book of General Principles and Particular Rules of the Hebrew Language*, was an eight-volume work completed in AD 1026.[8] 'Abū al-Faraj had a slightly different emphasis than his Karaite predecessors, but he added to ibn Nūḥ's focus by saying that his primary goal was faithful interpretation and reading of the Hebrew text. In other words, 'Abū al-Faraj was willing to focus on detailed morphology so that the biblical text would be read and interpreted correctly. Again, this emphasis of the Karaite grammarians matches the goal of this book. We want to devote time to these details so that we can more readily read God's word in the original Hebrew and, therefore, interpret it more faithfully.

The Karaites also influenced later grammarians. Geoffrey Khan mentions two works from the eleventh century, *Light of the Eye* (מאור עין) and *Book of Rules Regarding the Grammatical Inflections of the Hebrew Language* (*Kitāb al-'Uqūd fī Taṣārīf al-Luġa al-'Ibrāniyya*) that carried forward the grammatical approach of the Karaites.[9] As grammarians continued to teach these detailed principles, they developed mnemonics to aid in memorizing verbal forms. The concept of mnemonics was also present in 'Abū al-Faraj's work, but these memory aids became prominent in these eleventh century works.[10] Khan notes that these mnemonics were reminiscent of the Masoretic system of abbreviations for the Masorah Parva.[11] The decision to use mnemonics in

---

6. Khan, "Grammarians: Karaite," *EHLL*, 2:78.
7. Khan, "Morphology in the Medieval Karaite Grammatical Tradition," *EHLL*, 2:711.
8. Khan, "Grammarians: Karaite," *EHLL*, 2:79.
9. Nadia Vidro, *Verbal Morphology in the Karaite Treatise on Hebrew Grammar Kitāb Al-'Uqūd Fī Taṣārīf Al-Luġa Al-'Ibrāniyya*, Cambridge Genizah Studies Series 2 (Leiden: Brill, 2011); Geoffrey Khan, "Grammarians: Karaite," *EHLL*, 2:81.
10. Vidro, *Verbal Morphology in the Karaite Treatise*, §8.5.
11. Vidro, *Verbal Morphology in the Karaite Treatise*, §8.5. In the Masoretic Text, the Masoretes added notes in the margin called the Masorah Parva ("the small Masorah"). Since these notes were in the margin, they often used abbreviations or acronyms to convey their intended note. For further study of the masorah of the Masoretic Text, see Page H. Kelley, Daniel S. Mynatt, and Timothy G. Crawford, *The Masorah of Biblia Hebraica Stuttgartensia: Introduction and Annotated Glossary* (Grand Rapids: Eerdmans, 1998).

this present volume was not based on these Karaite grammarians. But note that this approach and methodology has roots in a longstanding grammatical tradition.

A prominent Rabbanite Hebrew grammarian was Saʿadya Gaon. Aharon Maman says, "Morphology constituted the core of Hebrew grammar in the Middle Ages."[12] In keeping with this focus on morphology, Gaon's approach consisted of analyzing words based on their morphological patterns to understand word usage in a particular context.[13] While Gaon did not seem to accept the concept of a verbal root, other Rabbanite grammarians espoused this view and analyzed verbs from the perspective of a verbal root with affixes.[14] Subsequent Rabbanite grammarians who analyzed morphology based on a verbal root include Yehuda ben Quraysh, Ḥay Gaon, Menaḥem ben Saruq, Dunash ben Labraṭ, Yehuda Ḥayyūj and Jonah ibn Janāḥ.[15] The Spanish grammarian Yehuda ben David Ḥayyūj solidified the concepts of a triconsonantal root that are still in use today.[16] For our purposes, understanding that the concept of a root has a rich history in grammatical discussion will help with how this book approaches the idea of a root and strong verb "shell" with consistent and predictable affixes.

One final grammarian to include here is Rabbi David Qimḥi (Radaq). According to Maman, Qimḥi employed the same morphological concepts as Ḥayyūj in his מכלול (*miklôl*).[17] Ḥayyūj focused on weak I-, II-, and III-ו/י roots and geminate roots, and to the degree that Qimḥi followed his methodology, we find helpful discussions in Qimḥi's מכלול.[18] Qimḥi also references ibn Janāḥ, another of the prominent Rabbanite grammarians. Because Qimḥi seems to rely upon this rich tradition, we have provided citations to Qimḥi's comments where they pertain to the topics discussed here.

Much has changed in the study of language since the medieval period, but these works were the precursors to how we approach Hebrew grammar and morphology today. We are not trying to replicate these medieval grammarians in every detail, but it is helpful to consider the rich tradition from which our current understanding of Hebrew arose.

---

12. Aharon Maman, "Morphology in the Medieval Rabbanite Grammatical Tradition," *EHLL*, 2:712.
13. Maman, "Morphology in the Medieval Rabbanite Grammatical Tradition," 2:712.
14. Maman, "Morphology in the Medieval Rabbanite Grammatical Tradition," 2:713.
15. Maman, "Morphology in the Medieval Rabbanite Grammatical Tradition," 2:713.
16. Maman, "Morphology in the Medieval Rabbanite Grammatical Tradition," 2:715–16, 718–19.
17. Maman, "Morphology in the Medieval Rabbanite Grammatical Tradition," 2:720.
18. Maman, "Morphology in the Medieval Rabbanite Grammatical Tradition," 2:718.

A Note on Resources

A recent treatment of Hebrew phonology and morphology is *The Development of the Biblical Hebrew Vowels: Including a Concise Historical Morphology* by Benjamin Suchard.[19] Suchard says, "Perhaps due to strong philological tradition in the scholarship of such languages as Arabic, Aramaic, and Hebrew, the field of comparative Semitics tends to be more tolerant of loosely formulated sound laws with unexplained exceptions and allows for nonphonetic factors to condition sound change."[20] Suchard's goal is to counter this tendency and to bring what he calls a "Neogrammarian" method to biblical Hebrew, showing that morphological vowel changes are driven by phonology.[21] He says, "This work aims to bring this Neogrammarian method to bear on the problems surrounding the development of vocalic phonemes from Proto-Northwest Semitic to Biblical Hebrew in an attempt to describe the changes affecting them with exceptionless sound laws."[22] This aim proposed by Suchard expresses what I hope will also be true of this book. I hope you will begin to see that vowel changes in weak verbs are a result of regular phonological conditions. We cannot say, with Suchard, that weak verbs are "exceptionless," but there is far more morphological consistency than is often assumed. Suchard focuses on vocalic sound changes that cannot be explained by other means whereas in this resource, the focus is on the regular patterns for identifying and parsing weak verbs. So, our emphases are slightly different. Even so, in Suchard's appendix, "A Concise Historical Morphology of Biblical Hebrew," he includes a section on weak verb morphology, and we will reference that section where it is fitting for our discussion.[23]

An alternative approach is that of Joshua Blau in his 2010 monograph, *Phonology and Morphology of Biblical Hebrew: An Introduction*.[24] Blau applies what he calls a "diachronic-comparative" linguistics approach to biblical Hebrew.[25] Whereas Suchard recognizes that biblical Hebrew is multilayered, he also views

---

19. Benjamin D. Suchard, *The Development of the Biblical Hebrew Vowels: Including a Concise Historical Morphology*, Studies in Semitic Languages and Linguistics 99 (Leiden: Brill, 2020).
20. Suchard, *The Development of the Biblical Hebrew Vowels*, 2.
21. The Neogrammarian Hypothesis states that morphology is driven by phonology and that when a certain sound change happens in one place because of the surrounding conditions, that same sound change will occur in other places in the language when those same conditions are met. In other words, sound change happens due to certain phonetic conditions and those sound changes are preserved in the morphology of the word.
22. Suchard, *The Development of the Biblical Hebrew Vowels*, 3.
23. Suchard, *The Development of the Biblical Hebrew Vowels*, 248–53.
24. Joshua Blau, *Phonology and Morphology of Biblical Hebrew: An Introduction*, LSAWS 2 (Winona Lake, IN: Eisenbrauns, 2010).
25. Blau, *Phonology and Morphology of Biblical Hebrew*, 5.

the unifying effect of the Tiberian Masoretic vocalization as what essentially makes biblical Hebrew a consistent language for investigation.[26] Blau is more inclined to explain the phonological and morphological changes within the diachronic layering of the Hebrew Bible by comparing the historical layers to comparative texts from the same periods. The net effect is that Blau argues for morphological change from a slightly different perspective than Suchard, but still offers important and helpful insights into the morphological patterns of weak verbs. So, while these approaches vary rather significantly, we will cite both throughout this book without a wholesale adoption of the particular approach of either. What I hope to show is that the morphological patterns we see in weak verbs are consistent and predictable within each weak verb type whether or not we can precisely define the historical derivation.

A third work to which we will refer is Eric Reymond's *Intermediate Biblical Hebrew Grammar: A Student's Guide to Phonology and Morphology*, another extensive treatment of Hebrew morphology.[27] Reymond employs a methodology that seems to embrace diachronic linguistics but also recognizes the consistency of the Masoretic Text. Reymond relies heavily on historical bases as the morphological derivative of inflected forms (e.g., **qatl*, **qitl*, or **qutl* for segolate nouns), but he also comments that "the vocalization of the text as we have it today in the MT has likely been made uniform to a degree that largely masks most dialectical and many chronological differences."[28] Reymond provides a good balance of diachronic explanations from Proto-Semitic while also recognizing the value of the Masoretic Text. Reymond's discussions are often quite similar to Blau's, but he considers that linguistic leveling may have had an effect on Hebrew morphology and some forms cannot be explained by diachronic linguistics and comparative Semitics alone. Reymond's work is another monograph that we will cite often to direct readers to a more in-depth discussion of the patterns observed and derivations proposed in this book. As such, all of these highly technical works on Hebrew morphology (Suchard, Blau, and Reymond) are cited in footnotes to provide the reader with more nuanced discussions if there is a desire to do further research.

---

26. Suchard says, "the Hebrew Bible's temporal heterogeneity does not affect the phonological homogeneity of Tiberian Hebrew" (Suchard, *The Development of the Biblical Hebrew Vowels*, 21).

27. Eric D. Reymond, *Intermediate Biblical Hebrew Grammar: A Student's Guide to Phonology and Morphology*, RBS 89 (Atlanta: SBL Press, 2018).

28. Reymond, *Intermediate Biblical Hebrew Grammar*, 14. Aaron Hornkohl calls this "linguistic leveling," saying, "It is likely that a further portion [of the dialectical differences] is masked by the Tiberian vowel points, which reflect a remarkably uniform pronunciation that cannot possibly have been shared by all texts of the Hebrew Bible at the place and time each was composed" (Aaron D. Hornkohl, *Ancient Hebrew Periodization and the Language of the Book of Jeremiah: The Case for a Sixth-Century Date of Composition*, Studies in Semitic Languages and Linguistics 74 [Leiden: Brill, 2014], 19).

In addition to these technical monographs, I have also included citations to Gesenius (GKC), Joüon-Muraoka (JM), and Rabbi David Qimḥi (Qimḥi). The citations to Gesenius and Joüon-Muraoka were chosen because they (1) address these topics in significant detail and (2) are considered respectable reference grammars. These citations should be used for further research and study of the patterns we observe in weak verbs. As we said in the section on historical background, the citations of Qimḥi are provided to tie these discussions back to the rich history of investigating the details of phonological and morphological patterns in the Hebrew Bible. With citations to these resources, from medieval to modern, readers who desire to pursue these topics further should be well equipped.

For digital resources in this project, I have used several morphology databases. Since all electronic morphology databases are created by scholars who may approach Hebrew morphological tagging differently, I sometimes had to refer to different tagging systems to find certain forms (e.g., not all systems mark verbs as "jussive"). Also, some systems may differ in how they label roots. When a byform is possible, some tagging systems will label one byform whereas others will label a different root (e.g., תלא/תלה). These are not extremely common "problems" with searching databases, but in order to be as accurate as possible, I consulted multiple morphology databases. Throughout the book and in relevant footnotes, I have specified which tagging database I used for a particular search. Here is a list of the databases used and where one can access them for further study.

Morphology Database	Module Name	Software
Groves-Wheeler Westminster Morphology	*BHS*-W4 *BHS*-T	Accordance Bible Software
ETCBC (WIVU)[29]	MT-ETCBC	
	BHS/WIVU	Logos Bible Software
SESE (Stuttgart Electronic Study Edition)[30]	*BHS* OT	
Lexham Morphology (*Lexham Hebrew Bible*)	LHB	

---

29. WIVU is an acronym for Werkgroep Informatica, Vrije Universiteit, the group led by Eep Talstra to develop this morphology database. ETCBC stands for Eep Talstra Center for Bible and Computer, the current name given to this database, named in honor of Eep Talstra when he retired in 2012. These are the same morphology databases. The ETCBC module in Accordance Bible Software contains syntactical tags as well as morphological tagging.

30. The SESE is an adaptation of the WIVU database that allows for slightly different searching in Logos Bible Software.

The Methodology

When I began my Hebrew studies in 2005, Dr. T. J. Betts was my professor at The Southern Baptist Theology Seminary. We used Russell Fuller and Kyoungwon Choi's grammar, *Invitation to Biblical Hebrew: A Beginning Grammar*. I did not know at that time there were various methods for learning Biblical Hebrew, and so I just did what I was told as we progressed through the course. Fuller and Choi's grammar is what I have come to call a "morphology-heavy" approach to Biblical Hebrew. By that, I mean they teach students how to recognize the changes to all the jots and tittles on the page, by teaching them how to write all the jots and tittles on the page. Another way to summarize the approach is "if you can write it, then you can read it." So, when we arrived at weak verbs, we learned all of the minute details for how to compose weak verbs. We learned what weak verb forms *should* look like—e.g., what changes when a I-ו follows a *pataḥ* preformative vowel, what changes when a guttural consonant rejects a *dagesh forte*, etc. At the time, I did not know the value of what I was learning. I simply did what I was told.

As I progressed in Hebrew classes, there was certainly a steep uphill learning curve for me with translation, but I found myself not asking the same questions as other students when parsing verbs. Some students who had learned from a "paradigm-heavy" approach seemed to be paralyzed in the mental Rolodex of paradigms when asked to parse verbs, especially weak verbs. On the other hand, I found myself saying in my head, "Of course that is a *hiphil* with an $aw \rightarrow ô$ contraction of the I-ו." This internal dialogue was no pat on my own back; I had plenty of other struggles. And yet, because I had been taught the detailed morphological changes that are rather consistent within the individual weak verb types, I was able to recognize the patterns even when they differed from the strong verb morphology.

In order to reach this understanding of weak verb morphology, the approach that Fuller and Choi present is one that teaches students to create (to compose by writing) nouns and verbs in all their various types. We learned to create weak verbs with all their idiosyncrasies and peculiarities. In order to anticipate the changes in weak verbs, this method requires a precise knowledge of the standard, strong verb morphology. If a student misses elements of strong verb morphology, then understanding weak verbs will be a challenge. Because of the need to know the strong verb perfectly, in Part 1 of this book, we will "review" Fuller and Choi's method for creating strong verbs so that our discussions of weak verb morphology will make sense. In order to say that the *hiphil holem-vav* preformative vowel of I-ו verbs in the imperfect is the product of an *aw* → *ô* contraction (יֹשִׁיב [יֹשֵׁב]), we have to first know that there should have been a *pataḥ* as the "original" preformative vowel (*יַוְשִׁיב).

We will talk more about the methodology in Part 1, but for now, it is important to know that it is worth the effort to learn the strong verb morphology *precisely* so that you can make sense of the consistent changes in weak verb morphology. We will not create weak verbs in this book. Rather, we will discuss weak verb morphology by referring to what the verbal root "originally" had before the morphological change we see in the Hebrew Bible. Or, we will say, "The R₂ (i.e., the second root consonant) *should* have a *dagesh forte*." These kinds of statements will presume a precise knowledge of what the strong verb morphology was before any changes caused by the weaknesses of weak verbs. For those interested in the full "creating weak verbs" methodology, I would recommend *Invitation to Biblical Hebrew* by Fuller and Choi.

Terminology

There is no small disagreement among Hebrew scholars regarding the "correct" terminology to use when describing verbal forms. Some conventions use "perfect," "imperfect," "imperfect + *vav*-consecutive," while others use *qatal*, *yiqtol*, and *vayyiqtol*, respectively. It is important to clarify the terminology I will use throughout this book. However, I am not making an argument for which is best or even which is "correct." I simply follow the conventions I learned as a Hebrew student and want to accommodate other systems where it is helpful.

The following sections provide the definitions of common terms we will use and how I will refer to them.

Roots and Root Consonants

We will speak of verbal roots as the consonantal "skeleton" that communicates the base meaning of a verb.[31] Most verbal roots are triconsonantal, but there are good historical arguments for some biconsonantal roots as well. Additionally, biblical Hebrew has quadrilateral roots (four consonants), but they are rare.[32] The concept of a root derives from early Jewish grammarians who used the term שׁוֹרֶשׁ ("root") to refer to the consonantal base of Hebrew words.

In this book, the concept of a root and root consonants will be important as we consider the "shell" that can be superimposed on any three root consonants. Most Hebrew verbs can be created by adding a consistent pattern of

---

31. *IBHS*, §21.1a.; cf. GKC, §30. For an excellent introduction to Hebrew roots, see Tamar Zewi, "Roots: Modern Notions," in *EHLL*, 3:427–31.

32. GKC, §30p; JM, §60.

affixes before and/or after the root consonants. In order to work backwards and parse these verbs as we see them in their final form in the Hebrew Bible, we will need to dissect a word into its root and affixes, separating the base "skeleton" for lexical purposes (definition) and the affixes for inflectional purposes (function).

Throughout this book, we will refer to root consonants of the verbal skeleton as the R_1 (first root consonant), R_2 (second root consonant), and R_3 (third root consonant). These will read from right-to-left, of course ($R_3 R_2 R_1$).

Stems

The verbal stem is the pattern of pronunciation with affixes that give a verb its "varied shades of meaning."[33] Medieval Hebrew grammarians called these *binyanim* (בִּנְיָנִים) or "buildings" since they "built" upon the base root to provide nuanced meanings (intensive, causative, passive, etc.). The base stem in the Hebrew verbal system is the *qal* (קַל; "light"). In other methodological systems, the *qal* may be called the G-stem or the *paʿal* from the pedagogical root פעל. The other six stems we will work with are often called "derived" stems because they are derivative of the base stem *qal*. Using the root פעל for the spelling of the stem names, these derived stems are *niphal*, *piel*, *pual*, *hithpael*, *hiphil*, and *hophal*.

Conjugations

In this book, we will use the term conjugation to refer to the affix patterns that indicate tense, aspect, and mood (TAM) and identify person, gender, and number (PGN) in the verbal form. Gesenius and Joüon-Muraoka use the term conjugation to refer to the verbal stems listed in the previous section.[34] I cannot make the argument here as to which nomenclature is best, nor does it matter. I simply want to provide clarity with how we will refer to the phonological and morphological adjustments to the verbal root that provide TAM and PGN for a verbal form. The conjugations we will use are the perfect, imperfect, imperative, infinitive (absolute and construct), and participle. Some secondary, though no less important, conjugations are the jussive, cohortative, *vav*-consecutive imperfect (*vayyiqtol*), and *vav*-consecutive perfect (*veqatal*).[35]

---

33. GKC, §39c.
34. GKC, §39c; JM, §40a. Both Gesenius and Joüon-Muraoka admit that they use the term "conjugation" to refer to the *binyanim* for lack of a better term and that it also has a different meaning in Hebrew than in Greek, Latin, or English.
35. There is debate about whether the jussive and cohortative are distinct conjugated forms or just contextual functions of the imperfect (*yiqtol*). In this book, we will treat the jussive and cohortative as unique morphological forms since some weak verbs distinguish the long and short imperfect. These forms

Preformatives and Suformatives

For the various affixes that attach directly to the verbal root, we will use the terms preformatives and suformatives.[36] Preformatives, as the name suggests, come at the front of the verbal root. Suformatives attach at the end of the verbal root. Using this definition, we will consider both the ה of the *hiphil* stem and the איתן letters of the imperfect conjugation to be examples of "preformatives."[37] These are morphological affixes that occur at the beginning of the verbal root and are part of the final verbal form. Examples of suformatives would be the endings of the perfect (suffixed conjugation; ־תִּי, ־תָּ, ־תְּ, ־נוּ, etc.) or the *shureq* of many plural verbs (יִקְטְלוּ; *qal* impf 3mp). Preformatives and suformatives are the elements attached to the verbal root that make up the final verbal form before any other prefixes or suffixes are added.

Vocalic Suformative/Ending

With suformatives, we will further distinguish between vocalic suformatives and syllabic suformatives. Vocalic suformatives are suformatives that are *only* a vowel. For example, the וּ added to the end of a perfect 3cp verb (קָטְלוּ) or the imperfect mp verbs (יִקְטְלוּ; תִּקְטְלוּ) is a vocalic suformative because it is *only* a vowel added to the verbal form. The *hireq yod* on the end of the imperfect 2fs is also a vocalic suformative since the entire suformative is *only* a vowel (תִּקְטְלִי). I also consider ־ָה of the perfect 3fs to be a vocalic suformative (קָטְלָה). It is true that when these vocalic suformatives are added to the verbal root that they constitute a final syllable in conjunction with the R_3. The distinction we will make in this volume is that the vocalic suformative is only a vowel when considered individually.

The concept of a vocalic suformative is important in verbs because we will employ a vowel adjustment rule that a "vocalic ending causes reduction of the

---

display a morphological distinction that, in a book on weak verb morphology, is important to maintain. In addition to these morphological distinctions from the imperfect, their contextual function and clause position certainly help us to recognize these forms as jussive or cohortative. For an introduction to the advanced conversation on jussives and cohortatives, see Ahouva Shulman, "Jussive," in *EHLL*, 2:437–40; Steven Fassberg, "Cohortative," in *EHLL*, 1:476–77; Scott Callaham, "Mood and Modality: Biblical Hebrew," in *EHLL*, 2:687–90; and their associated bibliographies.

36. For the sake of consistency in this volume, we will use the terms preformative and suformative even for the affixes of the verbal stems. We will reserve the terms prefixes and suffixes for elements added before or after the final verbal form (e.g., pronominal suffixes or prefixed interrogative ה). While this convention may be a bit idiosyncratic, I believe that it helps students to consistently identify what morphological distinctives are part of the verbal form itself versus what elements may be secondary additions like pronominal suffixes, conjunctive ו, or interrogative ה.

37. Some may distinguish between preformatives/suformatives that are part of the verbal conjugation and prefixes/suffixes that are part of the verbal stem. For this volume, we will follow the definitions provided in these paragraphs.

R₂ vowel." For example, whenever we see a vocalic sufformative, the thematic vowel (R₂ vowel) will reduce to a vocal *shewa*. This may not seem like a big deal, but if that second root letter is a guttural consonant, then we will want to know that it will become a composite *shewa* ($\circ$, $\circ$, $\circ$) instead of a simple vocal *shewa* (תִּבְעֲטוּ) *qal* impf 2mp בעט, 1 Sam 2:29). We will discuss this more in the chapter on II-guttural verbs, but this morphological adjustment begins with knowing that a vocalic sufformative normally produces the reduction of the stem vowel associated with R₂.

Syllabic Sufformative/Ending

We will use the term "syllabic sufformative" to refer to an ending on a verbal root that is an entire syllable. Some describe these endings as those that "begin with a consonant," and that would also be an accurate way to describe them. As opposed to vocalic sufformatives in which the ending itself is only a vowel, syllabic sufformatives constitute an ending that is an entire syllable in itself. Examples of syllabic sufformatives are several of the sufformatives in the perfect conjugation (־תִּי, ־תָּ, ־נוּ, etc.). The imperfect 2fp and 3fp also have a syllabic sufformative (־נָה). Notice that all of these begin with a consonant and constitute an entire syllable when considered separately from the triconsonantal verbal root.

Syllabic sufformatives will require special attention in weak verbs when a verbal form takes a helping vowel as a phonological buffer between the verbal root and the sufformative (e.g., נְפוּגוֹתִי *niphal* pf 1cs פוג, Ps 38:9). Additionally, we will see in III-ה verbs that vocalic sufformatives in the imperfect attach directly to R₂ whereas syllabic sufformatives will use a helping vowel (י$\circ$) as a buffer to the sufformative. Both examples will require a knowledge of the distinction between vocalic sufformatives and syllabic sufformatives. This is just a preview of why this terminology is important. We will address these concepts in more detail in later chapters, so there is no need to remember these examples perfectly now.

Prefixes and Suffixes

Prefixes and suffixes are the terms most often used to specify the affixes on a verbal root. We will use the terms preformatives and sufformatives to refer to those affixes and reserve the terms prefixes and suffixes to refer to elements added before or after the final verbal form. For example, the interrogative ה would be considered a prefix added to the beginning of a final verbal form (e.g., הֲיִפָּלֵא *niphal* impf 3ms פלא + הֲ, Gen 18:14). If a verb has an interrogative ה, that prefix will attach before the preformative. Other prefixed elements may be the *vav*-consecutive or *vav*-conjunctive. Similarly, suffixes may attach to verbal forms *after* sufformatives (e.g., עֲבָדוּם *qal* pf 3cp עבד + 3mp suffix, Gen 15:13). Again, prefixes and suffixes are most often understood to be the affixes on a verbal root, but we will use those terms to refer to anything added to the beginning or end of a *final* verbal form.

Weak Verb Types

One will find that weak verbs can be categorized in different ways. Some grammars follow the system that uses the root פעל and will refer to פ״נ or ל״ה verbs for those roots with a נ as the first root letter or a ה as the third root letter, respectively. Other systems will use the nomenclature R_1, R_2, and R_3 (R_1-guttural verbs; R_2-ו/י verbs; etc.). In this book, we will use Roman numerals to define the weak verb type (I-guttural; II-ו/י; III-ה; etc.). There is nothing superior to this nomenclature. It is simply how I have come to refer to the weak verb types.

Other weak verb types do not fit neatly into this nomenclature. Geminate verbs, for example, we will refer to as "geminate verbs" rather than ע״ע verbs. The פעל nomenclature indicates that the R_2 (פעל) has been doubled (ע״ע). In the system of Roman numerals we will use, there is not a clean way to refer to geminate verbs other than to call them geminate verbs.

Another weak verb type to define is what I will call I-א ōPV verbs. These are a subset of I-guttural verbs that specifically have a I-א. In the imperfect conjugation of I-א ōPV verbs, the א quiesces and the verbal form takes a *holem* (ō) as the **p**reformative **v**owel (PV). There are only a few I-א verbs that morph in this way, and so they deserve their own unique nomenclature. The most common example of this weak verb type is אמר that in *vayyiqtol* forms becomes וַיֹּאמֶר. This admittedly idiosyncratic nomenclature (I-א ōPV) is simply my attempt to name these verbs in a memorable way based on their characteristic *holem* preformative vowel.

PART 1

A Strong Verb Methodology

CHAPTER 1

A Strong Verb Methodology

1.1 Introduction

It may seem odd to begin a study of weak verb morphology with a chapter on the strong verb system. This is necessary, however, because this methodology for learning weak verbs presupposes mastery of a *specific approach* to strong verb morphology. This approach teaches the student to overlay "shells" on consonantal roots rather than requiring rote memorization of verbal paradigms.[1] Using this method, the student quickly learns to anticipate verbal forms by applying known morphological principles.[2] The operative pedagogical principle is that if you can "create"/"write" the verbal form, then you can "parse"/"read" the verbal form. This methodology should provide significant confidence when parsing and will hasten the student's progress to Hebrew fluency.

We will begin by first unpacking two summary charts, namely, the *qal* paradigms and the derived stems chart. Next, we will introduce the steps to create Hebrew strong verbs. What is presented here is a methodology to help solidify what the weak verb forms would look like hypothetically, *prior to* any morphological adjustments due to the weakness. In later chapters, we will discuss the morphological changes due to specific weaknesses, but first, we must know what the strong verb pattern should be that led to the weak verb change. Finally in this chapter, we will discuss general vowel changes we can observe by applying the rules of vowel adjustment.

---

1. For an in-depth presentation of this approach see Fuller and Choi, *Invitation to Biblical Hebrew*, 133–62.
2. In the following chapters on weak verbs, we will assume a knowledge of these strong verb characteristics. For example, we will use the term "originally" (that is, in the strong verb morphology) or say "the R_1 takes a silent *shewa*," or that "I-guttural verbs often flip an R_1 silent *shewa* to a composite vocal *shewa* in their final forms." Any comments about what verbs *should* look like refers to these strong verb characteristics.

1.2 The *Qal* Paradigms

We will not spend much time on the *qal* paradigms. Table 1.1 provides the paradigms that must be mastered in order to progress with this methodology. The purpose of the *qal* paradigms in this methodology is to provide the distinctive morphology of the verbal conjugations and their respective PGN. For example, the perfect 1cs will end with the sufformative -תִּי whether it is a *qal*, a *niphal*, a *piel*, etc. Regardless of the verbal stem, the *qal* paradigms are where we observe these morphological distinctives. Likewise, the imperfect 1cs will begin with א across all verbal stems, but the *qal* paradigms provide this information.

We will use the *qal* paradigms later in this chapter to create strong verbs. If the *qal* paradigms are a little rusty for you, then you may want to devote some time to memorizing Table 1.1 perfectly. I tell my students that I should be able to bust into their dorm room at 2:00 am and ask for the *qal* perfect 2fs and they immediately say, "קָטַלְתְּ" without any hesitation. I would, of course, never do that, but that is the degree to which the *qal* paradigms should be memorized.

Table 1.1: *Qal* Paradigms

	Perfect	Imperfect	Imperative	Cohortative	Jussive	Participle	
3ms	קָטַל	יִקְטֹל			יִקְטֹל	Active	
3fs	קָטְלָה	תִּקְטֹל			תִּקְטֹל	קֹטֵל	ms
2ms	קָטַלְתָּ	תִּקְטֹל	קְטֹל		תִּקְטֹל	קֹטְלָה	fs
2fs	קָטַלְתְּ	תִּקְטְלִי	קִטְלִי		תִּקְטְלִי	קֹטְלִים	mp
1cs	קָטַלְתִּי	אֶקְטֹל		אֶקְטְלָה		קֹטְלוֹת	fp
3mp (3cp)	קָטְלוּ	יִקְטְלוּ			יִקְטְלוּ	קֹטֶלֶת	t-form
3fp		תִּקְטֹלְנָה			תִּקְטֹלְנָה	Passive	
2mp	קְטַלְתֶּם	תִּקְטְלוּ	קִטְלוּ		תִּקְטְלוּ	קָטוּל	ms
2fp	קְטַלְתֶּן	תִּקְטֹלְנָה	קְטֹלְנָה		תִּקְטֹלְנָה	קְטוּלָה	fs
1cp	קָטַלְנוּ	נִקְטֹל	Long Form Imperative קָטְלָה	נִקְטְלָה		קְטוּלִים	mp
						קְטוּלוֹת	fp
		Inf Abs	קָטוֹל	Inf Cstr	קְטֹל		

A few comments are worth adding here. First, the left column identifies PGN for the perfect, imperfect, imperative, cohortative, and jussive. For participles, you will want to refer to the far-right column for gender and number. Second, for participles, I have only included absolute participles and not construct participles. Again, the *qal* paradigms here are for reference and are not intended to be a full discussion of every *qal* form. You may want to refer to the *qal* paradigms in your introductory grammar to get the fullest review of these forms. Finally, the long form imperative is included here because of its distinctive morphology with the final הָ‎ֹ. I am not trying to designate a separate function of the imperative, but because of its distinct morphology (הָ‎ֹ), it is worth including.

1.3 The Derived Stems Chart

As we begin learning the derived stems chart, first remember that the derived stem names (*niphal, piel, pual, hithpael, hiphil, hophal*) are built on the pedagogical root פעל. Next notice the transliterated ע (') in the stem names, and that some middle עs have a doubled transliteration ("). These unique spellings indicate that the stems *piel, pual,* and *hithpael* have a *dagesh forte* (doubling *dagesh*) in the R$_2$. Thus, a helpful strategy for learning the derived stems chart is to learn to spell the names of the stems, including the transliterated ע. Memorizing the stem name spellings will give you a jump start to mentally retrieve the shells when needed for parsing. If we look at an example, נְ◌ַ◌ is the shell for the *niphal* perfect, the first shell in the *niphal* column. If you take the shell נְ◌ַ◌, the thematic vowel *patah*, and overlay them on the root פעל, you get נִפְעַל, the name of the stem.

The dotted circles represent any root consonant of a triconsonantal root. We will discuss later that some verbal roots may originally derive from biconsonantal roots, but for our purposes, we will overlay the shells in Table 1.2 on three root consonants even for supposed biconsonantal roots (e.g., *hiphil* impf shell [יַ◌ִ◌] on שׁוב—יָשׁוּב). We designate the dotted circles as "R$_1$," "R$_2$," and "R$_3$." This again, corresponds to the respective root consonants in a verbal root from right-to-left. This nomenclature also corresponds to the weak verb types that we will call I-נ/י, II-gutturals, etc.

Notice that the shaded boxes in the derived stems chart have the stem names *and* the thematic vowel symbols (e.g., A-e/E-a for the *hithpael*). We will speak more about this in a moment, but for now, know that this system of symbols identifies vowel classes (a, e, i, o, u). In the upper right corner of the chart, you can see the Hebrew vowels to which those letters correspond. To use this chart effectively, memorize the thematic vowel[3] symbols for each derived stem.

---

3. The thematic vowel is what we will call the vowel under the second root consonant (R$_2$ vowel).

Table 1.2: The Derived Stems Chart

	Niph'al			
	A/E-a			
perfect	נׇOO	A (or a) = *pataḥ* (ַO)		
imperfect	OOׇO	E (or e) = *tsere* (ֵO) I (or i) = *ḥireq-yod* (יִO)		
imperative	הOׇO	O = *ḥolem* (ֹO)		
infinitive	הOOׇ/ןOOׇ	○ = any root consonant		
participle	נׇOO	○ ○ ○ R₃ R₂ R₁		
	Pi''el	**Pu''al**	**Hithpa''el**	
	A-e/E	**A/A**	**A-e/E-a**	
perfect	OOׇO	OOֻO	הOOתׇO	
imperfect	OOׇO	OOֻO	OOתׇO	
imperative	OOׇO		הOOתׇO	
infinitive	OOׇO		הOOתׇO	
participle	מOOׇO	מOOֻO	מOOתׇO	
	Hiph'il	**Hoph'al**		
	A-i/I-e	**A/A**		
perfect	הOOׇO	הOOׇO		
imperfect	OOׇO	OOׇO		
imperative	הOOׇO			
infinitive	הOOׇO			
participle	מOOׇO	מOOׇO		

Next observe that the shell for the imperfect conjugation in each stem has a י as the preformative consonant. This י serves as a placeholder for *any* of the preformative letters in the imperfect paradigm (איתן; a.k.a. אֵיתָן [*ēytān*] letters). For example, if we were to compose a *hiphil* imperfect 2ms, the appropriate shell *from the chart* is OOׇO. However, we know from the *qal* imperfect paradigm that the preformative for the 2ms is a ת (תִּקְטֹל). Hence, we must adjust the shell from ○○ִ֯י to ○○ִ֯תּ for the *hiphil* imperfect 2ms. For learning the chart, simply use the י as a placeholder rather than trying to memorize a different shell for each of the אֵיתָן letters.

Finally, you may notice that the *pual* and *hophal* do not have imperative or infinitive shells. These forms are so rare in the Hebrew Bible, it is not worth putting brain energy into memorizing them.[4]

1.4 The Meaning of the Thematic Vowel Symbols

Table 1.3: Strong Verb Thematic Vowel Symbols

	qal	Nonstative Verb A/O כתב A/E נתן A/A שלח	Stative Verb E/A מלא A-e/A כבד A/A גדל O/A קטן
Perfect **Imperfect** **Imperative**	*niphal*	A/E-a	
	piel	A-e/E	
	pual	A/A	
	hithpael	A-e/E-a	
	hiphil	A-i/I-e	
	hophal	A/A	
Infinitives	absolute	O	*niphal*; *piel*(!)[5]
		E	*hiphil* [○ִ֯]; *hithpael*; *piel*(!)
	construct	E or [I]	*hiphil* [יִ֯○]; *piel*; *hithpael*; *niphal*
Participles		A	*niphĀl*; *puĀl*; *hophĀl* [○ָ]
		E or [I]	*piEl*; *hithpaEl*; *hiphIl* [○ֵ or יִ֯○]

---

4. For those interested in the statistics, for the *pual*, no imperatives are found in the Hebrew Bible, only one infinitive construct occurs (עֻנּוֹתוֹ [with 3ms suffix], Ps 132:1), and only one infinitive absolute occurs (גֻּנֹּב, Gen 40:15). For the *hophal*, none of these forms occur in the Hebrew Bible. These searches are based on the ETCBC morphology database.

5. The exclamation point beside the *piel* is simply to highlight that the thematic vowel for the *piel* infinitive absolute can be *holem* (O) or *tsere* (E).

The purpose of Table 1.3 is to assist the student's mastery of the thematic vowel symbols. This chart will prove essential to gain full facility in using this method to learn the Hebrew verb. In our previous discussion of Table 1.2, we observed these symbols for the derived stems located below the stem names in the shaded boxes. For the *qal*, Hebrew students do not often learn the nuances of the different thematic vowels that can appear. It is usually best simply to memorize the paradigm and move forward. However, even the *qal* has a variety of thematic vowels depending on the type of verb and various other factors. The top row of Table 1.3 shows the variety of thematic vowels for the *qal*. These are here mainly for reference. The primary benefit of Table 1.3 will be the derived stem thematic vowel symbols.

Students must memorize both the content and meaning of this system. To enable full comprehension let us take a closer look at the *hiphil* thematic vowel symbols as an example. We have chosen the *hiphil* because its complexity gives us an example of each element.

E.g., *Hiphil*
← Perfect / Imperfect and Imperative →

$$\text{A-i/I-e}$$

Lower case = 3rd persons   Lower case = Feminine Plurals
(3ms, 3fs, 3cp)   (2fp, 3fp)

First, notice that all letters to the left of the slash represent the thematic vowel(s) for the perfect conjugation. So, in the *hiphil*, we would expect to see the R_2 vowel in the perfect to be primarily a *pataḥ* (A). The lower-case letter on the left side of the slash ("i"—*hireq yod*) represents all perfect third person forms (3ms, 3fs, 3cp). Indeed, that is what we find in the *hiphil* perfect paradigm (הִקְטִיל [3ms]; הִקְטִילָה [3fs]; הִקְטִילוּ [3cp]).[6]

The symbols on the right side of the slash represent the thematic vowel(s) for the imperfect and imperative conjugations. The capital "I" (again, *hireq yod*) represents most of the forms, but on the right side of the slash, the lower-case letter ("e"—*tsere*) represents the thematic vowel for the feminine plurals of the imperfect or imperative. Again, this is the pattern we see in the paradigm

---

6. In this symbolism, the upper case and lower case letters represent the same Hebrew vowel. Thus, the upper case "I" represents a *hireq yod* just the same as the lower case "i" represents a *hireq yod*. The difference in case for the English symbol is to differentiate the third person forms in the perfect conjugation, not to differentiate the vowel represented.

(e.g., *hiphil* imperfect 3ms with *hireq yod*—יַקְטִיל; *hiphil* imperfect 2/3fp with *tsere*—תַּקְטֵלְנָה).

In the chapters on weak verbs, we will say things like "the original thematic vowel shifts to a *pataḥ* even though we expect to see a *tsere*." The ideas of "original" and "expectation" refer to these symbols. We may also say, "the R₂ takes a *hireq yod*," and that also refers to this system. Table 1.3 lists the thematic vowel symbols for the *qal* and also repeats the thematic vowel symbols for the derived stems in the perfect/imperfect and imperative. The thematic vowels for the derived stems are also listed in Table 1.2. These are repeated in order to have a complete thematic vowel chart. There is no difference in the derived stem thematic vowels between the two tables.

Now that we have our bearing on the perfect, imperfect, and imperative thematic vowel symbols, we must also address the thematic vowels for the infinitives and the participle. Table 1.3 also provides these thematic vowels below the derived stems, under the thicker line. You may notice that these are listed in an inverse relationship to the perfect, imperfect, and imperative. For the infinitives and participles, the table lists the thematic vowel and then lists the derived stems that take that thematic vowel.

A few things need to be clarified about this portion of the chart.

First, observe that the Hebrew vowel associated with the English letter is the same. Nothing changes there.

Second, notice that for the infinitive absolute, the *piel* stem is repeated, marked by the exclamation point in parentheses. This is done to draw your attention to the fact that the *piel* infinitive absolute may have a *holem* thematic vowel or it may have a *tsere* thematic vowel. Both are possible.

Third, for the infinitives, notice that the *hiphil* has bracketed vowels, a *tsere* (◌ֵ) in the infinitive absolute and *hireq yod* (◌ִי) in the infinitive construct. There is no reason to memorize this if you know the *hiphil* "*tsere* forms." These are forms in the *hiphil* that take a *tsere* thematic vowel even if a *hireq yod* is expected. These can be memorized with the mnemonic J.I.I.V.E. (**J**ussive; **I**mperative 2ms; **I**nfinitive absolute; **V**av-Consecutive all get an **E** [*tsere*] thematic vowel). I call these the "jive" forms though I realize the mnemonic is spelled with two I's. If you know these J.I.I.V.E. forms for the *hiphil*, then there is no need to memorize which infinitive takes which vowel. Just expect the *hiphil* to get a *hireq yod* thematic vowel unless it is one of the J.I.I.V.E. forms. In that case, it gets a *tsere* R₂ vowel.

The last element to address in Table 1.3 is the thematic vowel for the participle. These may be the easiest ones on the chart, and it takes us back to where we began. All you need to do is learn to spell the stem names and you will have the thematic vowel for the participles. Table 1.3 has the thematic vowel letter bold and capitalized to highlight which letter of the stem name is the thematic vowel for participles. The one caveat to mention here is that for participles, the "Ā" represents a long *qamets* rather than a short *pataḥ* as it has before. Hence, it is spelled in this table with the macron. This long *qamets* is also written in brackets in the table to remind you of this last point.

1.5 A Method for Building Hebrew Verbs

With the *qal* paradigms, the derived stems chart, and the thematic vowel symbols under our belt, we will now use this information to build strong Hebrew verbs. In the ensuing chapters, we will not build weak verbs, but our discussions about weak verbs will assume you understand the concepts for superimposing "original" shells on weak roots and then accounting for expected morphological adjustments.

The process for building Hebrew verbs can be summarized in three steps. The first step is to identify the shell for the specific verb stem and conjugation you are creating. For our example, we will create a *piel* imperfect 3fs using the root בצר.[7] From Table 1.2, we need to find the *piel* imperfect shell and that would be יֹ֯֯֯. We then superimpose that shell on the root—יְבַצֵּר. The second step is to identify the thematic vowel. Since we are composing a *piel*, we use the vowel symbols A-e/E and find that the thematic vowel for the imperfect is E. This directs us to overlay a *tsere* as the R₂ vowel—יְבַצֵּר. The final step is to determine the distinguishing marks of the PGN that we are composing. In this example, we are creating a 3fs. To finish composing this verb, we must refer to the *qal* paradigm. Regardless of the stem, the distinguishing marks for PGN come from the *qal* paradigm. When we look to the *qal* imperfect 3fs to find those distinguishing marks, we see that the preformative consonant should be a ת rather than the י placeholder of the derived stems chart. And so, in step three, we replace the י placeholder with the ת of the 3fs form we are composing—תְּבַצֵּר. If there were sufformatives as part of the distinguishing marks, then we would overlay those as well, but in this example, there are no sufformatives. After those three steps, we find that the *piel* imperfect 3fs of בצר is תְּבַצֵּר.

Here is the process in a "steps" format.

---

[7]. I chose the uncommon root בצר because that form occurs in the Hebrew Bible, and we can check it to confirm the method works. The verb we are creating occurs in Jer 51:53.

Piel Imperfect 3fs בצר

יְבַצֵּר	יְ◌ַ◌ּ◌	Step 1—Shells
יְבַצֵּר	A-e/**E**	Step 2—Thematic Vowel
תְּבַצֵּר	תִּקְטֹל	Step 3—*qal* 3fs distinguishing marks

There are many additional nuances to this method, including things like metathesis in the *hithpael* when the ת of the shell is adjacent to a sibilant[8] or accounting for the *hiphil tsere* forms (J.I.I.V.E.). For all those nuances, I would refer you to chapters 23–25 of Fuller and Choi's grammar.[9] Again, the point here is not to grasp all the intricate nuances. Rather, what is important is that you understand the idea of shells, thematic vowels, and distinguishing marks of the PGN in order to compose what a strong verb *should* look like.

1.6 Examples

In this section, we will build two example verbs. Both are straightforward examples to demonstrate the process. We will use the simplified "steps" layout for these.

Niphal Participle fs רצח (Judg 20:4)

נִרְצָח	נִ◌ְ◌ָ◌	Step 1—Shells
נִרְצָח	Ā (niph**Ā**l)	Step 2—Thematic Vowel
נִרְצָחָה	קְטָלָה	Step 3—*qal* distinguishing marks

In this example, the shell is pretty straight forward. Remember that the thematic vowel of the participle can be determined from the spelling of the stem name. And finally, the distinguishing suffformative from the *qal* paradigm gives us the fs participle ending, ◌ָה. Remember that the thematic vowel Ā in the participle is a long *qamets* that will not reduce to a vocal *shewa* like in the *qal* paradigm.

---

8. Avihai Shivtiel, "Metathesis" in *EHLL*, 2:634–35; JM, §17b; GKC, §19m.
9. Russell T. Fuller and Kyoungwon Choi, *Invitation to Biblical Hebrew: A Beginning Grammar* (Grand Rapids: Kregel, 2006), 141–162.

Hiphil Imperfect 2mp שבת (Exod 12:15)

יַשְׁבֵּת	○○ֵ○ַי	Step 1—Shells
יַשְׁבִּית	A-i/I-e	Step 2—Thematic Vowel
תַּשְׁבִּיתוּ	תִּקְטְלוּ	Step 3—*qal* 2mp distinguishing marks

The derived stem and conjugation shell is again straight forward. For the thematic vowel, we exclude everything to the left of the slash since that represents the perfect conjugation. On the right side of the slash, we disregard the lower case "e" since that represents the feminine plurals. Therefore, the thematic vowel is the historically long י○ִ. Finally, for the 2mp distinguishing marks from the *qal* paradigm, we have both a preformative (ת) and a sufformative (ו) that must be superimposed on the verb.

Hopefully these examples adequately illustrate the concept of building verbs by overlaying shells and other distinguishing marks onto any verbal root. This will be how we approach weak verbs. If we say that the *piel* "originally" had a *dagesh forte* in the R₂ of the *piel* participle, we will be referring to the *piel* participle shell (○○ַ○ְמ). For weak verbs that have a guttural letter in the R₂, we will have to account for that *dagesh forte* since the gutturals reject *dagesh forte*. But first, we must know that the *dagesh* was supposed to be there by memorizing the derived stem shells.

1.7 Parsing—Working Backwards

Building verbs provides an avenue to practice all the detailed vowel points of the strong verb, but parsing is the end goal. We *build* verbs so that we can more easily *parse* them. In this method for strong verbs, parsing uses the same "steps," but works backwards. By backwards, I mean that we observe a final form and then consider (1) what shell we see, (2) what thematic vowel confirms the parsing, and then (3) what distinguishing marks of the *qal* paradigm provide the PGN of the parsing.

We will use the same table layout to see the steps for parsing but flip it around to represent "working backwards."

Perhaps the trickiest aspect of our first example is recognizing the *hiphil* imperfect shell (○○ֵ○ַי) when we are looking at a final form that has already superimposed the *qal* 1cp distinguishing mark (נ), obscuring the י placeholder of the shell. You may be inclined initially to parse this as a *niphal*, but the *niphal* does not have a *patah* as the preformative vowel nor does it have

נַזְבִּירָה

Step 1—Shells?	◌◌◌נַ	◌◌◌יַ	*hiphil* impf
Step 2—Thematic vowel?	ִי◌	A-i/I-e	ִי◌ confirms the *hiphil* shell
Step 3—*Qal* distinguishing marks?	נַ◌◌◌ָה	נִקְטְלָה	cohortative 1cp
Hiphil cohortative 1cp זכר			

a *hireq yod* as the thematic vowel. Recognizing these things will take some practice, but once you begin to think of Hebrew verbs in this way, seeing all the various "pieces" of the verb parsing will become much easier.

קֻטְּלוּ

Step 1—Shells?	◌◌ֻ◌		*pual* pf
Step 2—Thematic vowel?	◌ֻ	A/A	These symbols for the *pual* are A/A, but the ◌ֻ obscures the thematic vowel
Step 3—*Qal* distinguishing marks?	◌◌◌וּ	קָטְלוּ	pf 3cp
Pual perfect 3cp קטל			

Here, the shell is straightforward. Once we know the shell, we already know the expected thematic vowel (A/A). In this example, the thematic vowel reduces because of a vocalic ending (see §1.8 below) and obscures the expected *pataḥ* thematic vowel, but that does not affect the parsing. Finally, the *qal* paradigm leads us to the perfect 3cp because of the *shureq* sufformative.

As you can hopefully see, this method of building verbs facilitates recognition of the components necessary to parse verbs. While this method is just one way to approach Hebrew verbal morphology, it is the one on which we will base the rest of our discussions of weak verbs. It is not imperative that you master this method for building strong verbs, but it may be helpful to refer to this chapter when we begin weak verb morphology.

1.8 Vowel Adjustment Rules

One final thing to address in this introductory methodology is vowel adjustment rules. We cannot possibly address all the details here, so I would again commend to you Fuller and Choi.[10] However, we need to cover enough here to make sense of later discussions related to expected vowel changes.

We will refer to the following general vowel adjustment rules in our discussions of weak verbs. These rules anticipate the expected vowel for a given syllable type.[11]

1. A closed accented syllable prefers a long vowel.
2. An open pretonic syllable requires a long vowel.
3. A closed unaccented syllable requires a short vowel.
4. An open accented syllable prefers a short vowel.
5. An originally open propretonic syllable reduces the vowel to a vocal *shewa*.

These five rules can be simplified with the following mnemonic.

CAPL—**C**losed **A**ccented **P**refers **L**ong
OPRL—**O**pen **P**retonic **R**equires **L**ong
CURS—**C**losed **U**naccented **R**equires **S**hort
OAPS—**O**pen **A**ccented **P**refers **S**hort
OOPPS—**O**riginally **O**pen **P**ro**P**retonic *reduces the short vowel to a Vocal* **S**hewa

In the vowel adjustment rule labeled OOPPS, the term "originally" means that the syllable would have been open and propretonic prior to the reduction of the vowel to a vocal *shewa*. The final forms we see in the Hebrew Bible will have already reduced. And so, we expect to see a vocal *shewa* in a syllable that is at least two syllables in front of the accented syllable. Take, for example, the word דְּבָרִים. The initial syllable, prior to its reduction to a vocal *shewa* would have been a vowel—*דָּבָרִים.[12] With the accent over the ר, the first syllable would be what we will call "originally" open propretonic.

---

10. Fuller and Choi, *Invitation to Biblical Hebrew*, chapter 6. Kutz and Josberger, *Learning Biblical Hebrew* also uses a similar methodology for vowel adjustment rules, but with simpler terminology (see pp. 63–80).

11. See GKC, §27 and JM, §28 for a much more detailed discussion of expected vowel changes. See Fuller and Choi, *Invitation to Biblical Hebrew*, 25 for these summarized rules of syllables.

12. The reconstruction here with *pataḥ* is based on the system of "proto-Hebrew" used by Fuller and Choi. In their system, proto-Hebrew is a pedagogical tool for building biblical Hebrew forms. In proto-Hebrew, original long vowels were short vowels, and so in this reconstructed form, the *qamets* of the lexical form is *pataḥ*. This is only a pedagogical tool and not an attempt to argue for a literal diachronic change in Hebrew.

רִ֫ים*		בַּ		דְּ
CAPL		OPRL		OOPPS
רִים		בְּ		דְּ

The division of these syllables shows how the initial syllable would be labeled as an "originally" open propretonic syllable. The top form is theoretical (hence the asterisk). The bottom form shows the reduction of that "originally" open propretonic syllable to a vocal *shewa*.

A second vowel adjustment rule we need to address is what I call the verbal adjustment rule. This rule says that a vocalic sufformative on a verb will result in the reduction of the R_2 thematic vowel. A more concise way to say it is, "Vocalic sufformative = R_2 vowel reduction." One could also say that for verbs, thematic vowels in the pretonic position experience vowel reduction. Like the other vowel adjustment rules, this one will have already been applied when we see final forms in the Hebrew Bible. For example, the *qal* perfect 3fs and 3cp, both apply this rule (קָטְלָה; קָטְלוּ). However, most students just memorize the final form. When we discuss weak verb morphology, we will say "the vocalic sufformative causes the thematic vowel (R_2) to reduce." This vowel adjustment rule provides context for those comments.

1.9 Conclusion

In this chapter, we have summarized a methodology for building Hebrew strong verbs to give context for how we will talk about weak verbs. The overarching idea is that there are consistent patterns and "shells" that help us parse verbs. In strong verbs, these shells will be remarkably consistent.[13] With weak verbs, we will see changes to these shells that often make parsing more difficult. We need to know how the "original" shell should have appeared so that our explanation of changes in weak verbs makes sense. Our system for discussing weak verbs will initially superimpose the strong verb shell onto the weak verb root and then make adjustments based on other morphological principles.

A quick example will make the concept more concrete. With I-ו/י weak verbs, we will discuss a series of contractions. To recognize the origin of these contractions, we must know what the "original" shell should have been. The *hiphil* imperfect 3ms of ילד in Gen 17:20 has a *holem vav* for the preformative vowel (יוֹלִיד). If we know that this *holem vav* was the result of an *aw* → *ô*

---

13. Gesenius uses phrases like "unvarying analogy" and "incomparably more regular and systematic" when referring to the strong verb patterns in biblical Hebrew (GKC, §39c).

contraction, then we can "unravel" the form and recognize the superimposed shell from Table 1.2 on the weak verb root (*יַוְלִיד; ◯◯ִ◯ִ֯י). If we can recognize the original shell, then parsing this form as a *hiphil* imperfect becomes considerably easier. But first, we must know what the original shell should have been. That is what this chapter has sought to provide.

PART 2

Weak Verb Morphology

CHAPTER 2

Introduction to Weak Verbs

2.1 Introduction

With the summary of strong verbs completed, we now move to the discussion of weak verbs. In this chapter, we will introduce the general morphological characteristics for various types of weak verbs. We are not trying here to zero in on specific weak verbs (though some of these characteristics only apply to certain weak verb types). Rather, we want to introduce the phonological and morphological principles associated with weak verbs so that when we discuss them in specific chapters, they will be somewhat familiar. In some ways, this chapter constitutes a summary of the chapters that follow. The general principles and characteristics in this chapter will be what drive the specific morphological changes we see in each type of weak verb as we progress through the rest of the book. The material in this chapter should be mastered (memorized) in order to gain proficiency in the identification of weak verbs and weak verb morphology.

2.2 Types of Weak Verbs

A weak verb is any verb with one or more root consonants that may occasion a different morphological pattern than is expected in the original *qal* paradigm or derived stems chart for the strong verb.[1] In this sense, it is best not to think of weak verbs as the exceptions. Rather, they constitute verbs in the language that might be classified as "irregular."[2] If we consider an analogy from English, we may say that the "strong" form of the past tense is to add "-ed" to the verb (e.g., guard → guarded). But then English also has verbs like "swim" that becomes "swam," "fall" that becomes "fell," and "go" that becomes "went." It turns out that English probably has as many verbal irregularities as Hebrew. But for

---
1. Reymond, *Intermediate Biblical Hebrew Grammar*, §5.12, p. 194; JM, §71.
2. JM, §71a, n. 3.

a native speaker, these morphological changes are entirely "normal." In other words, once the student learns the irregularity, these "exceptions" are no longer a problem. And so Hebrew weak verbs are indeed "irregular" in that they do not match the standard *qal* paradigm and derived stems chart for the strong verb, but they do display considerable regularity within each type of weak verb.

The following chart lists the types of weak verbs we will consider. This table lists the weak verbs in the order that we will cover them. This order will begin with the weaknesses associated with the first root consonant (I-guttural; I-א ōPV; I-ו/י; I-נ), and then move to weaknesses related to the second (II-guttural; II-ו/י) and third (III-ה, III-guttural; III-א) root consonants, respectively. Geminate verbs will fall after II-ו/י because some of their forms have analogous morphological features.

Table 2.1: Types of Weak Verbs

Weak Verb Type	Alternate Names	Example(s)
I-guttural	R₁-guttural; פ guttural	עבד
I-א ōPV[3]	R₁-א; פ״א	אבה, אפה, אבד, אכל, אמר (אחז)
I-ו/י	R₁-ו/י; פ״ו/י	ישב
I-נ	R₁-נ; פ״נ	נפל
II-guttural	R₂-guttural; ע guttural	צעק
II-ו/י	R₂-ו/י; ע״ו/י; biconsonantal	קום
Geminate Verbs	ע״ע	סבב
III-ה	III-ו/י; R₃-ו/י; ל״ה	גלה
III-guttural	R₃-guttural; ל guttural	שלח
III-א	R₃-א; ל״א	מלא

The first column lists the names of the weak verb types as we will use them in this book.

The second column provides alternative names for these weak verb types. Not all grammars use the same terminology, and if you decide to do further

---

3. I-א ōPV verbs is what I am calling that special class of I-א verbs that take a *holem* as the preformative vowel. Grammars name this set of verbs differently. I have chosen I-א ōPV as a descriptive title to help remember their distinctive morphology with the *holem* (ō) as the **p**reformative **v**owel.

study on weak verbs, you may need to consider how other grammars will refer to them.

Note that not all grammars consider verbs with one or more guttural consonants to be weak.[4] However, since guttural consonants affect verbal morphology such that it differs from that of the standard strong verb, we will cover them in this book.

2.3 General Characteristics of Weak Verbs

In this section, we will outline the general characteristics of weak verb morphology that we will apply more specifically as we look at each weak verb type in the rest of the book. Nearly all the idiosyncrasies we see in specific weak verb situations will be some form of the following general characteristics.

2.3.1 Characteristics of Gutturals

The guttural consonants trigger a number of predictable weak verb spelling features. If we understand these characteristics, then weak verbs with gutturals are not actually exceptions, but follow their own set of rules. These characteristics will guide our discussions of the weak verbs with guttural consonants.

The following characteristics are generally true of gutturals.[5]

1. Gutturals (and ר) reject a *dagesh forte*.
2. Gutturals (excluding ר) take *hatef shewas* (ֲ, ֱ, ֳ), not simple vocal *shewas* (ְ).
3. Gutturals prefer /a/ sounds under them and before them, usually a *pataḥ* (ַ).
4. The gutturals ע, ח, ה at the end of a word take a furtive *pataḥ* when not immediately preceded by another a-class vowel. Furtive *pataḥ* represents a vocalic glide into the final guttural consonant. (e.g., רוּחַ—*rûaḥ*; שָׁלוֹחַ—*šālôaḥ*).
5. Guttural א may become quiescent (silent).

---

4. E.g., Joshua Blau covers what he calls I-, II-, and III-Laryngeals/Pharyngeals in a section of his book separate from "weak verbs" (Blau, *Phonology and Morphology of Biblical Hebrew*), §4.3.7, pp. 237–40. Similarly, Gesenius covers "Verbs with Gutturals" in §§62–65, "The Weak Verb" in §§66–67, and then "The Weakest Verbs" in §§68–78. Joüon-Muraoka also covers guttural verbs separately from verbs with "weak" consonants (JM, §§67–70 for guttural verbs and §§71–82 for weak verbs).

5. For further study on gutturals, see Geoffrey Khan, "Guttural Consonants: Masoretic Hebrew" in *EHLL*, 2:165–69; GKC, §§22–23; JM, §§20–25.

When considering the guttural letters, we understand ר as a semi-guttural. It will sometimes act like a guttural, but it most often will not. In fact, the primary guttural characteristic that ר exhibits is the rejection of a *dagesh forte*.

These guttural features are not unique to weak verbs. In fact, some advanced grammars do not include guttural verbs as "weak" verbs. Blau discusses them in a separate section on "phonological variations."[6] Joüon and Gesenius also address guttural verbs separately from weak verbs.[7] These grammars define weak verbs only as those that may lose one of their root consonants rather than verbs that differ from the standard strong verb shells. However, since many introductory grammars treat guttural verbs as weak verbs,[8] and since their morphology differs from that of the standard strong verb, we will cover them in this volume.

2.3.1.1 Gutturals Reject *Dagesh Forte*

A common feature of guttural consonants is that they do not take a *dagesh forte*.[9] This characteristic will affect verbal roots in derived stem shells that have a *dagesh forte*. Hence, the *piel* (○○̇○), *pual* (○○̇○), and *hithpael* (הִת○○̇○) with a guttural letter in the R_2 position will look different from our strong verb because the guttural in second root position rejects the *dagesh forte*. Likewise, the *niphal* imperfect, imperative, and infinitive will demonstrate morphological adjustments when the guttural letter is in the R_1 position due to those shells having a *dagesh forte* in the first root letter (e.g., *niphal* impf ○○̇○יִ).

When gutturals reject *dagesh forte* we often see lengthening of the preceding vowel by way of compensation (compensatory lengthening).[10] Hence, if a *piel* verb has a guttural in the R_2 position, we can anticipate a lengthened R_1 vowel with certain guttural consonants.

בֵּרֵךְ ← *בֵּרֵךְ

---

6. Blau, *Phonology and Morphology of Biblical Hebrew*, §4.3.7, pp. 237–40.
7. JM, §§67–70; GKC, §§62–65.
8. E.g., Gary D. Pratico and Miles V. Van Pelt, *Basics of Biblical Hebrew Grammar*, 3rd ed. (Grand Rapids: Zondervan, 2019); Fuller and Choi, *Invitation to Biblical Hebrew*; Karl V. Kutz and Rebekah L. Josberger, *Learning Biblical Hebrew: Reading for Comprehension: An Introductory Grammar* (Bellingham, WA: Lexham Press, 2018). Allen Ross calls them "irregular verbs," but includes guttural verbs with the other so-called weak verbs (Allen P. Ross, *Introducing Biblical Hebrew* [Grand Rapids: Baker, 2001]).
9. There are a few exceptions with ר and א. For ר, see JM, §23a; GKC §22s. For the so-called *dagesh* א, see GKC, §14d on *mappiq* and JM, §20a, n. 2.
10. Another way to explain this is that without the *dagesh forte*, the preceding vowel is left in an open pretonic syllable that requires a long vowel. See §1.7; GKC, §22c; JM, §20b.

With other guttural consonants, the R₂ guttural will imply the *dagesh* (virtual doubling).¹¹

בֵּעֵר* ← בִּעֵר

In this example, the ע will not display the *dagesh forte*, but we also do not see compensatory lengthening of the *hireq* in the R₁ position. Since the *dagesh forte* in the second root consonant is a distinguishing mark of the *piel*, students may struggle trying to parse these verbs without the distinctive *dagesh*. However, knowing that gutturals reject the *dagesh forte* and sometimes imply it will ease the tension when parsing verbs with gutturals. We will address more specific situations in which the *dagesh* is rejected or implied (virtual doubling) in Chapter 6.

2.3.1.2 Gutturals Take Composite *Shewas*

Another characteristic of gutturals is that they do not take simple vocal *shewas*. Gutturals prefer *ḥatef shewas*.

Consider the *qal* imperative 2ms with a guttural in the R₁ position.

אְמֹר* ← אֱמֹר

The first form is technically correct if we consider the "shell" from the *qal* paradigm (קְטֹל ← ○ְ○ֹ○). However, that is not what we will see in the 58 occurrences of the *qal* imperative 2ms of אמר in the Hebrew Bible. Since gutturals prefer *ḥatef shewas*, אֱמֹר is what we find in the Hebrew Bible.

Also consider that sometimes a guttural consonant that should have a silent *shewa* may "flip" to a composite *shewa*.¹²

יְעְבֹר* ← יַעֲבֹר

Admittedly, there are more things going on in this example than just the flip to a *ḥatef shewa*, but we will address those later. The element to highlight here is that the ע should have a silent *shewa* based on the *qal* paradigm "shell" (○ִ○ְ○ֹי). However, like the ע in segolate nouns with gutturals (נַעֲרִי; נַעַר with a 1cs suffix), it will "flip" that silent *shewa* to a *ḥatef shewa*.¹³ When this happens

---

11. To say that the guttural "implies" the *dagesh* is a way to describe that fact that the preceding syllable retains a short vowel. Gesenius calls this "virtual doubling" (GKC, §22b–c). In the example given, notice that the R₁ *hireq* does not lengthen and hence the syllable is technically open. Even so, it retains a short vowel in a pretonic open syllable whereas it should reduce as a pretonic open syllable in verbs. Essentially, the first syllable is acting like it is closed (i.e., acting like the guttural has the *dagesh forte*), but the *dagesh forte* is not visible. Hence, we say it is "implied." See also JM, §18b; §20a; and §69a.

12. JM, §22.

13. GKC, §22m; JM, §21f.

in verbs, the preformative vowel will often take the corresponding short vowel as you can see in the final form (יַעֲבֹר). We will cover this characteristic in more detail in Chapter 8 on I-guttural verbs.

2.3.1.3 Gutturals Prefer /a/ Sounds Around Them

We also find in weak verbs that gutturals prefer a-class vowels under and before them. Here are a few places where we can expect to see a preference for a-class vowels related to the guttural letters.

I-Gutturals

In the previous example (יַעֲבֹר), notice that when the guttural flips the silent *shewa* to *hatef shewa*, the preformative vowel takes the corresponding short vowel to get the a-class vowel (*patah*) before it. This shift will not always occur, but that is why we say that gutturals "prefer" a-class vowels rather than "require" them.

II-Gutturals

In II-guttural verbs, the *qal* thematic vowel (the vowel associated with the second root consonant) will often shift to an a-class vowel (*patah*) in the imperfect and imperative even if the thematic vowel preference of a specific derived stem prescribes an /e/ or /o/ vowel as the following example demonstrates.

qal imperative 2ms of בחר

בְּחֹר* ← בְּחַר

In this example, the *qal* paradigm form of the imperative 2ms should have a shell, ○○֫○, with a *holem* thematic vowel. However, due to the influence of the guttural in the second root position, that o-class vowel changes to *patah*. The final form we see in the Hebrew Bible is בְּחַר with *patah* (Exod 17:9; 2 Sam 24:12; 1 Chr 21:10).

III-Gutturals (ח and ע)

III-guttural verbs are most affected by the gutturals preferring a-class vowels under *and before them*. If a III-guttural verb prefers a-class vowels before it, then we must consider a shift to the thematic vowel. Where we expect to see an /e/ thematic vowel according to our strong verb chart (Table 1.2), we will now see an a-class vowel. This phenomenon is mostly limited to III-ח and III-ע verbs.[14]

---

14. III-א verbs tend to push thematic vowels to /e/ (see §11.3). III-ה verbs are really III-ו/י verbs (see §9.1). A true III-ה verb will have a *mappiq* (e.g., גבה) and will behave like III-ח and III-ע (see §10.1, n. 1).

piel perfect 3ms of בקע

בִּקֵּעַ ← *בִּקֵּע

Here, the expected thematic vowel is a *tsere* (A-e/E). However, due to the *ayin* in the third root position, and the preference for a-class vowels with gutturals, the thematic vowel changes to *pataḥ*. If you know this characteristic of guttural letters, then you can anticipate the vowel change and you are not caught off guard when you see a *pataḥ* as the thematic vowel of a *piel* perfect in which you were expecting *tsere*.

2.3.1.4 The Gutturals ה, ח, ע at the End of a Word May Take a Furtive *Pataḥ*

This characteristic of weak verbs is related to the desire for guttural letters to have /a/ sounds under and around them. In some weak verbs (III-gutturals ending with ה, ח, and ע), the final guttural will sometimes get a furtive *pataḥ* if it is not immediately preceded by another a-class vowel. There are primarily three places where this happens with verbs.

1. Historically Long Thematic Vowels
הִשְׁמִיעַ	*hiphil* pf 3ms שמע	Isa 30:30
שָׁלוּחַ	*qal* pass ptc ms שלח	Jer 49:14

2. Nonfinite Verbal Forms
שְׁלֹחַ	*qal* inf cstr שלח	Num 22:15
שֹׁלֵחַ	*qal* ptc ms שלח	Exod 9:14

3. Finite Verb Pausal Forms[15]
בִּקֵּעַ	*piel* pf 3ms (pausal) בקע	Job 28:10

2.3.1.5 Guttural א Quiesces with a Silent *Shewa*

The final characteristic of gutturals to consider here is that א likes to quiesce when it has a silent *shewa*.[16] Phonologically, this makes sense because the silent consonant with a silent *shewa* effectively produces zero sound. One will

---

15. Pausal forms are forms that have a heavy disjunctive accent, typically an *athnaḥ* or *silluq*. In the example given here, the heavy disjunctive accent is the *athnaḥ* (◌̰). Pausal forms will often reveal or retain an "original" vowel. In the case of III-guttural verbs, the pausal form withstands the pressure of the guttural and retains the expected *tsere*. However, for the III-guttural to get the /a/ sound it prefers, the furtive *pataḥ* slides into place.

16. The quiescent א is an א that has lost all vowel markings and is entirely unpronounced as a voiceless guttural stop. See JM, §24c and GKC, §23a; §27g for more detailed discussion on the quiescent א.

recognize the quiescent א because it has no vowel or *shewa* associated with it (e.g., קְרָאתִי).

We will address the details of quiescent א when it appears in various weak verbs, but one that you are likely already familiar with is the *qal* imperfect of אמר. Rather than treating it like a I-guttural and shifting the expected silent *shewa* to a vocal *shewa* (*יֶאֱמֹר), אמר is one of a set of I-א verbs in which the א quiesces and takes a *holem* as the preformative vowel (I-א ōPV verbs; §8.5).[17] This final verb form produces the familiar וַיֹּאמֶר (with *vav*-consecutive). Notice the א has no vowel associated with it. This feature is unique to the I-א ōPV verbs, but it is nothing new to the characteristics of the guttural א.

Another example of the quiescent א in verbs is found in III-א verbs. In the *qal* perfect paradigm, the pointing under the third root consonant is often a silent *shewa*. In many III-א verbs, this א will quiesce—מָלֵאתִי; קָרָאתִי. In some cases, when the א quiesces, the preceding vowel will lengthen by compensation.[18] This compensation proves to be true even when the א is the last consonant in the word. Consider the *qal* perfect 3ms מָצָא where the vowel under the second root consonant lengthens to *qamets* rather than the expected *patah* (e.g., קָטַל).

2.3.2 Nun (נ) with Silent *Shewa* May Assimilate

The consonant נ may assimilate when it has a silent *shewa*.[19] We will encounter this phenomenon most frequently with I-נ weak verbs.[20] If you recall the strong verb paradigms, many of them, in both the *qal* and the derived stems, have a silent *shewa* under the first root consonant. When that first consonant is a נ, it may assimilate into the following consonant as a *dagesh forte*.

qal imperfect 3ms נטע
יִנְטַע ← *יִטְטַע ← *יִטַּע

Keep in mind that assimilation is the process of a consonant becoming the same as (or similar to) a nearby sound.[21] The middle form in the example above shows the נ assimilating to the ט. In cases like this, the two identical

---

17. JM, §73b–e.
18. GKC, §23a.
19. JM, §72b.
20. The III-נ in נתן will also often assimilate the final נ of the root when with a silent *shewa*. This phenomenon usually happens in the perfect conjugation with syllabic sufformatives (e.g., נָתַתִּי *qal* pf 1cs נתן, Gen 9:3). Other III-נ verbs tend to retain the III-נ in a silent *shewa* position except with the perfect 1cp or the imperfect feminine plurals when the sufformative begins with a נ (e.g., נִשַּׁעְנוּ *niphal* pf 1cp שׁען, 2 Chr 14:10; תִּשְׁבֹּנָּה *qal* impf 3fp שׁבן, Ezek 17:23).
21. Steven Fassberg, "Assimilation: Pre-Modern Hebrew" in *EHLL*, 1:223–24; Blau, *Phonology and Morphology of Biblical Hebrew*, §3.3.5.4, pp. 93–94.

consonants are written as a single consonant with *dagesh forte*. For ease, we will often speak of the נ "assimilating *as dagesh forte*" or "becoming *dagesh forte*."

2.3.3 *Vavs* and *Yods* in Weak Verbs[22]

ו and י are Hebrew consonants that demonstrate several morphological peculiarities.[23] Weak verbs with ו and י will likely be some of the more difficult forms we cover. The details of how ו and י behave can seem complicated, but once you get used to seeing their general tendencies, many of their final forms will become familiar. In general, the following characteristics can be expected.

2.3.3.1 *Vavs* and *Yods* May Drop Out

There is not a comparable situation in Hebrew morphology outside the weak verbs to serve as an analogy for ו and י dropping out. Depending on where the ו or י occurs in the verbal root (R_1, R_2, or R_3), it may be prone to drop out.[24] Additionally, this dropping out may depend on the conjugation. For most II-ו/י (biconsonantal) verbs, the perfect and the participle will often drop the middle ו or י vowel letter, but the other conjugations will retain it. We will address the specifics of these later but knowing that a ו or י may drop out will be half the battle when you are trying to parse a verb that has lost one of the distinguishing consonants of the verbal root.

qal perfect 3ms בוא

בוא ← בָּא

Notice in this example that the perfect conjugation of the II-ו/י verb בוא drops the middle ו and the thematic vowel becomes *qamets*. Again, while this may seem odd now, it is consistent for II-ו/י verbs.

Another place where ו and י may drop out is when they occur in the R_1

---

22. Throughout my Hebrew training, I have used modern Hebrew pronunciation, and therefore, I pronounce ו as *vav*. I realize that for morphological discussions, there is a phonological dissonance to call this consonant *vav*. The /v/ phoneme is not a semivowel that may contract, whereas /w/ will contract. In our discussions on Hebrew contractions (see e.g., §2.3.3.2 below), you will see the contraction transliterated as *aw → ô*. I recognize this dissonance, but have chosen to retain "*vav*" when writing out the consonant name (e.g., in *vav*-consecutive or *holem vav*). To help alleviate this dissonance to some degree, I have used the Hebrew character ו as often as possible so that if you learned classical pronunciation, you will read "*waw*" when you see the character ו.

23. GKC, §24; Blau, *Phonology and Morphology of Biblical Hebrew*, §3.4, pp. 96–105.

24. We will use the terminology of "dropping" since the ו or י is no longer visible in the final form at all (JM, §26a). However, see Blau (*Phonology and Morphology of Biblical Hebrew*, §3.4, pp. 96–105) and Reymond (*Intermediate Biblical Hebrew Grammar*, §5.16, p. 204) for evidence that these are diphthong and triphthong contractions where the long vowel superseded the contraction and became the only vowel remaining.

position.²⁵ This again feels abnormal compared to the strong verb paradigms, but it is consistent for certain weak verb types.

qal imperfect 3fs יֵשֵׁב

תֵּשֵׁב ⟵ *תִּוְשֵׁב

Notice that the י of the lexical form (יֵשׁב) becomes a ו in the hypothetical form on the right. This is why we call these I-ו/י verbs; the "original" consonant could be a ו or a י even though it is always a י in the lexicon.

Secondly, notice that the ו drops from the hypothetical form. In the final form the *hireq* preformative vowel has lengthened to *tsere*. This lengthening is the indicator that the original ו is missing. So, even though the consonant drops, there is still a morphological indicator it has done so. Those subtle indicators can help with identifying the root when parsing.

2.3.3.2 *Vavs* and *Yods* May Contract into Vowels

The second characteristic of ו and י is that they may contract into historically long vowels.²⁶ This concept should be partially familiar to us from the way inseparable prepositions may appear at the beginning of words.²⁷ When a preposition is added to a word that begins with י *and* a vocal *shewa*, that leaves two consecutive vocal *shewas* (Form 2 below). Hebrew does not allow this and initiates what my professor called a "*shewa* fight."²⁸ The *shewa* fight produced Form 3 below and set up the phonological scenario where a *hireq* followed by a *yod* with a silent *shewa* is prone to contract into the historically long *hireq yod* (Form 4).

בִּיהוּדָה ⟵ *בְּיְהוּדָה ⟵ *בְּיְהוּדָה ⟵ בְּ + יְהוּדָה
    4   3   2   1

This is a rather long way to explain Hebrew contractions, but the point is to show that they are not a feature of weak verbs that appear unexpectedly. Rather, contractions operate under principles that Hebrew students have encountered since learning the inseparable prepositions.

---

25. The I-ו will not be visible in the lexical form of I-ו/י verbs like the example, יֵשׁב. In the lexical form, original I-ו verbs will display the I-י.

26. GKC, §24b; JM, §26a–c. Hebrew may at times retain dipthongs or triphthongs with ו and י. For example, /ay/ at the end of סִינַי or the 1cs pronominal suffix on plural nouns like דְּבָרַי, "my words." The contractions we will discuss represent occasions when diphthongs resolve into a single vowel. This is sometimes called monophthongization. For an introduction to diphthongs and contractions, see Amnon Bruck, "Diphthongs: Pre-Modern Hebrew," *EHLL*, 1:738; Blau, *Phonology and Morphology of Biblical Hebrew*, §2.9.5, pp. 70–71; §3.4.2–§3.4.3, pp. 96–97.

27. GKC, §24c.

28. Fuller and Choi, *Invitation to Biblical Hebrew*, 35; cf. GKC, §28a; JM, §26b.

The following chart displays the more important contractions and should be memorized. We will study these in more detail in Chapter 4.[29]

Table 2.2: Common Contractions

יֹ◌ ← יְ◌	$aw \rightarrow ô$
וֹ◌ ← וְ◌	$uw \rightarrow û$
י◌ ← י◌	$ay \rightarrow ê$ (tsere)
י◌ ← י◌	$ay \rightarrow ê$ (segol)
י◌ ← י◌	$iy \rightarrow î$

2.3.4 Hebrew Tends to Avoid the Writing of Two Identical Consecutive Consonants

This weak verb feature applies to a specific type of weak verb called geminate verbs. Geminate verbal roots have identical second and third root consonants (e.g., הלל, סבב).[30] Since Hebrew prefers not to write the same identical consonant consecutively, these verbs can appear with only one of the geminate consonants represented, but with a *dagesh forte* as the following example illustrates.[31]

qal perfect 3cp סבב
סָבְבוּ ← סַבּוּ

The presence of the *dagesh forte* is not always permitted, and sometimes the verbal forms will place a *dagesh forte* in the first root consonant (transposition of gemination; *qal* imperfect 3mp—יִסֹּבּוּ), but the basic principle that Hebrew will avoid writing identical consecutive consonants will help you understand the appearance of the root in these verbal forms. We will address geminate verbs in Chapter 8.

2.3.5 Many Preformative Vowels Shift to A-Class Vowels

Based on the *qal* paradigm, we know that the *qal* preformative vowel for the imperfect is a *hireq* (יִקְטֹל) in most forms (not the 1cs). We also know in

---

29. For these contractions, and as I write them out in transliterations throughout the book, I have used SBL academic transliteration style in order to distinguish the resulting historically long vowels (SBL Press, *The SBL Handbook of Style*, 2nd ed. [Atlanta, GA: SBL Press, 2014], 56–57). Note the meaning of the transliterations in the grammatical abbreviations in the front matter.
30. JM, §82.
31. GKC, §67.

the *hiphil* and *niphal* perfect, the preformative vowels are *hireq* (הִoo and נִoo, respectively). However, in most weak verbs, the preformative vowel tends to shift to an a-class vowel, most often a *patah*. The place this will be most noticeable is in the *qal* imperfect. Since the *qal* paradigm is the first verbal paradigm students learn and it has the *hireq* preformative vowel in the imperfect, students naturally assume the *hireq* is "normal." However, historically, preformative vowels were a-class vowels and those will often resurface in certain weak verbs. For example, the *qal* imperfect 3ms of the II-ו root קוּם is יָקוּם with a *qamets* as the preformative vowel instead of the *hireq* of the standard *qal* paradigm (יִקְטֹל). Similarly, the *niphal* perfect 3ms of the strong root שׁמר would be נִשְׁמַר with the *hireq* preformative vowel. However, in a weak root like פוץ (II-ו), the *niphal* perfect 3cp is נָפֹצוּ (Gen 10:18) with the a-class preformative vowel. Like all of these general characteristics, we only want to introduce the idea here. We will discuss these details as they appear in later chapters.

2.4 The Strong Verb Equation

I have adapted the following discussion from Karl Kutz and Rebekah Josberger, and it is what they call the "Strong Verb Equation."[32] They use a mathematical analogy to show that two sides of an equation do not need to *look* exactly the same in order for both sides to be equal.

$$(2 + 2) = (2 + 1 + 1)$$

qal imperfect 2fs קטל = *qal* imperfect 2fs ישב

תִּקְטְלִי = תֵּשְׁבִי

If we take this mathematical analogy and apply it to weak verbs, we are showing that a weak verb formula (2+1+1) will not always look identical to our strong verb formula (2+2), and yet both verbs have the same sum total. In the example above, notice that both formulas add up to four. They are equal in sum. However, due to certain weak verb characteristics (1+1), both verbs or formulas do not necessarily *look* identical.

This is a good analogy to help conceptualize weak verb morphology. Weak verbs are not a radically new set of verbs that appear without any analogy to the strong verb. There are always similarities. However, because of the weak verb morphological features outlined in this chapter, enough differences exist

---

32. Kutz and Josberger, *Learning Biblical Hebrew*, 300–01.

that students are often frustrated with the proper identification of weak verb forms. If you know the strong verb system precisely, and add to it the weak verb characteristics introduced in this chapter, then you will be able to notice where the weak verb morphology differs from the strong verb even though you are looking at the same parsing on both sides of the "equation."

The following acronym attempts to provide some guidance on how approach the parsing weak verbs in the Hebrew Bible.

F.O.C.U.S.
1. **F**ind all the *similarities* you can between the weak verb and what you know from the strong verb paradigm and charts.
2. **O**bserve the *differences* between the weak verb and the strong verb paradigms.
3. **C**onsider the *general characteristics* of weak verbs in this chapter to determine what morphological changes have affected the spelling of the weak verb.
4. **U**se the *strong verb paradigms and derived stems chart* to narrow down the parsing of your weak verb.
5. **S**ay a prayer of thanksgiving that you just parsed a weak verb.

The key to this entire process is *knowing the strong verb paradigms and derived stems chart with absolute precision*. This knowledge will help you complete the steps of the F.O.C.U.S. acronym above.

In class, I often use the analogy of detecting counterfeit money. It has been said that those who are trained to find counterfeit money do not look at all the various types of counterfeit money. They study, in detail, what genuine bills *should* look like. Then, when they encounter divergences from genuine bills, they recognize them. They must learn the feel of the money, the look of the money, the detailed holographic images in the money, and also the various features that show up when the bill is held up to a light. If the strong verb is something as simple as the feel of the bill, then the weak verb characteristics in this chapter are all the minute details that help you recognize a "genuine" *piel* imperfect 3fs of ברך. We are not saying that weak verbs are "counterfeit verbs," but the illustration is helpful. If you know weak verb morphology at this level of detail, then recognizing weak verb forms will become significantly easier and increase both your fluency in the language and your joy in reading the Hebrew Bible.

CHAPTER 3

I-Guttural Verbs

3.1 Introduction

The first group of weak verbs that we will cover are what we will call I-guttural verbs. These roots are part of a group of verbs called guttural verbs because they have one or more guttural consonants in the verbal root. We will encounter the other guttural verbs (II- and III-guttural verbs) later in the book. While the guttural consonants will cause some vowel changes in the stem shells, all of the root consonants remain, and so determining preformatives and sufformatives *around* the root should be manageable.

The main things to keep in mind for all guttural verbs are the characteristics of gutturals from Chapter 2 (§2.3.1). These characteristics will guide the changes we observe in guttural verbs. It may be good to review the characteristics of gutturals before diving into this chapter.

As we focus in on I-guttural verbs, the primary guttural characteristics we will encounter are that (1) gutturals reject *dagesh forte* and (2) gutturals often take composite *shewas*. In a particular subset of I-guttural verbs, which we will refer to as I-א ōPV verbs, the א will quiesce with a silent *shewa* in the imperfect.[1]

3.2 Strong Forms of I-Guttural Verbs

Like most weak verbs, there are stems and conjugations in which the guttural in the first root position does not cause any changes. These include the *piel*, *pual*, and *hithpael*, the *qal* perfect, *qal* imperative 2fs and 2mp, *qal* participle, and *qal* infinitive absolute. None of these stems or conjugations display morphological changes in I-guttural verbs that differ from the strong verb shells. Note the following representative examples:

---

1. We will cover these in more depth in §3.5, but I-א ōPV verbs are verbs like אמר that get a *holem* (ō) as the **p**reformative **v**owel (PV). The name given to this subset of I-א verbs is my attempt to label them in a descriptive, memorable way.

יְחַפֵּשׂ	*piel* impf 3ms חפשׂ	Gen 31:35
מְחֻשָּׁקִים	*pual* ptc mp חשׁק	Exod 27:17
יִתְעַצֵּב	*hithpael* impf 3ms עצב	Gen 6:6
חָשַׂכְתָּ	*qal* pf 2ms חשׂךְ	Gen 22:12, 16
עִבְרִי	*qal* impv 2fs עבר	Isa 23:10
חִזְקוּ	*qal* impv 2mp חזק	Deut 31:6
חֹלֵם	*qal* ptc ms חלם	Gen 41:1
עָנוֹשׁ	*qal* inf abs ענשׁ	Exod 21:22

In all these forms, the strong verb shell patterns are unaffected by the morphological characteristics related to gutturals.

3.3 Gutturals (including ר) Reject *Dagesh Forte*

As we have seen previously, gutturals reject *dagesh forte* (cf. §2.3.1.1).[2] This principle includes the semi-guttural ר.[3] The only place that the standard *qal* paradigms or derived stems shells have a *dagesh forte* in the R_1 position is in the *niphal* imperfect, imperative, and infinitive.[4] As a reminder, here are those shells with the R_1 *dagesh forte*.

imperfect   יִּׂ〇〇
imperative   הִּׂ〇〇
infinitive[5]   הִּׂ〇〇

Since the alternative shell for the *niphal* infinitive (הִּׂ〇〇) appears in both the absolute and construct, this *dagesh forte* issue may appear with either of the *niphal* infinitives (הֵרָאוֹת inf **cstr** ראה, Lev 13:14; הֵרָאֹה inf **abs** ראה, 1 Sam 3:21).

When a guttural consonant rejects a *dagesh forte*, it often lengthens the preceding vowel by way of compensatory lengthening.[6] In this case, preformative *hireq* lengthens to a *tsere*. The progression looks something like this.

niphal imperfect 3ms עבר

יֵעָבֵר ← יִּעָבֵר*

---

2. GKC, §22b.
3. GKC, §22q; JM, §20a.
4. Blau, *Phonology and Morphology of Biblical Hebrew*, §4.3.7.1.1, p. 237; Reymond, *Intermediate Biblical Hebrew Grammar*, §5.13, p. 196.
5. This is only one form of the *niphal* infinitive shell, but it is the one with the R_1 *dagesh forte* that affects the I-guttural morphology.
6. Reymond, *Intermediate Biblical Hebrew Grammar*, §3.13, p. 196; GKC, §63h.

None of the standard verb shells in Table 1.1 have a *tsere* preformative vowel, and so we must determine why the *tsere* is there. Understanding (1) that gutturals reject *dagesh forte* and (2) the principle of compensatory lengthening allows one to "work backwards" (§1.6) to discover the standard *niphal* shells.

3.4 Gutturals Take Composite Vocal *Shewas*

The second thing to consider is that gutturals take composite (*ḥatef*) *shewas* instead of simple vocal *shewas*.[7] This happens most often when the standard verb shell has a simple vocal shewa under the R_1. Additionally, when an expected silent *shewa* in the strong verb shell is under the R_1, the *shewa* may "flip" to a composite vocal *shewa*. I-guttural verbs display both morphological changes.[8]

3.4.1 I-Gutturals Take Composite *Shewas* Rather Than a Simple Vocal *Shewa*

The forms that belong in this category have a simple vocal *shewa* under the R_1 in the original strong verb shell. These forms include the *qal* imperative (קְטֹל) and infinitive construct (קְטֹל). When the R_1 is a guttural letter, this simple vocal *shewa* becomes a composite *shewa* (עֲמֹד, Deut 5:31).[9] The composite *shewa* will be a *ḥatef patah* (ֲ) except for I-א verbs that will take a *ḥatef segol* (ֱ). The progression from a theoretical "strong" form to the final form with a vocal *shewa* may be represented as such:

$$\text{עֲבֹד} \leftarrow \text{*עְבֹד}$$

Examples from the Hebrew Bible include the following.

עֲבֹר	*qal* impv 2ms	עבר	Exod 17:5
חֲטֹא	*qal* inf cstr	חטא	Exod 9:34
הֲרֹג	*qal* inf cstr	הרג	Exod 2:15
אֲכֹל	*qal* inf cstr	אכל	Gen 43:32
אֱרֹב	*qal* impv 2ms	ארב	Judg 9:32

---

7. GKC, §10f, §22l. We will use the term "simple" vocal *shewa* (ְ) to refer to vocal *shewas* that are not "composite" vocal *shewas* (ֲ, ֱ, ֳ).
8. This is the aspect of I-guttural verbs that Joüon covers almost exclusively (JM, §68).
9. GKC, §63a; JM, §68a.

3.4.2 I-Gutturals Take a Composite *Shewa* Instead of a Silent *Shewa*

When I-guttural verbs have a silent *shewa* in the R_1 position in the original shell, the silent *shewa* may change to a composite vocal *shewa* (usually *hatef patah* [ֲ]). Because gutturals also prefer a-class vowels near them, the preformative vowel in the *qal* will also change to a *patah* (יַעֲבֹד *qal* impf 3ms עבד, Gen 25:23). For stative verbs, the preformative vowel and *hatef shewa* will be *segol* and *hatef segol*, respectively (יֶחֱזַק *qal* impf 1cp חזק, 1 Kgs 20:23). For both stative and nonstative 1cs forms (with א preformative), the preformative vowel and *hatef shewa* will be *segol* and *hatef segol* (אֶעֱבֹר *qal* impf 1cs עבר, Gen 30:32). Finally, any o-class verbs (/O thematic vowel) with a I-א will get a *segol* and *hatef segol* combination (תֶּאֱסֹף *qal* impf 2ms אסף, Deut 28:38).[10]

These forms may be helpful to see in a table format.

Table 3.1: Vowel Dissimilation of I-Guttural Verbs

Nonstative Verb	*qal* imperfect 3ms עמד	יַעֲמֹד
Stative Verb	*qal* imperfect 3ms חזק	יֶחֱזַק
Nonstative/Stative Verb imperfect 1cs	*qal* imperfect 1cs	אֶעֱמֹד (standard) אֶחֱזַק (stative)
Nonstative/O Verb with I-א	*qal* imperfect 3ms אסף	יֶאֱסֹף

The *qal* is the most complicated stem when it comes to shifting the simple vocal *shewa* to the composite *shewa*. The other stems more consistently follow the vowel class of the preformative vowel from the derived stems shells. For example, since the *hiphil* perfect shell has a *hireq* as the preformative vowel (הִקֹּטֹ), the *hatef shewa* will stay within that E/I vowel class. Hebrew does not have a "*hatef hireq*," so the only E/I vowel class composite *shewa* is the *hatef segol* (ֱ).[11] Indeed, that is the form we find in the *hiphil* perfect of I-guttural verbs: הֶעֱזִיב ← *הִעְזִיב. This phenomenon will also be true of the *niphal* perfect (נִקֹטֹ), one form of the *niphal* infinitive absolute (נִקֹטֹ), and the *niphal* participle (נִקֹטֹ), all with a *hireq* preformative. The *niphal*, however, is less consistent than the *hiphil* (e.g., נֶעֱבַדְתֶּם *niphal* pf 2mp עבד, Ezek 36:9; נֶעֱזָבוֹת *niphal* ptc fp עזב, Ezek 36:4; but see נַעֲלָמִים *niphal* ptc mp עלם, Ps 26:4).

---

10. For details of all these changes, see GKC, §63 and JM, §68.
11. Blau says that this shift to the *segol* in the preformative is due to partial assimilation (*Phonology and Morphology of Biblical Hebrew*, §3.3.3.3.3, p. 84). Cf. GKC, §63o–p.

Similarly, but with an a-class vowel, *hiphil* imperfect, imperative, infinitive, and participle exhibit a *pataḥ/ḥatef pataḥ* pattern in the preformative vowel and R₁, respectively (אַעֲבִיר *hiphil* impf 1cs עבר, Exod 33:19; תַּחֲרִים *hiphil* impf 2ms חרם, Deut 7:2). Again, these *shewas* follow the vowel class of the preformative vowel in the strong verb shell.

Finally, the *hophal*, which takes a *qamets ḥatuf* preformative vowel in the original shells (○○◌ְהָ; ○○◌ְיָ; ○○◌ְמָ), will "flip" the R₁ *shewa* to a *ḥatef qamets ḥatuf* (מָעֳמָד *hophal* ptc ms עמד, 1 Kgs 22:35). For *hophal* verbs with a I-guttural and a II-ו/י, it seems that the II-ו/י weakness takes precedence over the I-guttural and these preserve the original I-guttural in the R₂ position (הוּעַד *hophal* pf 3ms עוד, Exod 21:29; cf. §7.5). The same is true for verbs that are both I-guttural and geminate in the *hophal* (הוּחַל *hophal* pf 3ms חלל, Gen 4:26; יוּאָר *hophal* impf 3ms ארר, Num 22:6; cf. §8.4.5).

Here are a few more representative forms from the Hebrew Bible. Notice in these examples the consistency of the derived stems taking the *ḥatef shewa* of the same vowel class as the preformative vowel.

נֶחֱרֶפֶת	*niphal* ptc t-form	חרף	Lev 19:20
נֶעֱצָב	*niphal* pf 3ms	עצב	2 Sam 19:3
הֶעֱשַׁרְתִּי	*hiphil* pf 1cs	עשר	Gen 14:23
יַחֲטִיאוּ	*hiphil* impf 3mp	חטא	Exod 23:33
מַחֲרִיב	*hiphil* ptc ms	חרב	Judg 16:24
יָחֳרַם	*hophal* impf 3ms	חרם	Lev 27:29

While this may seem complicated, remember that you will be looking at final forms when parsing. In other words, you will not need to anticipate that the *niphal* perfect will flip the silent *shewa* under the I-guttural to a *ḥatef segol*. You will only need to recognize that the *segol* is in the E/I vowel class and understand that the strong verb preformative was a *hireq* (in that same vowel class). This will lead you to the *niphal* shell, ○○◌ְנ.

Again, keep in mind that all root consonants remain. Once you identify the root, the fact that the normal silent *shewa* has changed to a composite vocal *shewa* will likely not affect your parsing at all. If you can parse the word by using the root, preformatives, and sufformatives, then feel free to disregard the *shewa* gymnastics.

3.4.2.1 Why Is There Not a Composite *Shewa*?

One further element to consider with I-guttural verbs is that in certain situations, you will not see a composite *shewa* in the final form, but rather a full vowel.[12] This happens when the verbal form has a vocalic sufformative and the R₂ vowel reduces to a vocal *shewa*.[13] The form is thus left with two consecutive vocal *shewas* in the R₁ and R₂, resulting in what we are calling a "*shewa* fight."[14] This example with עמד demonstrates the progression.

qal imperfect 3mp עמד

יַעַמְדוּ ← יַעֲמְדוּ* ← יַעֲמֹד* ← יַעְמֹד*
Final Form   Vocalic Sufformative   "Flip" to Composite   "Strong" Form
Shewa Fight   = R₂ Reduction   *Shewa*

3.4.3 I-Gutturals May Retain a Silent *Shewa*

In some cases, the I-gutturals may keep the silent *shewa* of the original shell. However, when the I-guttural verb keeps the silent *shewa*, *the preformative vowel will still shift based on what the shewa would have been if the I-guttural had flipped.*

qal imperfect 3ms חסר (Deut 8:9)
תֶּחְסַר* ← תֶּחֱסַר* ← תֶּחְסַר
    3   2   1

Form 1 is the "strong" form of the *qal* imperfect with the *hireq* preformative from the original paradigm. In Form 2, *if* the I-guttural flipped the *shewa* to a *hatef segol*, the preformative vowel would follow suit, becoming a *segol* also. Form 3 shows the ח in first root position retaining the silent *shewa*, but with the preformative vowel changing as if the *shewa* had flipped. The silent *shewa* is retained, but this pathway shows where the *segol* preformative vowel originated.

This same phenomenon will be true across verbal stems and with different guttural letters whenever the I-guttural retains the silent *shewa*.

---

12. GKC, §63g.
13. JM, §22c.
14. Reymond calls this an epenthetic vowel, which is the more technical term for the resulting vowel of a *shewa* fight (*Intermediate Biblical Hebrew Grammar*, §5.13, p. 196). This only happens when the expected silent *shewa* of the stem shell "flips" to a composite *shewa*. Some I-guttural verbs retain the silent *shewa* and therefore do not warrant the *shewa* fight (יֶחְזְקוּ Isa 28:22; see also §3.4.3). For "*shewa* fight," see Fuller and Choi, *Invitation to Biblical Hebrew*, 14, n. 5.

Some I-guttural verbs may retain the R₁ composite *shewa*. This may happen when the syllable retains the prosodic accent as a pausal form and therefore does not reduce the thematic vowel with a vocalic sufformative (יַעֲבֹדוּ *qal* impf 3mp עבד, Gen 15:14). Additionally, doubly weak I-guttural and III-ה verbs will not display this epenthetic vowel since the vocalic sufformative attaches directly to the R₂ (יַעֲלוּ *qal* impf 3ms עלה, Exod 19:13). The *hiphil* stem never reduces the R₂ vowel, and so even with vocalic sufformatives, it will also retain the *hatef shewa* in I-gutturals (יַחֲלִיפוּ *hiphil* impf 3mp חלף, Isa 40:31). Finally, there may simply be forms that retain the *hatef shewa* in the I-guttural without a clear explanation (יֶחֱזְקוּ *qal* impf 3mp חזק, 2 Sam 10:11).

The following examples provide the progressions to highlight the change in the preformative vowel.

נֶהְפַּךְ	*niphal* perfect 3ms הפך	Exod 7:15	נֶהְפַּךְ ← נֶהֱפַךְ* ← נֶהְפַּךְ*
יָאסֹר	*qal* imperfect 3ms אסר	1 Kgs 20:14	יָאסֹר ← יֶאֱסֹר* ← יֶאְסֹר*
נֶעְלַם	*niphal* perfect 3ms עלם	Lev 5:3	נֶעְלַם ← נֶעֱלַם* ← נֶעְלַם*
הַעְתַּרְתִּי	*hiphil* perfect 1cs עתר	Exod 8:25	הַעְתַּרְתִּי ← הַעֲתַרְתִּי* ← הַעְתַּרְתִּי*
הָחְבָּאוּ	*hophal* perfect 3cp (pausal) חבא	Isa 42:22	הָחְבָּאוּ ← הָחֳבָּאוּ* ← הָחְבָּאוּ*

3.5 I-א ōPV Verbs

While we are covering I-guttural verbs, it is important to cover a subset of I-א verbs. We will call this subset I-א ōPV verbs and only six roots fit into this category.[15] We will refer to these as I-א ōPV verbs because their distinctive morphology involves a shift to an o-class preformative vowel (*holem*). They can be memorized using this mnemonic (or a variety of others that Hebrew professors have proposed):

He *said* (אמר): "I am *willing* (אבה) to *seize* (אחז) and to *eat* (אכל) what I *bake* (אפה) even if I *perish* (אבד)."

Table 3.2: I-א ōPV Verbs by Occurrence

Verb	Definition	Total Occurrences[16]	*Qal* Imperfect
אמר	"to say"	5,307x	250x
אכל	"to eat"	810x	298x
אבד	"to perish"	186x	40x
אחז	"to seize"	110x	12x
אבה	"to want/be willing"	54x	11x
אפה	"to bake"	13x	2x

---

15. For more on these forms, see Reymond, *Intermediate Biblical Hebrew Grammar*, §5.13, p. 196; Blau, *Phonology and Morphology of Biblical Hebrew*, §4.3.8.2, p. 240; Suchard, *Development of Biblical Hebrew Vowels*, §4.2.2; GKC, §68; JM, §73.

16. These statistics of occurrences in the Hebrew Bible are based on the WIVU/ETCBC morphology and include all conjugations. The *qal* imperfect is the conjugation in which these verbs display this particular "weakness."

The weaknesses that these verbs display involve the preformative vowel shifting to a *holem* and dissimilation[17] of the thematic vowel depending on the form.[18] Many scholars attribute the appearance of the *holem* preformative vowel to what is known as the Canaanite Shift.

3.5.1 The "Canaanite Shift"

The Canaanite shift is the name given to the phenomenon of long /a/ vowels changing to long /o/ vowels.[19] In these I-א ōPV verbs, the *qal* imperfect preformative vowels "shift" from what we would expect to be a historical /a/ vowel to an /o/ vowel. The theoretical progression assumes the preformative vowels were historically /a/ (*יְאָמַר) as we have seen elsewhere. When the I-א quiesced in the silent *shewa* position, the preformative vowel lengthened to a long *qamets* (*יָאמַר) according to the principle of compensatory lengthening. This long /a/ vowel then "shifted" during the historical development of the language to the long /o/ *holem* (יֹאמַר).[20]

יֹאמַר	←	*יָאמַר	←	*יְאָמַר
Canaanite Shift to *Holem*		Quiescent א and Compensatory Lengthening		Historical /a/ Preformative

This preformative vowel shift occurs with the *qal* imperfect forms of these six verbs (e.g., *qal* imperfect 3fs תֹּאמַר). The preformative and suffixative consonants will remain unchanged.

One form to note is the *qal* imperfect 1cs.[21] In this form, both the

---

17. Dissimilation is "a linguistic process in which one of two nearby similar sounds changes with regard to one or more of these sounds' shared features" (Steven Fassberg, "Dissimilation" in *EHLL*, 1:766–67). For our purposes here, dissimilation describes the fact that the thematic vowels for this subset of I-א verbs are inconsistent and change depending on the phonetic context (see §3.5.2 below).

18. Qimḥi observes several exceptions when אח in the imperfect does not get *holem* preformative vowel (e.g., וַיֶּאֱהַב, Judg 16:3, and תֶּאֱהַב, Eccl 7:18). Qimḥi further comments that several other verbs "share with these this peculiarity only occasionally, e.g. אהב *qal* impf 1cs אהב, Mal 1:2," (Qimḥi, §35b).

19. Blau, *Phonology and Morphology of Biblical Hebrew*, §3.5.9.2, p. 136; John Huehnergard, "Canaanite Shift" in *EHLL*, 1:395.

20. It is difficult to accept the following explanation wholesale, but it is helpful for understanding the derivation of the long *holem* in these forms. Blau comments that the Canaanite Shift happened on stressed /a/ vowels that became stressed /o/ vowels (Blau, *Phonology and Morphology of Biblical Hebrew*, §3.3.4.2.1, p. 87). For these I-א ōPV verbs, the stress indeed falls on the preformative in the *vav*-consecutive forms. However, all other forms, pausal forms and standard forms, shift to the *holem* preformative vowel even when it is unstressed. As with other weak verbs, the theoretical derivation is only conjectural. The important thing to know is that the final forms get a *holem* as the preformative vowel.

21. Blau, *Phonology and Morphology of Biblical Hebrew*, §3.3.4.2.1, p. 87.

preformative consonant and the first root consonant are א. Since א does not take a *dagesh forte* to represent doubling, only one א remains in the final spelling of the form. The morphological progression may be represented like this. The gray font follows the preformative so that you can easily see that the א of the root has dropped out.

אֹמַר	←	*אֹאמַר	←	*אַאמֹר	←	*אַאְמֹר	←	*אֲאֱמֹר
Drop I-א of the Root		Dissimilation of Theme Vowel		"Canaanite Shift"		Quiescent א Compensatory Lengthening		"Strong" Form

When parsing, you will not need to explain this progression, but you will need to be able to recognize that אֹמַר is a *qal* imperfect 1cs of אמר, that has dropped the I-א consonant.[22] Be careful not to confuse this form with the *qal* active participle ms. The thematic vowel will distinguish them (אֹמַר *qal* impf 1cs [*pataḥ* theme vowel]; אֹמֵר *qal* act ptc ms [*tsere* theme vowel]).

This same preformative vowel phenomenon will be true of the cohortative 1cs. אמר occurs twice as a cohortative, once in Gen 46:31 and again in Ps 42:10. The form in Ps 42:10 has the preformative *holem* written fully (אוֹמְרָה). אכל occurs as a cohortative four times (אֹכְלָה, Gen 27:25; Deut 12:20; אֹכֵלָה as a pausal form in Gen 27:4, 7), and אחז occurs once as a cohortative (אֹחֲזָה, Song 7:9).

3.5.2 Dissimilation of Thematic Vowels

The dissimilation of thematic vowels for I-א ōPV verbs will almost never be the deciding factor on parsing these forms. But for a complete morphological study of these weak verbs, the following table provides the anticipated dissimilation of these thematic vowels. A change in thematic vowel may be occasioned by prefixing the *vav*-consecutive or by the verb appearing as a pausal form.[23]

---

22. Recognizing this form may take some time and exposure to become comfortable, but it is not a form you will encounter often. The *qal* imperfect 1cs of אמר only occurs seventeen times in the Hebrew Bible. The *qal* imperfect 1cs of אכל only occurs ten times. No other I-א ōPV verbs occur as a *qal* imperfect 1cs.

23. Qimḥi, §35d. A pausal form is a verbal form with a "heavy" disjunctive accent, most often a *silluq* or an *athnaḥ*. In Table 3.3, I have used the *athnaḥ* as the representative disjunctive accent.

Table 3.3:[24] I-א ōPV Verbs Thematic Vowel Dissimilation

	Standard	*Vav*-Consecutive
Nonpausal Forms	יֹאמַר	וַיֹּאמֶר
	יֹאכַל	וַיֹּאחֶז
	יֹאבַד	וַיֹּאכַל
	(יֹאחֵז)	וָאֹמַר (1cs only)
Pausal Forms	יֹאמֵר	וַיֹּאמֵר
	יֹאכֵל	וַיֹּאכֵל
	יֹאבֵד	

There is no need to memorize this table, but it can be helpful to have on hand for reference.

3.6 Conclusion

For I-guttural verbs, the primary characteristics of gutturals that we must account for are (1) gutturals reject *dagesh forte* and (2) gutturals often take composite *shewas*. In a specific subset of I-guttural verbs (I-א ōPV verbs), we see the characteristic that the guttural א may quiesce. It is important to remember that the spelling features described in this chapter are neither random nor haphazard. Weak verbs with guttural consonants inflect based on a few consistent and predictable patterns. I-guttural verb forms may look different from strong verbs, but after learning a few morphological principles, I-guttural verbs will soon become easier to identify and therefore easier to read.

---

24. This table is adapted from Fuller and Choi, *Invitation to Biblical Hebrew*, 203.

CHAPTER 4

I-ו/י Verbs

4.1 Introduction

In this chapter, we will consider I-ו/י verbs as two separate types of weak verbs. We will first address originally I-ו verbs and then originally I-י verbs. For both originally I-ו and I-י verbs, the lexical form will have a י in the R_1 position. For example, ישב, יצא, יטב, and יצר are all I-ו/י verbs. The way to know if they were originally a I-ו or originally a I-י is to observe their morphology in certain inflected forms.

It is slightly unfortunate that the י took precedent in the lexical root because the majority of I-ו/י verbs are originally I-ו roots. One way to remember which lexical forms are originally I-י verbs is to memorize this mnemonic. As one would expect, there are some exceptional forms, but this mnemonic will guide you to the most common original I-י roots.

> It is *good* (יטב) and *right* (ישר) to *advise* (יעץ) a parent to *nurse* (ינק) a baby when he *wakes* (יקץ) and *wails* (ילל). Then use your *right hand* (ימן) to burp him so that he can *sleep* (ישן).[1]

With originally I-י verbs, the original י is usually retained as a *hireq yod* in the imperfect (e.g., יִיטַב *qal* impf 3ms יטב, Deut 4:40).

Some I-ו/י verbs show what we may call a mixed morphology. For example, יבש inflects with characteristics of a I-י verb in the *qal* (e.g., יִיבַשׁ *qal* impf 3ms, Isa 19:7), but in the *hiphil*, it inflects like a I-ו (e.g., הוֹבַשְׁתָּ *hiphil* pf 2ms, Ps 74:15). We will not focus on these idiosyncratic examples.

---

[1] This mnemonic is adapted from Kutz and Josberger, *Learning Biblical Hebrew*, 327, n. 1. I added יעץ to the mnemonic based on Fuller and Choi, *Invitation to Biblical Hebrew*, 241. Jouön's list includes seven verbs as "primitive" I-י verbs: ימן, ילל, יקץ, יטב, ישר, ינק, יבש (JM, §76d). While determining exactly which roots are true primitive I-י or I-ו verbs is tricky, knowing the most common original I-י verbs with this mnemonic will aid with recognizing morphological patterns.

Knowing, with precision, whether a verb is *originally* a I-י or a I-ו is overall unnecessary for parsing purposes. Knowing what morphological phenomena have led to the final form will be what aids the recognition and parsing of I-ו/י verbs.

4.1.1 Contractions

One of the main things to learn with all ו/י verbs is the concept of contraction (cf. §2.3.3.2).² Contractions may occur with both the semivowels, ו and י. For our purposes, we will discuss only the vowel contractions that are produced when certain vowels are adjacent to a ו or י and produce the familiar historically long vowels associated with the ו and י (יֹ; יֶ; יֵ; וֹ; וּ).³ A thorough knowledge of these contractions will help us to "unravel" the ו/י final forms so that we can discover the original verbal shell of the strong verb derived stems.

The following table should be memorized for ו/י contractions.

Table 4.1: Common Contractions

וֹ ← וְ	$aw \rightarrow \hat{o}$
וּ ← וְ	$uw \rightarrow \hat{u}$
יֵ ← יְ	$ay \rightarrow \hat{e}$ (tsere)
יֶ ← יְ	$ay \rightarrow \hat{e}$ (segol)
יִ ← יְ	$iy \rightarrow \hat{\imath}$

4.1.2 I-ו/י General Principles

For I-ו/י verbs, the general principles relate to ו or י with a *shewa* in the strong verb shell. The first general principle to note is that the original ו/י may contract. Notice in the contractions in Table 4.1, the original ו/י has a silent *shewa*. The absence of a vowel sound under the ו or י creates the phonological conditions for contraction. A second general principle is that the original ו may drop out.

---

2. This phenomenon may also be called fusion or coalescence.
3. Historically long vowels are what we will call the vowels that are comprised of a vowel and consonant combination such that the vowel itself is the vowel-consonant combination. The historically long vowels are *tsere yod* (יֵ), *segol yod* (יֶ), *hireq yod* (יִ), *holem vav* (וֹ), *shureq* (וּ), and *qamets he* (הָ). These are sometimes called vowel markers or *matres lectionis*.

The overarching principle for I-ו/י verbs can be summarized like this: The original ו or י consonant in I-ו/י roots will often contract to a historically long vowel and will sometimes drop out. As we work through I-ו and I-י verbs, respectively, we will see this principle in action.

Finally, anytime we see the ו or י with a vowel or *dagesh forte* (or both), the form is strong, namely, the ו or י serves as a consonant in the word and not a vowel.[4] Here are some examples of those strong forms with consonantal ו or י. In each of these, there is no contraction or loss of the original I-ו/י. These appear just like strong forms even though they are technically weak roots.

יְיַשֵּׁר	*piel* impf 3ms ישר	Prov 3:6	
מְיֻשָּׁר	*pual* ptc ms ישר	1 Kgs 6:35	
יִוָּלֵד	*niphal* impf 3ms ילד	Gen 17:17	ילד *is an original I-ו*
יִיָּרֶה	*niphal* impf 3ms ירה	Exod 19:13[5]	
אֶתְוַדַּע	*hithpael* impf 1cs ידע	Num 12:6	ידע *is an original I-ו*

4.2 Original I-ו Verbs

In I-ו verbs, the original ו will contract, and other times it will drop out.[6] In both cases, this will generally happen when the original ו has either a silent or vocal *shewa* in the strong verb shell.

4.2.1 Original I-ו Contracts

In the following sections, we will discuss the derived stems in which the I-ו will contract according to the typical contractions in Table 4.1. We will find in the examples provided in each section that these contractions are rather consistent within each derived stem.

4.2.1.1 *Niphal*

In the *niphal* perfect and participle, the R_1 consonant has a silent *shewa* in the strong verb shell (נְOOO). This shell produces the conditions for a I-ו to contract. Remember that in many weak verbs, the historical preformative vowels were a-class vowels (§2.3.5). This means that the *niphal* (*naphal**) is

---

4. GKC, §69i.
5. ירה is not in the I-י mnemonic, but here inflects like an original I-י. This is the only occurrence of the *niphal* impf of ירה in the HB, and so the form is unique.
6. JM, §75a; Qimḥi, §36a.

set up for the *aw* → *ô* contraction in its final forms.⁷ The tables of examples in this section show the progression of the contractions to help solidify that concept.

   נוֹתַר ← *נוְתַר *niphal* pf 3ms יתר Exod 10:15
    ô ← *aw*
   נוֹלָדִים ← *נוְלָדִים *niphal* ptc mp ילד Gen 48:5
    ô ← *aw*

This phenomenon only occurs in the *niphal* perfect and participle. In the *niphal* imperfect, imperative, and infinitive, the R₁ has a *dagesh* and will most often be a strong form. If you look at the derived stems chart (Table 1.1) you may think that one of the options for the *niphal* infinitive would fit this phenomenon having a silent *shewa* under the R₁ consonant (נְOOO). However, this shell only applies to the *niphal* infinitive absolute and there are no *niphal* infinitives absolute of I-ו/י verbs in the Hebrew Bible.

4.2.1.2 *Hiphil*

In the *hiphil*, the I-ו would have a silent *shewa* throughout all conjugations. Once the historical preformative vowel becomes /a/ (הַOOO—'*haphil*'), the final forms will experience the *aw* → *ô* contraction.

   הוֹלִיד ← *הַוְלִיד *hiphil* pf 3ms ילד Gen 11:27 (2x)
    ô ← *aw*
   יוֹרִישׁ ← *יַוְרִישׁ *hiphil* impf 3ms ירשׁ Josh 3:10
    ô ← *aw*
   הוֹרֵד ← *הַוְרֵד *hiphil* impv 2ms ירד Judg 7:4
    ô ← *aw*
   הוֹעִיל ← *הַוְעִיל *hiphil* inf cstr יעל Jer 7:8
    ô ← *aw*
   מוֹכִיחִים ← *מַוְכִיחִים *hiphil* ptc mp יכח Prov 24:25
    ô ← *aw*

Note that the contraction can be written defectively with *holem* instead of *holem vav*. (e.g., וַתֹּסֶף *hiphil* impf 3fs יסף, Gen 4:2; אֹסִף *hiphil* impf 1cs יסף, Gen 8:21).

---

7. Suchard, *The Development of Biblical Hebrew Vowels*, §4.2.3, p. 250.

4.2.1.3 *Hophal*

In the *hophal*, the concept of contraction is the same, but now it is the $uw \rightarrow \hat{u}$ contraction.[8] For the *hophal*, the morphology adjusts to what we may call a *huphal*.[9] Again, remember to think more in terms of vowel classes and not actual vowels. This will help you to understand the $uw \rightarrow \hat{u}$ contraction as still within the *hophal* stem. Due to infrequency, we did not learn strong verb shells for the *hophal* imperative or infinitive, so the following examples only include the perfect, imperfect, and participle.

הוּרַד ← *הֻוְרַד ← *הָוְרַד   *hophal* pf 3ms ירד   Gen 39:1
$\hat{u}$ ← uw [*huphal*] ← *hophal*

תּוּקַד ← *תֻּוְקַד ← *תָּוְקַד   *hophal* impf 3fs יקד   Lev 6:2
$\hat{u}$ ← uw [*huphal*] ← *hophal*

מוּצָק ← *מֻוְצָק ← *מָוְצָק   *hophal* ptc ms יצק   1 Kgs 7:23
$\hat{u}$ ← uw [*huphal*] ← *hophal*

4.2.2 Parsing—Working Backwards

Now that we understand that these vowel changes are a result of contraction, it is important to know how to implement this information into parsing I-ו weak verbs. Understanding these contractions will allow you to work "backwards" and discover the original shells. For example, now that we have seen $aw \rightarrow \hat{o}$ as a standard contraction, we can work backwards and "unravel" the contraction.

הֳOOֹO ← *הוֹשִׁיב ← *הַוְשִׁיב ← הוֹשִׁיב
Hiphil Perfect Shell   Historic /a/ aw $\hat{o}$
　　　　　　　　　Preformative Back　　　　(Final Form)
　　　　　　　　　to /i/ (§2.3.5)

"Unraveling" the contraction will be an important part of the process for parsing I-ו verbs. As we have said before, this method requires memorizing the strong verb shells in addition to understanding contractions. By working backwards, these contractions will uncover the correct parsing.

---

8. Suchard, *The Development of Biblical Hebrew Vowels*, §4.2.3, p. 250; GKC, §69w; JM, §75a.

9. *Huphal* is not a unique Hebrew derived stem. The term is used here, and will be used throughout, only as a way to describe the morphology of the *hophal* when the preformative vowel is ו in the final form.

4.2.3 Original I-ו May Drop Out

In certain morphological situations, the I-ו will flee.[10] This change can occur when the ו has a silent *shewa* (e.g., *qal* impf) or even when it has a vocal *shewa* (e.g., *qal* impv and inf cstr).

4.2.3.1 *Qal* Imperfect

In the *qal* imperfect, the I-ו will flee with a silent *shewa* in the R_1 position. It does not contract.[11] When this happens, the key to recognizing that a I-ו is missing is that the preformative vowel lengthens by compensation.[12] The following progression demonstrates the loss of the original I-ו.

qal imperfect 3ms יש׳ב

יֵשֵׁב ← *יִוְשֵׁב ← *יִוְשֵׁב ← *יִיְשֵׁב

Lengthened Preformative Vowel	I-ו Drops Out	"Original" I-ו Restored	Lexical Form w/I-י
4	3	2	1

In Form 1, the lexical root יש׳ב has the *qal* imperfect shell superimposed on it. In Form 2, the original I-ו is restored but the same *qal* imperfect 3ms shell remains superimposed. In Form 3, the arrow shows the original I-ו "dropping out." Finally, Form 4 shows the lengthening of the preformative vowel to a *tsere*. Notice that by the time we get to Form 4, the י that remains is the י of the preformative and *not* the י of the root. The presence of the preformative will be more obvious outside of the third masculine forms when the preformative

---

10. GKC, §69b–c, f–h.

11. Reymond proposes that the preformative vowel (*tsere* in most cases) "would seem to be due to the contraction of an earlier diphthong, **yaytibu > *yēšeb*" (Reymond, *Intermediate Biblical Hebrew Grammar*, §5.14, p. 198).

12. Blau says the prefix-tense for original I-ו verbs (after loss of the original I-ו) should be **yašib* (יָשִׁב) with an a-class preformative vowel according to Barth's law (§4.3.8.4.12, p. 246). He argues the shift to the *tsere* preformative vowel in the final form (יֵשֵׁב) is due to vowel assimilation, and is preserved even in open propretonic syllables where one would expect the vowel to reduce to a vocal *shewa* (e.g., יְדָעֻנּוּ, Jer 17:9). For a discussion on whether original I-ו verbs originate from triconsonantal or biconsonantal roots, see Blau, *Phonology and Morphology of Biblical Hebrew*, §4.3.8.4, pp. 243–45. He points out that what appears to be biconsonantal evidences are the prefix-tense [imperfect] (יֵשֵׁב) and the infinitive construct (שֶׁבֶת) but he says these can be explained by the imperative שֵׁב, which also only has two root consonants. In a subsequent note (§4.3.8.4.1n, p. 244), he says that if the *qal* imperative was originally monosyllabic, then even with the initial ו, the R_1 phoneme would be unstable (וְשֵׁב) (see the discussion of the I-ו dropping in the *qal* imperatives of I-ו verbs in §4.2.3.2 of this book). Blau also points out in the same note that due to the exclamatory nature of imperatives, they may have tended to be shortened anyway. Regardless of the position one holds on the origin of these forms, we see that the original I-ו effectively drops out in the final forms in the Hebrew Bible.

is א, ה, or נ. The best way to recognize that an original I-ו is missing is the lengthening of the preformative vowel.

For most of these weak verbs, we are trying to decipher how we arrived at the final form. We do not necessarily need to memorize the diachronic development, but we do need to be able to "unravel" the verbal form so that we can decipher the strong verb shell from which it derived. In this example, the thing to recognize is not a contraction, but rather compensatory lengthening of the preformative vowel. You can then "unravel" this morphological change backwards through the steps above and arrive at a root of ישׁב and a shell of ○○◌ֹ֯, namely, the *qal* imperfect 3ms.

4.2.3.2 *Qal* Imperative

In the *qal* imperative, there are two ways to consider how we arrive at these final forms. The primary way we can construct the imperative is to remove the preformative from the imperfect. If we use ישׁב with the second person forms for the imperative, all we do is remove the preformatives and we have the I-ו imperatives. Table 4.2 demonstrates this with the representative root ישׁב.

Table 4.2: I-ו Imperative Progression

	Qal Imperative	*Qal* Imperfect
2ms	שֵׁב ←	תֵּשֵׁב
2fs	שְׁבִי ←	תֵּשְׁבִי
2mp	שְׁבוּ ←	תֵּשְׁבוּ
2fp	שֵׁבְנָה ←	תֵּשֵׁבְנָה

The second way to think about I-ו imperative verbs is to consider that a I-ו with a vocal *shewa* will drop out.[13] We may even consider this the "rule" for I-ו verbs in the imperative even though they can be explained pedagogically by dropping the preformative in the imperfect. If we begin these forms with the I-ו root (וּשׁב), then the *qal* imperative shell will leave a vocal *shewa* in the I-ו position (וְשֵׁב). Hence, this would leave the form שֵׁב for the 2ms imperative, which matches Table 4.2 above.

שֵׁב ← *וְשֵׁב

---

13. Gesenius calls this aphaeresis in the imperative and infinitive construct (GKC, §69b.1.B). See also JM, §75a.(3).

The reason we need this new rule is because we will see the I-ו drop out in the infinitive construct even when there are no preformatives in an analogous form. It is likely that historically all of these forms were related in some way, but for pedagogical explanations, we simply need to see that what would have been a I-ו with a vocal *shewa* is now gone. Hence, a second way to think about the I-ו *qal* imperatives is that the I-ו with a vocal *shewa* will drop out.

Either of these pathways for learning the I-ו imperatives will work. The key, as before, is to be able to recognize that שֵׁב is from the root ישׁב (וְשׁב) and "unravel" that form knowing that the I-ו has fled.[14]

4.2.3.3 *Qal* Infinitive Construct

The *qal* infinitive construct of I-ו verbs is similar to *and* different from the previous examples. In the *qal* infinitive construct, the I-ו will also drop out. If we overlay the original *qal* infinitive construct shell (קְטֹל; ○ְ○○) on the weak root, the I-ו would have a vocal *shewa* (וְשֵׁב). This creates the conditions similar to the 2ms imperative above. However, with the infinitive construct, not only does the original I-ו flee, but the form adds a ת to the end and then mimics a segolate vowel pattern (segolization).[15] The following progression is not an argument for the historical development of the infinitive construct. It simply illustrates the explanation given here.

שֶׁבֶת	←	*שֶׁבְת	←	*שִׁבְתְּ	←	*שֵׁב	←	וְשֵׁב	←	○ְ○○
Final Form		Segolization		ת Added		Original I-ו Dropped		Shell Superimposed		Original Shell

---

14. In imperative forms that are connected to another word by a *maqqef*, the *tsere* vowel will reduce to a *segol* in a closed and unaccented syllable (e.g., שֶׁב־שָׁם *qal* impv 2ms ישׁב + *vav*-conjunctive, Gen 35:1). Qimḥi, 36d.

15. Grammarians have a variety of explanations for the infinitive construct. Gesenius argues these forms come from an original base *šibh* with an added "feminine ending (ת)" that lengthens the vowel pattern to a segolate pattern as compensation for the loss of the I-ו (GKC, §69c). Gesenius also comments, however, that the weak form שְׁבָה for the infinitive construct has a ground-form *šibt* that appears with suffixes—שִׁבְתִּי (GKC, §69m; cf. Suchard, *The Development of the Biblical Hebrew Vowels*, §4.2.3, p. 250). Joüon comments that the original form of the *qal* infinitive construct is *šib* with a feminine ת making it *šibt* with subsequent segolization (JM, §75a.[3]). Reymond (*Intermediate Biblical Hebrew Grammar*, §5.14, p. 199) simply comments that the infinitive is from the *qilt* base resulting in a segolized form. Blau (*Phonology and Morphology of Biblical Hebrew*, §4.3.8.4.13, pp. 246–47) and Suchard (*Development of Biblical Hebrew Vowels*, §4.2.3, p. 250) also reference the feminine ending (ת) and an original form *šibt* that changed to *šabt* by Philippi's Law and then resulted in segolization (שֶׁבֶת).

There are some attested forms where the feminine תָ is retained in the *qal* infinitive construct of I-ו verbs even when the initial ו is elided (e.g., לְדֵעָה from ידע in Exod 2:4). First Samuel 4:19 has an exceptional form of the infinitive construct of ילד as לַת. Gesenius explains this is likely due to the lack of segolization and the assimilation of the R₃ ד into the feminine ת (GKC, §69m). Since the ת is at the end of the word, it will not display the *dagesh forte* common to assimilation.

Infinitive Construct

שֶׁבֶת	qal inf cstr ישב	Gen 13:6 (2x)	
רֶשֶׁת	qal inf cstr ירש	Lev 20:24	
דַּעַת	qal inf cstr ידע	Deut 4:35	*pataḥ segolization with guttural* ע
לֶדֶת	qal inf cstr ילד	Zeph 2:2	

4.2.4 *Vav*-Consecutives and Jussives of I-ו Verbs

When *vav*-consecutives are added to imperfects (*vayyiqtol*) of I-ו verbs, they often display a retraction of the accent to the preformative consonant.[16] This occurs primarily in the *qal* and in the *hiphil* but is also possible in the *niphal*.[17]

Form 1 is the final form of the imperfect 3ms of יֵשׁ. In Form 2, the *vav*-consecutive has been added, but the accent remains on the final syllable to show the progression. Form 3 demonstrates the retraction of the accent to the preformative consonant. Notice in the final form that when the accent retracts, the final syllable is closed and unaccented and requires a short vowel. It therefore shortens the *tsere* thematic vowel to a *segol* (וַיֵּשֶׁב).

qal imperfect 3ms + *vav*-consecutive ישב

יֵשֵׁב ← וַיֵּשֵׁב* ← וַיֵּשֶׁב
  3   2   1

Unlike the apocopated III-ה verbs (cf. §9.4.2), the jussives of I-ו verbs do not display this accent retraction as often. Out of 219 I-ו/י jussives in the tagged *Lexham Hebrew Bible*, only three display the retraction of the accent. These three seem to be exceptions and not the general rule for I-ו/י verbs.

Vav-Consecutives

וַתֵּלֶד	qal impf 3fs ילד + *vav*-cons	Gen 4:1	
וַיֵּדַע	qal impf 3ms ידע + *vav*-cons	Gen 8:11	*pataḥ thematic vowel with III-guttural* ע
וַיּוֹלֶד	hiphil impf 3ms ילד + *vav*-cons	Gen 11:10	*some hiphil forms also retract the accent*
וַתֵּרֶד	qal impf 3fs ירד + *vav*-cons	1 Sam 25:23	

---

16. Reymond, *Intermediate Biblical Hebrew Grammar*, §5.14, p. 199; "Appendix," p. 284; GKC, §69v.

17. Because the *niphal* imperfect shell has a *dagesh forte* in the R₁, the I-ו/י *vav*-consecutive does not regularly retract the accent. In fact, it only occurs with יחל in Gen 8:10, 12 and in 1 Sam 13:8. The two occurrences in Gen 8:10, 12 are worth noting. Gen 8:10 has וַיָּחֶל whereas Gen 8:12 has וַיִּיָּחֶל (Qimḥi, §36f). Genesis 8:12 looks more like what we would expect from the *niphal* shell with a י as the R₁. The thing to notice in these forms, however, is the retraction of the accent in the *vav*-consecutive forms.

Jussives

יֵשֵׁב   *qal* jussive 3ms ישב   Gen 44:33   *cf.* יֵשֵׁב *without accent retraction in Lam 3:28*

תֵּרֶד   *qal* jussive 3fs ירד   2 Kgs 1:10

4.3 Original I-ו and II-צ Verbs (I-וצ Verbs)

There are a few verbs that have an original I-ו and II-צ that morph differently than the patterns we have presented in this chapter.[18] It is debated whether these were original I-י or original I-ו verbs.[19] These verbs include יצת, יצע, יצק, יצב, יצג, and יצר.[20] Joüon offers the mnemonic פ״יצ בְּקָעַ״ת גֵּר where the letters of "valley of sojourner" (בְּקָעַ״ת גֵּר) represent the R_3 of the I-וצ verbs.[21] A different mnemonic using the meanings of these verbs may be something like this.

> After you *fashion* (יצר) a fire pit, *place* (יצג) the wood into the pit and *pour out* (יצק) lighter fluid on it so that it will *catch fire* (יצת) with only one match. Then, *take your stand* (יצב) beside it and enjoy the warmth before *spreading out your bed* (יצע) in the tent for the night.

In originally I-ו verbs with צ in the second root position, rather than contracting the I-ו with the preformative letter, they will *often assimilate* the I-ו. Assimilation makes these verbs behave much like I-נ verbs that we will discuss later. The assimilation of a consonant letter (especially נ) is not foreign to biblical Hebrew even though we do not often see it with ו.[22]

qal impf 1cs יצק, Isaiah 44:3
אֶצֹּק ← *אֶוְצֹק

In this example, the I-ו assimilates, leaving the *dagesh forte* in the II-צ. Since the *dagesh forte* closes the initial syllable, and since it is unaccented, the preformative vowel *segol* remains.[23]

---

18. JM, §77. Joüon calls these פ״יצ verbs, maintaining the designation from the lexical form with I-י. However, these forms morph as if the R_1 was an original I-ו.

19. Reymond, *Intermediate Biblical Hebrew Grammar*, §5.14, p. 199.

20. Joüon comments that יצב has a true root of נצב, which makes sense of the assimilation (JM, §77b[1]). More tentatively, he comments that יצת and יצג could be נצת and נצג, respectively (JM, §77b[4] and [6]). Cf. the list in Qimḥi, §361.

21. JM, §77a(1).

22. Blau, *Phonology and Morphology of Biblical Hebrew*, §1.19.2, p. 57.

23. The retention of the short vowel follows the vowel adjustment rule that a closed and unaccented syllable requires a short vowel (cf. §1.7).

hiphil impf 2mp יצת

תָּצִּיתוּ ← *תַּוְצִיתוּ

Again, the I-ו assimilates instead of contracts. In the *hiphil*, we might expect the *pataḥ* preformative vowel to contract to a וֹ in the $aw \rightarrow ô$ contraction from Table 4.1. However, in these I-צו verbs, the original I-ו will assimilate.[24]

Like other original I-ו verbs, these verbs *may also drop* the original I-ו.

qal imperative 2ms יצק, 2 Kings 4:41

צָק ← *וְצָק* ← *יְצָק*

qal infinitive construct יצק, Exodus 38:27

צֶקֶת	←	*צָקְתְ	←	*צָק	←	*וְצָק
Segolization		ת Added		I-ו Drops		Original Form

The morphological phenomena in the imperative and infinitive construct are the same as what we have seen already in this chapter. However, they do not occur consistently within this certain class of verbs.[25] These forms involve a mixture of patterns that do not need to be memorized. You will be parsing final forms as you see them in the Hebrew Bible. Knowing that a special class of I-צו verbs morph with slight variation will at least give you a category to think through when parsing these forms.

4.4 הלך

הלך inflects like a I-ו verb in the *qal* and *hiphil*.[26] In the *qal* imperfect, these forms drop the original ה and the preformative vowel will lengthen as in the I-ו verbs. In the *qal* imperative and infinitive construct, the forms will drop the original I-ה. In the *hiphil*, the forms morph as if they were a I-ו and the ו contracts to a וֹ. Table 4.3 shows these representative forms.

In each of these progressions, I have begun with the root הלך and then shifted to the I-ו to show how הלך is like the I-ו verbs. Historically, this step is only conjectural. Gesenius proposes that the better explanation is that the form originated with the *hiphil* but shifted by analogy with the *qal* imperfect of I-א verbs to an /o/ preformative vowel.[27] Regardless of the historical explanation,

---

24. It is important to note that the very common root יצא is *not* one of these I-צו verbs even though it has an R₂ צ. In the *hiphil*, יצא inflects with the expected $aw \rightarrow ô$ contraction.
25. E.g., see יְצֹק (*qal* imperative 2ms יצק) in Ezek 24:3 that behaves like a strong form.
26. Blau, *Phonology and Morphology of Biblical Hebrew*, §4.3.8.4.16, p. 247; §3.3.5.5.1, p. 94; GKC, §69x; JM, §75g.
27. GKC, §69x.

Table 4.3: הלך

יֵלֵךְ	← *יְלֵךְ ← *יְהְלֵךְ	*qal* imperfect 3ms
לֵךְ	*הְלֵךְ ← *לֵךְ ←	*qal* imperative 2ms
לֶכֶת	*הְלֵךְ ← *לֵכְתְּ ←	*qal* infinitive construct
הוֹלִיד	*הַהְלִיד ← *הוֹלִיד ←	*hiphil* perfect 3ms

the final forms are what you want to be aware of and in the *qal* and *hiphil* הלך displays characteristics of original I-ו verbs.

On rare occasions, הלך inflects with the I-ה even in the *qal* imperfect, infinitive construct, and imperative. Here are some of those representative forms.

יַהֲלֹךְ	*qal* impf 3ms	Ps 58:9
תַּהֲלֹךְ	*qal* impf 3fs	Exod 9:23; Ps 73:9
אֶהֱלֹךְ	*qal* impf 1cs	Job 16:22
הֲלֹךְ	*qal* inf cstr	Exod 3:19; Num 22:13–16; Eccl 6:8–9
הִלְכוּ	*qal* impv 2mp	Jer 51:50

Outside of the *qal* and *hiphil*, הלך inflects with the I-ה. While these forms do not completely align with the I-ו morphology, they are easily parsed since the original root letters are all present.

יְהַלֵּךְ	*piel* impf 3ms	Ezek 18:9
מְהַלֵּךְ	*piel* ptc ms	Ps 104:3
יִתְהַלֵּךְ	*hithpael* impf 3ms	Gen 5:22
נֶהֱלַכְתִּי	*niphal* pf 1cs	Ps 109:23

4.5 יכל

Another verb we should consider is יכל ("to be able"). יכל is a I-ו/י verb. However, it inflects differently than other I-ו/י verbs.[28]

יכל only occurs in the *qal*, so we will consider it by conjugation. The perfect displays an /o/ as the thematic vowel, sometimes written fully (יָכוֹל pf 3ms, 1 Sam 4:15) and sometimes written defectively (יָכֹל pf 3ms, Exod 40:35). Because the thematic vowel is not a true historically long vowel, it will reduce with vocalic sufformatives (יָכְלוּ pf 3cp, Num 9:6; יָכְלָה pf 3fs, Gen 36:7).

---

28. GKC, §69r; JM, §75i; Qimḥi, §36p.

Outside the third persons, the thematic vowel remains an /o/, but the verb only occurs as a 1cs or 2ms.

| יָכֹלְתִּי | pf 1cs | Gen 30:8; Judg 8:3; Ps 13:5; Ps 40:13 |
| וְיָכָלְתָּ | pf 2ms + *vav*-cons[29] | Exod 18:23 |

In the imperfect, יכל "contracts" like I-ו verbs, but with a *shureq* preformative vowel (יוּכַל impf 3ms, Isa 16:12). In three forms, the preformative vowel is written defectively as a *qibbuts* for no apparent reason (יֻכְלוּ impf 3mp, Josh 7:12; Jer 20:11; Ps 18:39). In all forms of the imperfect, the preformative vowel shifts to a /u/ vowel, most often *shureq*.

אוּכַל	impf 1cs	Num 22:6
תּוּכַל	impf 2ms	Gen 15:5
תּוּכְלִי	impf 2fs	Isa 47:12
נוּכַל	impf 1cp	Gen 24:50
תּוּכְלוּ	impf 2mp	Judg 14:13

יכל does not occur as an imperative in the Hebrew Bible, and the infinitive absolute is identical to the perfect 3ms. It occurs four times in the Hebrew Bible as יָכוֹל (Num 13:30; 22:38; 2 Chr 32:13; once written defectively as יָכֹל, 1 Sam 26:25). The key to distinguishing the infinitive absolute from the perfect 3ms will be the syntax. In each of the four occurrences of the infinitive absolute of יכל, it is an absolute object (cognate accusative) adjacent to the imperfect of יכל.

The infinitive construct occurs twice in the Hebrew Bible with a final ת and o-class vowel segolization (יְכֹלֶת, Num 14:16; Deut 9:28).

So, while יכל is a bit of an anomaly in the I-ו/י category, its frequency and patterns are easy enough to recognize. With the thematic vowel patterns addressed here, we could list the thematic vowel symbols for יכל as O/A.

4.6 I-י Verbs

For original I-י verbs (remember the mnemonic in the introduction), the *yod* will nearly always be present (as a vowel letter with י) when parsing.[30]

---

29. The *vav*-consecutive + perfect (*veqatal*) often shifts the accent to the sufformative. Here, that leaves the middle syllable closed and unaccented and so the thematic vowel reduces to a *qamets ḥatuf* (*vəyāḥoltā*).

30. Some forms may be written defectively without the original I-י as a contracted vowel marker (e.g., יָטַב *qal* impf 3ms יטב, Judg 19:6; 1 Sam 24:5; 1 Kgs 21:7; 2 Kgs 25:24).

With few exceptions, the presence of the original I-י will make the lexical root obvious. In both the *hiphil* and the *qal*, the original I-י will contract with the preformative vowel.

4.6.1 *Qal* Imperfect

In the *qal* imperfect, the original I-י contracts with the *hireq* preformative vowel to become *hireq yod* ($iy \rightarrow \hat{\imath}$).[31] The *qal* thematic vowel symbols for the I-י verbs are A/A.

יִיטַב	*qal* impf 3ms יטב	Gen 12:13	
תִּישַׁר	*qal* impf 3fs ישר	Judg 14:7	
תִּינְקוּ	*qal* impf 2mp ינק	Isa 66:11	

4.6.2 *Hiphil*

In the *hiphil*, the original I-י will also contract, but since the preformative vowel in the *hiphil* is a-class (○○◌ַי), the contraction will be $ay \rightarrow \hat{e}$ (יֵ◌ ← יַ◌).[32] Even in the *hiphil* perfect, the preformative vowel is a-class for I-י verbs (*hiphil* → *haphil*; ○○◌ַה ← ○○◌ִה) following the theory that historical preformative vowels were a-class (cf. §2.3.5).

תֵּיטִיב	*hiphil* impf 2ms יטב	Gen 4:7	
הֵיטֵב	*hiphil* inf abs יטב	Deut 17:4	*inf abs is a hiphil tsere form (J.I.I.V.E.; §1.3)*
הֵינִיקָה	*hiphil* pf 3fs ינק	Gen 21:7	
אֵימִנָה	*hiphil* cohortative 1cs ימן	Gen 13:9	*thematic vowel written defectively*

As with the original I-ו verbs, we must learn to "unravel" these contractions to arrive at the lexical root and recognizable shell. However, with original I-י verbs, the י of the root will most often be present in the contraction and so the verbal root should be more readily apparent. Here, the key will be knowing that the contraction יֵ◌ "unravels" to a recognizable shell (e.g., *hiphil* impf 2ms/3fs; ○○◌ַתְ ← *תַּיְטִיב ← תֵּיטִיב).

Some exceptions exist, but in each of these cases, the original I-י is present for parsing purposes and the "exception" is that these verbs look like strong forms. These should therefore be easy to parse when encountered.

---

31. GKC, §70a; JM, §76b.
32. GKC, §70b; JM, §76c.

יְיַשְּׁרוּ	*hiphil* impf 3mp ישר	Prov 4:25	
מַיְמִינִים	*hiphil* ptc mp ימן	1 Chr 12:2	

4.7 Mixed Forms: ירא and ירש

The verbal roots ירא and ירש are mixed forms.³³ They sometimes morph like I-ו verbs and sometimes morph like I-י verbs. The table below provides representative forms, but it is best to use this chart for reference rather than for memorization. The verb ירא will be most helpful to learn since it can often be confused with ראה in conjugated forms.³⁴ Apart from the potential confusion with ראה, when you see these mixed forms, you will be able to recognize whether they morph like a I-ו or a I-י based on their final forms rather than having to anticipate their unique morphology.

Table 4.4: I-ו/י Mixed Forms³⁵

ירא		
Original I-י	*Original I-ו*	
יִירָא		*qal* imperfect 3ms
יְרָא		*qal* imperative 2ms
יִרְאָה (irregular form)		*qal* infinitive construct
	יִוָּרֵא	*niphal* imperfect 3ms

ירש		
Original I-י	*Original I-ו*	
יִירַשׁ		*qal* imperfect 3ms
	רֵשׁ	*qal* imperative 2ms
	רֶשֶׁת	*qal* infinitive construct
	יִוָּרֵשׁ	*niphal* imperfect 3ms
	הוֹרִישׁ	*hiphil* perfect 3ms

---

33. Fuller and Choi, *Invitation to Biblical Hebrew*, 241–42.
34. See comment in GKC, §69q.
35. This table is adapted from Fuller and Choi, *Invitation to Biblical Hebrew*, 242.

These forms do not need to be memorized. All of the principles of this chapter are present in these mixed forms and so when you see the final form in the Hebrew Bible, you will be able to unravel the forms to an original verbal root and a distinguishing shell. Trying to predict or memorize how a mixed-form verb will morph in specific situations is unnecessary. Knowing the principles behind the final form, however, will lead you to the correct parsing.

4.8 Conclusion

I-נ/י verbs display a variety of morphological features unique to their weak verbal components. However, they can be rather neatly packaged into the concepts of (1) contraction or (2) dropping out. In both cases, a silent *shewa* will cause the I-נ/י to undergo the morphological change. With contractions, Table 4.1 will help you unravel the final forms to discover an original shell for parsing purposes. The I-נ dropping out is largely limited to the *qal* imperfect (with compensatory lengthening of the preformative vowel), *qal* imperative, and *qal* infinitive construct (with the addition of the final ת and segolization). With these morphological principles under your belt and with the strong verb shells at your disposal, parsing I-נ/י weak verbs is no longer a matter of recognizing a variety of "exceptions." Rather, it is a matter of recognizing the morphological phenomenon that consistently identify I-נ/י verbs.

CHAPTER 5

I-נ Verbs

5.1 Introduction

I-נ verbs can appear as strong forms when the נ has a vowel (נָתַן *qal* pf 3ms נתן; יְנַקֶּה *piel* impf 3ms נקה), a *dagesh forte* (יִנָּגֵשׁ *niphal* impf 3ms נגשׁ), or a vocal *shewa* in the perfect (נְפַלְתֶּם *qal* pf 2mp נפל). Alternatively, when the נ has a silent *shewa* in the original shell, it will often assimilate into the following consonant (יִשֹּׁק ← יִנְשֹׁק *qal* impf 3ms נשׁק, Gen 41:40).[1] This assimilation is the most common weakness for I-נ verbs.

I-נ verbs may also drop the first root letter in certain forms of the imperative and infinitive. The "new" principle of this chapter is that the I-נ drops when it receives a vocal *shewa* in the strong verb shell of these conjugations.[2] In both the imperative and infinitive construct, these I-נ conjugations begin to resemble the I-י verbs in the imperative and infinitive construct (cf. §4.2.3.2; §4.2.3.3).

Finally, when the I-נ has a silent *shewa*, but is followed by a guttural (e.g., נהג), the I-נ will *not* assimilate (e.g., *qal* impf 3ms יִנְהַג). Remember that gutturals do not admit *dagesh forte*, and so the I-נ does not assimilate into an R_2 guttural as one would anticipate.[3]

---

1. Blau, *Phonology and Morphology of Biblical Hebrew*, §4.3.8.3.1, p. 241; Reymond, *Intermediate Biblical Hebrew Grammar*, §5.13, pp. 197–98; Suchard, *The Development of the Biblical Hebrew Vowels*, §4.2.4, p. 250; GKC, §66d; §19c; JM, §72b; §17g.

2. Cf. the I-י verbs that drop the original י in an unstable, vocal *shewa* position (§4.2.3.2). Suchard, *The Development of the Biblical Hebrew Vowels*, §4.2.4, p. 250; GKC, §66a–c; JM, §72c–d. Reymond comments that since the imperative is closely related to the short-*yiqtol*, in which the I-נ is missing due to assimilation (יִתֵּן), it would make sense that the imperative would also not have the נ (Reymond, *Intermediate Biblical Hebrew Grammar*, §5.13, p. 198). Reymond's explanation for the imperative here is a more specific application of the principle that the imperative is formed by removing the preformatives of the imperfect (*yiqtol*). For infinitives, Reymond says that they have a "segolate-like" base (*qilt) in the *qal*.

3. Blau, *Phonology and Morphology of Biblical Hebrew*, §4.3.8.3.1, p. 241; Reymond *Intermediate Biblical Hebrew Grammar*, §5.13, p. 198. Blau mentions a few exceptions, one with the root נחת that occurs twice in Ps 38:3, once without assimilation (וַתִּנְחַת *qal* impf 3fs נחת + *vav*-cons) and once with

5.2 I-נ Assimilates

The assimilation of נ in Hebrew is comparable to the assimilation of "n" in English in certain contexts. The English prefix "in-" partially assimilates as "im-" before labials ("impossible" or "imbalanced") to improve efficiency of speech. Additionally, the English prefix "in-" assimilates to the next consonant in other phonological situations ("illogical" or "irreversible"). English allows identical consonants to be written consecutively more often than Hebrew, and so we do not think much about the assimilation of the "n" in the prefix in English. We simply learn "impossible" or "irreversible." In Hebrew, however, assimilation of the נ will often warrant a *dagesh forte* in the following consonant. The assimilation of the I-נ to the following consonant leaves two consecutive consonants, which is the ideal condition for a *dagesh forte*.

יִגַּשׁ	←	יִגְגַשׁ*	←	יִנְגַּשׁ*	←	יִקְטֹל
Assimilated *Nun* as *Dagesh Forte*		Assimilation		R₁ *Nun* with Silent *Shewa* in Shell		*Qal* Imperfect 3ms Shell

5.2.1 Qal

In the *qal* imperfect, the I-נ may assimilate into the second root consonant and appear as a *dagesh forte* in the second root consonant. Throughout the *qal* imperfect paradigm, the original shell has the R₁ with a silent *shewa* and so we can expect assimilation of the I-נ in all forms when the R₂ is not a guttural. Throughout this list of examples, notice the variation of o-class, a-class, and e-class thematic vowels (R₂ vowel). This observation should not distract you when parsing, but it is helpful to know that thematic vowels will vary with *qal* I-נ verbs. In the other conjugations of the *qal*, the I-נ will drop out (see §5.3) or the forms will appear as a strong form.

---

assimilation (נֵחַתּוּ *niphal* pf 3cp נחת). The assimilation in the second form is "hidden" in the ח. The נ that is present is the *niphal* preformative and so without two *nuns* written, the נ of the root (נחת) has clearly (virtually) assimilated into a guttural letter. Likewise, נחת appears as תֵּחַת/יֵחַת in Prov 17:10 and Jer 21:13, respectively, both showing that the I-נ did not assimilate into the ח, but instead caused compensatory lengthening of the preformative vowel. A second example given by Blau is the *niphal* perfect of נחם that attests to assimilation into the R₂ ח in *all* biblical Hebrew forms (see also Reymond, *Intermediate Biblical Hebrew Grammar*, §5.13, p. 198). A final exception Blau discusses is יִנְצֹרוּ. Blau accepts that these forms of נצר are dialectal and stylistic (*Phonology and Morphology of Biblical Hebrew*, §4.3.8.3.2 and note) since most of them are pausal forms that tend to prefer longer verbal forms. Indeed, נצר occurs also with assimilation (יִצֹּר in Prov 3:1), so Blau's "exception" seems to be related to pausal forms more than being a true exception. Gesenius comments on these forms that retain the I-נ before what he calls a "firm consonant" (GKC, §66f).

Qal Imperfect

3ms	יִשֹּׁק	נשק	Gen 41:40	*a-class thematic vowel*
	יִגֹּף	נגף	Exod 21:35	*o-class thematic vowel*
3fs	תִּדֹּר	נדר	Num 30:4	*o-class thematic vowel*
	תִּתַּךְ	נתך	Jer 42:18	*a-class thematic vowel*
2ms	תִּבֹּל	נבל	Exod 18:18	*o-class thematic vowel*
	תִּשָּׂא	נשא	Exod 20:7	*a-class thematic vowel*
2fs	תִּטְּעִי	נטע	Isa 17:10	*thematic vowel obscured by R₂ reduction*
1cs	אֶתִּץ	נתץ	Judg 8:9	*o-class thematic vowel*
	אֶתֵּן	נתן	Gen 12:7	*e-class thematic vowel*
3mp	יִפְּלוּ	נפל	Num 14:29	*thematic vowel obscured by R₂ reduction*
3fp	תִּטֹּפְנָה	נטף	Prov 5:3	*o-class thematic vowel*
2mp	תִּגְּעוּ	נגע	Gen 3:3	*thematic vowel obscured by R₂ reduction*
2fp	תִּפֹּלְנָה	נפל	Ezek 13:11	*o-class thematic vowel*
1cp	נִטֹּשׁ	נטש	Neh 10:32	*o-class thematic vowel*
	נִתֵּן	נתן	Gen 34:21	*e-class thematic vowel*

5.2.2 *Niphal*

In the *niphal* of I-נ verbs, the נ of the verbal root will assimilate, leaving the נ of the *niphal* shell in the perfect, participle, and one form of the infinitive absolute.[4] For example, נִגַּשׁ in Gen 33:7 shows the assimilated I-נ of the root נגשׁ as the *dagesh forte* in the ג whereas the נ that is written is the נ of the *niphal* shell. Table 5.1 provides a representative paradigm using נגשׁ, but not all of these forms are attested in the Hebrew Bible. Some of these forms may look similar (or identical) to the *piel* perfect. You will have to be careful to distinguish these contextually.

The thematic vowel symbol for *niphal* perfect of I-נ verbs is A/ with a *pataḥ*. If the I-נ verb is doubly weak with a III-ה, then the thematic vowel may be a י֫ ׄ or י ׄ depending on the root (נִקֵּיתִי pf 1cs נקה, Ps 19:14; נָסִיתִי pf 1cs נסה, 1 Sam 17:39). The *niphal* perfect thematic vowel lengthens to *qamets* in pausal forms (נִצָּבָה pf 3fs נצב, Prov 8:2) and reduces to a vocal *shewa* with vocalic sufformatives (נִכְּרוּ pf 3cp נכר, Lam 4:8).

The thematic vowel for the participle is the expected irreducible long *qamets* with only a few exceptions. Doubly weak III-ה verbs will add the participle ending directly to the R₂ consonant (נִצִּים ptc mp נצה, Exod 2:13).

---

4. According to the ETCBC/WIVU morphology, only one *qal* infinitive absolute of I-נ verbs has the נָ◌ֹ◌ shell (נָגוֹף) *qal* inf abs נגף, Judg 20:39).

Table 5.1: *Niphal* Perfect and Participle Representative Paradigm (נגשׁ)

	Perfect	Participle	
3ms	נִגַּשׁ	נִגָּשׁ	ms
3fs	נִגְּשָׁה	נִגָּשָׁה	fs
2ms	נִגַּשְׁתָּ	נִגָּשִׁים	mp
2fs	נִגַּשְׁתְּ	נִגָּשׁוֹת	fp
1cs	נִגַּשְׁתִּי		
3cp	נִגְּשׁוּ		
2mp	נִגַּשְׁתֶּם		
2fp	נִגַּשְׁתֶּן		
1cp	נִגַּשְׁנוּ		

Pronominal suffixes reduce the *niphal* participle thematic vowel to *pataḥ* rather than a long *qamets* (cf., נִדְּחָךְ, Deut 30:4 that shortens the vowel;[5] and נִדְחוֹ, 2 Sam 14:13 that reduces the thematic vowel even in a pausal form).[6] T-form participles follow the segolate vowel pattern (נִתֶּכֶת ptc fs נתך, Jer 7:20; and נִשֵּׂאת ptc fs נשׂא, Zech 5:7 with quiescent א segolization [see §11.4.3]). Finally, the doubly weak III-א root נבא reduces thematic vowels with participle suffformatives in both the absolute and construct (נְבִאִים ptc mp abs נבא, 22x in the HB; נְבִאֵי ptc mp cstr, Jer 23:26, 32). Most of these details can simply be used for reference and do not need to be memorized. The ability to recognize the assimilation of the I-נ, identify the root, and then parse the verb based on remaining preformatives and sufformatives will identify key features of the weak verbal forms.

5.2.3 *Hiphil*

In the *hiphil*, *every* verbal shell places the I-נ in a silent *shewa* position (cf. Table 1.2). Therefore, all conjugations assimilate the I-נ in the *hiphil*. The thematic vowels follow the normal pattern of A-i/I-e for I-נ verbs while the *hiphil* J.I.I.V.E. forms still get a *tsere* (cf. §1.3).[7] Additionally, all preformatives and sufformatives follow the strong verb shells for the *hiphil*. Table 5.2 provides a representative paradigm with נגשׁ as the root.

---

5. This short *pataḥ* is probably the result of thematic vowel reduction. With the 2ms pronominal suffix, if the R₂ vowel reduced to a vocal shewa, that would leave two consecutive vocal *shewas* (*נִדְּחָךְ), thus requiring a *shewa* fight (נִדְּחָךְ), resulting in the short vowel under the ד.

6. נִדְחִי in Isa 16:4 has a 1cs suffix but retains the long *qamets* thematic vowel.

7. Remember that the *hiphil* J.I.I.V.E. forms are the jussive, imperative 2ms, infinitive absolute, and *vav*-consecutive. These forms all get an "E" (ֵ) thematic vowel.

Table 5.2: *Hiphil* I-נ Representative Paradigm (נגש)

	Perfect	Imperfect	Imperative	Participle	
3ms	הִגִּישׁ	יַגִּישׁ		מַגִּישׁ	ms
3fs	הִגִּישָׁה	תַּגִּישׁ		מַגִּישָׁה	fs
2ms	הִגַּשְׁתָּ	תַּגִּישׁ	הַגֵּשׁ	מַגִּישִׁים	mp
2fs	הִגַּשְׁתְּ	תַּגִּישִׁי	הַגִּישִׁי	מַגִּישׁוֹת	fp
1cs	הִגַּשְׁתִּי	אַגִּישׁ			
3cp/3mp	הִגִּישׁוּ	יַגִּישׁוּ		**Infinitive**	
3fp		תַּגֵּשְׁנָה			
2mp	הִגַּשְׁתֶּם	תַּגִּישׁוּ	הַגִּישׁוּ	הַגֵּשׁ	absolute
2fp	הִגַּשְׁתֶּן	תַּגֵּשְׁנָה	הַגֵּשְׁנָה	הַגִּישׁ	construct
1cp	הִגַּשְׁנוּ	נַגִּישׁ			

5.2.3.1 Doubly Weak I-נ/III-ה Verbs

Verbs that are both I-נ and III-ה (as in נכה and נטה)[8] are especially challenging since only one root consonant remains in some inflected forms.[9] Since the I-נ in the *hiphil* assimilates, it will be recognizable only as the *dagesh forte* in the R_2. III-ה verbs with vocalic sufformatives attach the sufformative directly to the R_2 (see §9.2). For example, the *hiphil* imperfect 3mp of נכה is יַכּוּ (Mic 4:14). Hence, only the R_2 כ is left of the root. Other conjugations in which these doubly weak verbs have only one root consonant remaining are the *vav*-consecutive (*vayyiqtol*) and the jussive (the III-ה short forms [see §9.4.2]). These may be even a little more difficult since the R_2 becomes the final consonant. For נכה, the middle כ becomes a final ךְ, making it even more difficult to recognize. Since Hebrew does not admit a *dagesh forte* in a final consonant, even the I-נ is obscured in these forms. The *hiphil vav*-consecutive of נכה becomes וַיַּךְ (Exod 2:12). נטה provides a good example of the jussive with טַט (Ps 27:9; 141:4). The examples below show other forms with only one root consonant remaining. These examples are all *hiphil*.

---

8. According to the ETCBC/WIVU morphology database, there are 893 occurrences of these I-נ/III-ה verbs from 17 different roots. Five hundred of those occurrences are נכה, 214 are נטה, 44 are נקה, and 36 are נסה. Not all of these forms display this difficult morphology, but these are the main roots to be aware of.

9. This phenomenon also occurs in the *qal* for I-נ/III-ה doubly weak verbs, but it is far more common in the *hiphil*. Examples from the *qal* are almost exclusively the imperfect *vav*-consecutive (*vayyiqtol*) (וַיֵּט *qal* impf 3ms נטה + *vav*-cons, Exod 8:13; וַתֵּט *qal* impf 3fs נטה + *vav*-cons, Num 22:23; וַיִּטּוּ *qal* impf 3mp נטה + *vav*-cons, 1 Sam 8:3; וַיִּז *qal* impf 3ms נזה + *vav*-cons, 2 Kgs 9:33) or the jussive (טַט *qal* jussive 2ms נטה, Prov 4:5, 27).

הֻכּוּ	pf 3cp נכה	Gen 19:11
הַךְ	impv 2ms נכה	Exod 8:12
וַיַּז	impf 3ms + *vav*-cons נזה	Lev 8:11
הַטִּי	impv 2fs נטה	Gen 24:14
מַטֵּי	ptc mp cstr נטה	Mal 3:5

5.2.4 *Hophal*

Like the *hiphil*, the *hophal* shell places the I-נ in a position with silent *shewa* in all conjugations. Also, the *hophal* has a *qibbuts* as the preformative vowel in all conjugations.[10] The *hophal* does not occur in any imperative or infinitive construct forms of I-נ verbs.. Only two I-נ infinitives absolute occur in the Hebrew Bible, and both assimilate the I-נ and take a *tsere* thematic vowel (הֻגֵּד *hophal* inf abs נגד, Josh 9:24; Ruth 2:11). Both of these forms occur as an adverbial modifier with the *hophal* perfect 3ms of נגד (הֻגַּד) and so it is relatively easy to identify them as infinitives absolute. Table 5.3 provides a theoretical representative paradigm of נגשׁ even though not all forms are attested in the Hebrew Bible.

Table 5.3: I-נ *Hophal* Representative Paradigm (נגשׁ)

	Perfect	Imperfect	Participle	
3ms	הֻגַּשׁ	יֻגַּשׁ	מֻגָּשׁ	ms
3fs	הֻגְּשָׁה	תֻּגַּשׁ	מֻגָּשָׁה	fs
2ms	הֻגַּשְׁתָּ	תֻּגַּשׁ	מֻגָּשִׁים	mp
2fs	הֻגַּשְׁתְּ	תֻּגְּשִׁי	מֻגָּשׁוֹת	fp
1cs	הֻגַּשְׁתִּי	אֻגַּשׁ		
3cp/3mp	הֻגְּשׁוּ	יֻגְּשׁוּ		
3fp		תֻּגַּשְׁנָה		
2mp	הֻגַּשְׁתֶּם	תֻּגְּשׁוּ		
2fp	הֻגַּשְׁתֶּן	תֻּגַּשְׁנָה		
1cp	הֻגַּשְׁנוּ	נֻגַּשׁ		

Two other forms that deserve attention are I-נ/II-ו doubly weak verbs. Since in the II-ו verbs, the middle ו flips to a I-ו, the I-נ in these forms becomes irrelevant and just switches places with the middle ו (הוּנַף pf 3ms נוף, Exod

---

10. GKC, §66d. Cf. JM, §29c where he comments that an /o/ vowel often becomes *qibbuts* in what he calls a "sharp syllable." For Joüon, a sharp syllable is one that is closed by a doubled consonant (i.e., a *dagesh forte*) (JM, §6i, n. 2).

29:27 and הוּנַח pf 3ms נוח, Lam 5:5).[11] The I-נ in these forms does not assimilate since it effectively becomes the R₂ and takes the thematic vowel.

5.3 I-נ Drops Out

For I-נ verbs, there are several forms that will drop the I-נ. However, a few strong forms occur. O-class I-נ verbs tend to retain the strong form of the imperative and infinitives (לִנְסֹךְ, Isa 30:1; בִּנְפֹל, Isa 30:25; כִּנְבֹל, Isa 34:4; לִנְקֹם, Ezek 24:8; נְצֹר [impv], Ps 34:14).[12] Besides the o-class strong forms, I-נ verbs will also appear strong when the I-נ has a vowel in the original shell (נָסוֹעַ qal inf abs נסע, Gen 12:9; לְנַשֵּׁק piel inf cstr נשק, Gen 31:28). Additionally, for infinitives with pronominal suffixes, the I-נ tends to retain a short vowel and therefore does not drop the I-נ (בְּנָגְפּוֹ qal inf cstr נגף + 3ms suffix + בְּ, Exod 12:27).[13] Doubly weak I-נ and II-guttural verbs retain the I-נ in the imperative and infinitive (לִנְחֹל qal inf cstr נחל + ל, Num 34:18; Josh 19:49; נְעַל qal impv 2ms נעל, 2 Sam 13:17; נְהַג qal impv 2ms נהג, 2 Kgs 4:24).[14] Finally, other strong forms simply appear even where a morphological change is expected (e.g., לִנְגֹּעַ qal inf cstr נגע + ל, Gen 20:6). Thankfully, these strong forms are not missing the I-נ and so parsing should match the standard verb paradigm with distinctive shells and thematic vowels.

The *qal* imperative and infinitive construct may drop the I-נ depending on the thematic vowel class.[15] O-class I-נ verbs tend to retain the I-נ as a strong form, but a- and e-class I-נ verbs may drop the I-נ. Table 5.4 provides a summary of these trends.[16]

---

11. Interestingly, נוח also occurs as an "assimilated" form, but retains the original I-נ (הֻנִּיחָה *hophal* [*hiphil*?] pf 3fs נוח, Zech 5:11). The *BHS* text-critical apparatus and *HALOT* suggest this form should be read as a *hiphil*.

12. The idea of a verb being "o-class" has more to do with its historical relationship to other forms. Reymond compares the relationship of the imperative to the *yiqtol* since the *qal yiqtol* has the ō thematic vowel (*Intermediate Biblical Hebrew Grammar*, §5.13, p. 198). In each of these infinitives with prepositions, the ב with a silent *shewa* is a secondary morphological change resulting from a "*shewa* fight" between the vocal *shewa* of the imperative and infinitive shell (ΟΟؘ) and the expected vocal *shewa* of the inseparable preposition (לִנְפֹּל ← *לְנְפֹל). Because of this, we do not expect to see this נ assimilate.

13. However, compare the root נגש that still drops the I-נ both with a prefixed preposition (בְּגִשְׁתָּם *qal* inf cstr נגש + 3mp suffix + בְּ, Exod 28:43; 30:20; Num 4:19) and without (גִּשְׁתּוֹ *qal* inf cstr נגש + 3ms suffix, Gen 33:3). Without the prefixed preposition, the I-נ is in an unstable vocal *shewa* syllable and drops as might be expected. With the prefixed preposition, it seems more to be due to the specific nature of the root (see also נתן that drops the I-נ with and without prefixed prepositions).

14. Interestingly, these are the forms that also do not assimilate the I-נ into a subsequent guttural letter. Reymond, *Intermediate Biblical Hebrew Grammar*, §5.13, p. 198.

15. JM, §72c–e.

16. Qimḥi (§34e–f) notes the occurrences of גַּשׁ as the imperative form of נגש (e.g., גֶּשׁ־הָלְאָה in Gen 19:9), and the occurrences of *holem* in גֹּשִׁי (Ruth 2:14) and גֹּשׁוּ (Josh 3:9).

Table 5.4:[17] I-נ Qal Imperative/Infinitive Construct by Vowel Class

	Thematic Vowel Class		
	O	A	E
qal impv 2ms	נְפֹל	גַּשׁ	תֵּן
qal impv 2fs	נִפְלִי	גְּשִׁי	תְּנִי
qal impv 2mp	נִפְלוּ	גְּשׁוּ	תְּנוּ
qal impv 2fp	נְפֹלְנָה	גַּשְׁנָה	תֵּנָּה
qal inf cstr	נְפֹל	גֶּשֶׁת ← *גַּשְׁתְּ ← תֵּת	תִּנְתְּ* ← תְּתִתְּ* ← תֵּת
inf cstr with ל	לִנְפֹּל	לָגֶשֶׁת	לָתֵת

As we look at this table, note that in both examples for the a- and e-class verbs, the R₂ is a *begadkephat* letter that takes a *dagesh lene* (גַּשׁ; תֵּן).[18] This *dagesh* is *not* due to the assimilation of the I-נ. I-נ verbs without an R₂ *begadkephat* letter do not get that *dagesh lene* (e.g., שַׁל *qal* impv 2ms נְשַׁל, Exod 3:5). Because the *begadkephat* consonant begins the syllable, it will take the *dagesh lene*.

Also note that the a- and e-class infinitives construct add a ת and shift to a segolate vowel pattern (גֶּשֶׁת).[19] Again, the *dagesh* in the R₂ נ is a *dagesh lene*, not due to the assimilation of the I-נ. Compare these forms to the I-ו/י infinitives construct in Chapter 4.

5.4 לקח

You will recall from your introductory study of Hebrew that the verb לקח inflects like a I-נ weak verb in the *qal* stem, both assimilating the I-ל when with a silent *shewa* and also dropping the I-ל in the *qal* imperative and infinitive.[20]

---

17. This table is adapted from Fuller and Choi, *Invitation to Biblical Hebrew*, 232.
18. Remember that *begadkephat* is the mnemonic to recall the Hebrew consonts that take a *dagesh lene* when preceeded by a silent *shewa*.
19. Blau comments that the ת is a retention of the feminine ת in forms that become short (Blau, *Phonology and Morphology of Biblical Hebrew*, §4.3.8.3.3, pp. 241–42). Reymond attributes this to the infinitive having a theoretical *qilt base that includes the ת (Reymond, *Intermediate Biblical Hebrew Grammar*, §5.13, p. 198).
20. For advanced discussions related to לקח see Blau, *Phonology and Morphology of Biblical Hebrew*, §4.3.8.3.7, p. 243 and associated note; GKC, §66g; JM, §72j; Qimḥi, §34m.

Outside the *qal*, לקח does *not* assimilate its first root consonant (e.g., נִלְקַח *niphal* pf 3ms, 1 Sam 4:11, 22; Ezek 33:6).[21]

The shell of the *qal* imperfect has a silent *shewa* under the I-ל (*יִלְקַח) where assimilation is now expected, and the imperative and infinitive shells both have a vocal *shewa* under the I-ל such that it drops out (*לְקַח). Apart from assimilation or dropping, all other preformatives and sufformatives of the respective conjugations will be present for parsing.

The thematic vowel for לקח is A/A due to the III-ח guttural that prefers /a/ vowels (§10.3.1). The only variations in the thematic vowel for קח in the *qal* are (1) lengthening in an open pretonic syllable with pronominal suffixes (יִקָּחֶנָּה *qal* impf 3ms + 3fs suffix, Deut 20:7), (2) lengthening when a pausal form (תִּקָּחוּ: *qal* impf 2mp, Exod 12:5), and (3) reducing with vocalic sufformatives (נִקְחָה *qal* impf 1cp [cohortative], 1 Sam 4:3). When the thematic vowel reduces under the ק with a *dagesh forte* of the assimilated I-ל (as in the 1 Sam 4:3 example), the *dagesh forte* often flees according to the SQNMLVY rule (אֶקְחָה *qal* impf 1cs [cohortative], Gen 18:5).[22]

Like I-נ verbs, לקח drops the I-ל and adds a ת to the *qal* infinitive construct (קַחַת). For this pattern of inflection, the infinitive construct gets a segolate vowel pattern. However, since the R₃ of לקח is the guttural ח, what appears as a segolate pattern in קַחַת is formed with two *pataḥs*.[23]

The examples below provide representative forms from the Hebrew Bible.

Qal Imperfect

3ms	יִקַּח	Exod 33:7	*58x in the HB*
3fs	תִּקַּח	Lev 15:29	*6x in the HB*
2ms	תִּקַּח	Gen 7:2	*37x in the HB*
2fs	תִּקְחִי	Zeph 3:7	*the lack of a dagesh in the ק is due to the SQNMLVY rule*
1cs	אֶקַּח	Gen 14:23	*12x in the HB*
3mp	יִקְחוּ	Gen 14:24	*the lack of a dagesh in the ק is due to the SQNMLVY rule*
2mp	תִּקְחוּ	Gen 34:9	*the lack of a dagesh in the ק is due to the SQNMLVY rule*
1cp	נִקַּח	Exod 10:26	*5x in the HB*

---

21. The WIVU and SESE parsing databases produce six *hophal* forms of לקח that assimilate the I-ל of לקח (תֻּקַּח impf 3fs [Gen 12:15] and יֻקַּח impf 3ms [Gen 18:4; Isa 49:24, 25; Ezek 15:3; Job 28:2]). However, Gesenius (and others) explains that these are more likely *qal* passives (GKC, §53u) and so the overarching concept that לקח assimilates or drops the I-ל in the *qal* would still stand. The Groves-Wheeler Westminster morphology database parses these forms as *qal* passives.

22. SQNMLVY is a mnemonic to remember the consonants that may omit the *dagesh forte* when they also have a vocal *shewa*. The mnemonic stands for all sibilants (שׁ, שׂ, ס, צ), ק, נ, מ, ל, ו, י. When any of these consonants occurs with a *dagesh forte and* a vocal *shewa*, the consonant *may* omit the *dagesh forte* (GKC, §20m[b]; JM, §18m; Fuller and Choi, *Invitation to Biblical Hebrew*, 18, n. 5).

23. Compare this to the segolization pattern of the noun נַעַר with the guttural letter (GKC,

Qal Imperative

2ms	קַח	Gen 6:21	*87x in HB; long form impv* קָחָה *once in Gen 15:9*
	לְקַח	Exod 29:1	*strong form; 3x in HB (Exod 29:1; Ezek 37:16; Prov 20:16)*
2fs	קְחִי	1 Kgs 17:10	*4x in HB(1 Kgs 17:10; Isa 23:16; Isa 47:2; Jer 46:11)*
	לְקְחִי	1 Kgs 17:11	*strong form; 1x in HB*
2mp	קְחוּ	Gen 42:33	*35x in HB*

Qal Infinitive Construct

קַחַת	Jer 5:3	
לָקַחַת	Gen 24:48	*with* ל *preposition, not the R₁* ל *of the root*

5.5 נתן

נתן deserves its own section because it is doubly weak as a I-נ and a III-נ verb, both of which may assimilated in certain phonological contexts.[24] When the נ in the third root position terminates a nonfinal syllable (with silent *shewa*), it may assimilate to the following consonant as a *dagesh forte*. In most forms, נתן behaves as anticipated. Other forms of נתן, as we will see, are perhaps best memorized even if they have a reasonable explanation.

Once again, the נ in the third root position may assimilate to the following consonant as a *dagesh forte* in certain contexts (נָתַתִּי *qal* pf 1cs, Gen 1:29; נָתַנּוּ *qal* pf 1cp, Gen 34:16). The perfect conjugation is where this assimilation happens most often since it has syllabic suffformatives into which the III-נ may assimilate.[25] The imperfect 2fp and 3fp do not have extant forms in the Hebrew Bible, so we do not need to worry about the III-נ assimilating into those suffformatives.

Consistent with other I-נ verbs, the *qal* imperative drops the I-נ. The expected form is תֵּן although it can be תֶּן־ when joined to the following word with a *maqqef* (e.g., Gen 14:21; Exod 16:33; Num 17:11; etc.).[26] The *qal* imperative has a long form, תְּנָה (24x in HB) that also drops the I-נ. Finally,

---

§22h). These /a/ vowels in segolization are the application of the characteristic that gutturals prefer /a/ sounds under and before them (cf., §2.3.1.3).

24. For focused discussions of נתן, see Blau, *Phonology and Morphology of Biblical Hebrew*, §4.3.8.3.4, p. 242; GKC, §66h–i; JM, §72i; Qimḥi, §34l.

25. The vast majority of occurrences of נתן in the Hebrew Bible are in the *qal*. But because the perfect conjugation has the same suffformatives in all the verbal stems, the assimilation of the III-נ into the suffformative occurs in conjugations outside of the *qal* as well (e.g., נִתַּתֶּם *niphal* pf 2mp, Lev 26:25).

26. The *maqqef* shifts the accent to the following word leaving the syllable closed and unaccented, thus requiring a short vowel (CURS; §1.7).

the *qal* imperative 2fs and 2mp also drop the I-נ (תְּנִי [7x in HB] and תְּנוּ [28x in HB]).

The *qal* infinitive construct is a form that will give many Hebrew students problems initially. However, it appears so often (159x in HB), it will become easy to recognize in context. The standard form can be derived from this theoretical pathway.

$$\text{נְתֹן}^* \leftarrow \text{תֵּן}^* \leftarrow \text{תֵּנְתְּ}^* \leftarrow \text{תֵּתְּ}^* \leftarrow \text{תֵּת}$$
$$12345$$

In the initial step, the I-נ drops since נתן is an e-class root.[27] Dropping the I-נ leaves the form as תֵּן where the *dagesh* is a *dagesh lene* and the final ן has an implied silent *shewa* at the end of a CVC syllable (Form 2). When the ת is added to the end (Form 3), the III-נ now reveals its silent *shewa* and therefore assimilates into the final ת (Form 4). However, Hebrew will not allow a *dagesh forte* in the final ת and so the final form (Form 5) does not show evidence of the assimilated III-נ.[28] The final assessment is that the *qal* infinitives construct of נתן *with a pronominal suffix* always get the *dagesh* of the assimilated III-נ.[29] נתן can be complicated to explain for the infinitive construct. Hence, it is often best for students to memorize the infinitive construct as תֵּת.

The table below provides some representative forms along with their pathway to the final form in these affected conjugations.

---

27. נתן is the only I-נ e-class root (Blau, *Phonology and Morphology of Biblical Hebrew*, §4.3.8.3.3, p. 242). Joüon remarks that this aspect of נתן is only seen in פ״י verbs like יֵשֵׁב *qal* impf 3ms of ישב (JM, §72i).

28. Blau and Reymond posit that this form is derived from a hypothetical base *tint* (Blau, *Phonology and Morphology of Biblical Hebrew*, §4.3.8.3.3, p. 242; Reymond, *Intermediate Biblical Hebrew Grammar*, §5.13, p. 198). Suchard comments that these forms arose from the "biradical" imperative forms through the analogy of I-ו verbs (Suchard, *The Development of the Biblical Hebrew Vowels*, §4.2.4, p. 250). Gesenius goes further in saying, "the ground form *tint* is not lengthened to *tèneth* (as גֶּשֶׁת from נָגַשׁ), but contracted to *titt*, which is then correctly lengthened to תֵּת" (GKC, §66i; see also JM, §72i). No matter how we explain the derivative, the pronominal suffix forms seem to build on the base *תִּתְּ with a "hovering *dagesh*" that lands when the suffix is added (תִּתִּי inf cstr נתן + 1cs, Gen 29:19). A "hovering *dagesh*" is the name I use to describe the dagesh forte that (re)appears in a final consonant when suffixes are added. Without the suffix, the *dagesh* is "hovering" over the final consonant, but will not appear in the final consonant until a suffix is added (see Fuller and Choi, *Invitation to Biblical Hebrew*, 84).

29. Acccording to the ETCBC morphology database, the *qal* inf cstr occurs 159x in the Hebrew Bible, and 32 of those have pronominal suffixes. All 32 forms with suffixes have the *dagesh forte* of the assimilated III-נ.

Table 5.5: נתן Representative Paradigm

	Qal Perfect
2ms	נָתַתָּ ← *נָתַנְתָּ
2fs	נָתַתְּ ← *נָתַנְתְּ
1cs	נָתַתִּי ← *נָתַנְתִּי
1cp	נָתַנּוּ ← *נָתַנְנוּ
	Qal Imperative
2ms	תֵּן
2fs	תְּנִי
2mp	תְּנוּ
	Qal Infinitive Construct
	תֵּת ← *תֶּנְתְּ ← *נְתֵן

5.6 Conclusion

Some of the details of this chapter might make I-נ verbs seem more complicated than they are. The overarching principles are that I-נ verbs will assimilate the I-נ when it has a silent *shewa* and they will drop the I-נ in certain situations when it would have a vocal *shewa*, mainly the *qal* imperative and infinitive construct. Beyond those principles, I-נ verbs will appear like strong verbs. לקח is indeed idiosyncratic and נתן, in some conjugations, should simply be memorized. But even those roots demonstrate considerable consistency when they appear in the Hebrew Bible.

We are now at a point with weak verbs that we are beginning to see the consistency of morphological phenomena even across weak verb types. I-נ verbs dropping the נ when it has a vocal *shewa* is like the I-ו verbs that do the same. We still have a way to go to cover all of the morphological adjustments in weak verbs, but I hope that you are beginning to see that despite the level of detail in these discussions, weak verbs are not the exceptions to the strong verb paradigms. Rather, they inflect with predictable patterns according to their specific weak verb characteristics.

CHAPTER 6

II-Guttural Verbs

6.1 Introduction

We move now in our study of weak verbs to II-guttural verbs. As the name implies, these are verbal roots with a guttural in the R_2 position. The primary guttural characteristics that we will address here are (1) gutturals reject *dagesh forte*, (2) gutturals take composite *shewas* instead of simple *shewas*, and (3) gutturals prefer a-class vowels.[1]

Regarding the rejection of the *dagesh forte*, this will include the semi-guttural ר (גֵּרַ֫שְׁתָּ *piel* pf 2ms גרש, Gen 4:14).[2] Additionally, rejection of *dagesh forte* may not result in compensatory lengthening. Certain gutturals will "imply" the *dagesh forte* of the doubled stems (*piel*, *pual*, and *hithpael*), sometimes called virtual doubling. In this case, the *dagesh* will not be present, but the preceding vowel will remain short as if the syllable were still closed (מְרַחֶ֫פֶת *piel* ptc fs [t-form] רחף, Gen 1:2).[3]

II-guttural verbs will prefer composite *shewas* anytime the verb has a vocalic sufformative that results in the reduction of the R_2 vowel to a vocal *shewas* (cf. §1.7). The expected composite vocal *shewa* will most often become a *hatef patah* (יִשְׁחֲטוּ *qal* impf 3mp שחט, Lev 7:2).

Finally, some II-guttural forms will shift the thematic vowel to a *patah* even though a *tsere* or *holem* may be expected as the thematic vowel.[4] This will happen in the *qal* imperfect and imperative primarily, which means that the *qal* imperative 2ms and infinitive construct are no longer identical forms, making

---

1. JM, §69a.

2. ר is considered a semi-guttural because the only characteristics of gutturals it displays are the rejection of *dagesh forte* and (only sometimes) prefers /a/ sounds near it (GKC, §22q–s; JM, §23).

3. With מְרַחֶ֫פֶת, the *patah* under the ר should lengthen in what appears to be a pretonic open syllable. As it stands, it is a CV syllable and therefore open. However, the rejected *dagesh forte* seems to be "closing" the syllable such that the *patah* does not lengthen in a pretonic open syllable as one would expect. The explanation for an "implied *dagesh*" is just a way to describe the morphology and is not a technical morphological phenomenon. The point is that when the *dagesh* is rejected by some gutturals, it will not always cause lengthening of the preceding vowel (see Table 6.1).

4. GKC, §64b; JM, §69a(2).

them easily distinguishable for II-guttural verbs (מְחַץ *qal* impv 2ms מחץ, Deut 33:11; cf. אֱחֹז *qal* inf cstr אחז, 1 Kgs 6:6).

6.2 II-Guttural Verbs Reject *Dagesh Forte*

Guttural consonants (including ר) reject *dagesh forte*.[5] When they do this, the preceding vowel may lengthen. This spelling feature applies to the *piel*, *pual*, and *hithpael* stems with *dagesh forte* in the R_2 of the strong verb shell (○◌○; ○◌○; ○◌הִתְ).

When the short vowels lengthen, they will lengthen to a long vowel within the same vowel class. As such, *pataḥ* (◌) becomes *qamets* (◌), *ḥireq* (◌) becomes *tsere* (◌), and *qibbuts* (◌) becomes *ḥolem* (◌). The short vowel will not lengthen to a historically long vowel.

Consider the following examples:

piel perfect 1cs	בֵּרַכְתִּי ← *בִּרַּכְתִּי	Gen 17:20
piel imperfect 3mp[6]	יְבָרְכוּ ← *יְבָרְכוּ	Gen 24:60
hithpael perfect 3ms	הִתְבָּרֵךְ ← *הִתְבָּרֵךְ	Deut 29:18
hithpael imperfect 3mp	יִתְבָּרְכוּ ← *יִתְבָּרְכוּ	Ps 72:17
pual participle ms	מְבֹרָךְ ← *מְבֹרָךְ	Ps 113:2

II-guttural verbs may also reject a *dagesh forte* without causing compensatory lengthening. This is sometimes called virtual doubling. In these cases, the II-guttural will "hide" the *dagesh forte*, but the preceding vowel will not lengthen.[7]

Here are some representative forms for this phenomenon along with their progression from a hypothetical "strong" form to the final form in the Hebrew Bible.

piel imperfect 3fs	תְּכַחֵשׁ ← *תְּכַחֵשׁ	Gen 18:15
piel participle ms	מְצַחֵק ← *מְצַחֵק	Gen 19:14
piel infinitive construct	שַׁחֵת ← *שַׁחֵת	Gen 13:10
hithpael participle mp	מִתְלַחֲשִׁים ← *מִתְלַחֲשִׁים	2 Sam 12:19

---

5. GKC, §64e.

6. Notice in this form, the vocalic ending reduces the R_2 to a vocal *shewa*. The ר will only rarely behave like a guttural regarding *shewas*. Compare this form to the *hithpael* imperfect 3mp in Ps 72:17 a few rows down. The ר there does not take a composite *shewa* even though the R_2 has reduced.

7. Gesenius and Joüon call this "half-doubling" or "virtually strengthening" (GKC, §22b-c; §64d; JM, §69a[3]).

The next question to ask is whether we can anticipate which gutturals will reject the *dagesh forte* and lengthen the preceding vowel by compensation and which gutturals will imply or "hide" the *dagesh forte*. The following chart provides a symmetrical picture of what to expect from the II-gutturals regarding the *dagesh forte*. "R" identifies the forms that will "reject" the *dagesh forte* while "I" indicates the *dagesh forte* will be "implied."

Table 6.1:[8] II-Guttural Dagesh Rejection

	Piel	*Pual*	*Hithpael*
א	R	R	R
ה	I	R	I
ח	I	I	I
ע	I	R	I
ר	R	R	R

While this table is helpful for the majority of the II-guttural forms, there are some exceptions.[9] Even so, this is a table that would be worth memorizing. The symmetrical nature of the table makes it easy to memorize and it will also provide confidence when parsing in order to understand what happened to the distinctive *dagesh forte* of the *piel*, *pual*, or *hithpael* stems.

6.3 II-Guttural Verbs Take Composite *Shewa*

II-gutturals also take composite *shewas* when the thematic vowel reduces to vocal *shewa*. The composite *shewa* is most often *ḥatef pataḥ* (ֲ).

צָעֲקָה	*qal* pf 3fs צעק	Deut 22:24, 27
יִשְׁחֲטוּ	*qal* impf 3mp שחט	Lev 7:2 (2x)
זַעֲקִי	*qal* impv 2fs זעק	Isa 14:31
תְּכַחֲדִי	*piel* impf 2fs כחד	2 Sam 14:18
יְשַׁאֲלוּ	*piel* impf 3mp שאל	2 Sam 20:18
יִתְגָּעֲשׁוּ	*hithpael* impf 3mp געש	Jer 46:7

---

8. This table is adapted from Fuller and Choi, *Invitation to Biblical Hebrew*, 208, and is attributed there to Isaac Jerusalmi.

9. בֹּחַן (*pual* pf 3ms בחן, Ezek 21:18); דֹּחוּ (*pual* pf 3cp דחה, Ps 36:13). Gesenius discusses both forms in GKC, §64d.

Notice in these examples, the R$_2$ *shewa* is the result of a vocalic sufformative. With the guttural in the second root position, the *shewa* becomes *ḥatef pataḥ*.

6.4 Minor Implications of II-Gutturals

The issues of *dagesh forte* and vocal *shewa* are the primary things to know for II-guttural verbs, but there are a couple of other minor principles to keep in mind.

6.4.1 Thematic Vowels Often Become /A in the *Qal* Imperfect and Imperative

First, in the *qal* imperfect and imperative, the thematic vowel of the strong verb shifts to /A with II-guttural verbs. The list below provides some representative forms.

יִבְעַר	*qal* impf 3ms	בער	Exod 3:3
תִּצְעַק	*qal* impf 2ms	צעק	Exod 14:15
יִרְחַץ	*qal* impf 3ms	רחץ	Lev 1:9
מְחַץ	*qal* impv 2ms	מחץ	Deut 33:11
בְּחַר	*qal* impv 2ms	בחר	2 Sam 24:12

This thematic vowel adjustment only applies in the *qal* imperfect and imperative. Other stems and conjugations generally follow the expected thematic vowels.

הִבְאִישׁ	*hiphil* pf 3ms	באשׁ	Exod 16:24
יִגָּאֵל	*niphal* impf 3ms	גאל	Lev 25:30
אֶבָּהֵל	*niphal* impf 1cs	בהל	Job 23:15
תְּאַחֵר	*piel* impf 2ms	אחר	Deut 23:22
יַרְעֵם	*hiphil* juss 3ms	רעם	2 Sam 22:14

6.4.2 *Qal* Imperative 2ms and Infinitive Construct Are Distinguishable

Second, since the *qal* imperative gets a *pataḥ* thematic vowel, but the infinitive retains the normal *holem* (קְטֹל), the imperative 2ms and infinitive construct are now distinguishable. This is only an observation of II-guttural verbs and not something that you need to memorize. Syntactical context will help with parsing these forms as well.

Qal Strong Verbs	
qal imperative 2ms	קְטֹל
qal infinitive construct	קְטֹל

Qal II-Guttural Verbs	
qal imperative 2ms	בְּחַר
qal infinitive construct	בְּחֹר

6.5 Conclusion

II-guttural verbs may be one of the simpler weak verb types to understand. Like I-gutturals, these forms simply apply the characteristics of gutturals that we already know (cf. §2.3.1). In some sense, there is nothing "new" in this chapter. For II-guttural verbs, none of the original root consonants are missing and so recognizing the root should be manageable. Perhaps the trickiest aspect of II-guttural verbs will be the loss of the distinctive R_2 *dagesh forte* in the *piel*, *pual*, and *hithpael* stems. However, by memorizing Table 6.1 you can anticipate which forms will lengthen the preceding vowel by compensation and which forms will imply the *dagesh*. Like the other weak verbs, II-guttural vowel changes are not random and haphazard. Rather, they follow consistent and predictable patterns that make identification manageable.

CHAPTER 7

II-ו/י (Biconsonantal) Verbs

7.1 Introduction

Some grammars approach these verbs separately as II-ו verbs and II-י verbs.[1] For our purposes, we will address them together, but consider them with different vowel classes in the *qal* stem. Sometimes, an original II-ו will become a *shureq* thematic vowel as in (קוּם) יָקוּם. Other II-ו verbs will take an o-class thematic vowel like (בּוֹא) יָבוֹא. For original II-י verbs, the thematic vowel will be i-class as in (שִׂים) יָשִׂים. In the *hiphil* and *niphal*, II-ו/י verbs will follow more consistent thematic vowel patterns based on the stem.

Some II-ו/י verbs appear to be "strong" forms. These are most likely true II-ו verbs rather than biconsonantal roots. In other words, the middle ו of these roots was an original R₂ of a triconsonantal root.

יֶחֱוָרוּ	*qal* impf 3mp חור [pausal]	Isa 29:22
יִצְוָחוּ	*qal* impf 3mp צוח [pausal]	Isa 42:11
יִרְוַח	*qal* impf 3ms רוח	Job 32:20
יִגְוַע	*qal* impf 3ms גוע	Job 34:15

In each of the above examples, the II-ו is consonantal whereas with other II-ו lexical roots, the II-ו will contract as the thematic vowel in these same conjugations. Rather than considering these as exceptions to the II-ו/י morphology, it is best to see these are true triconsonantal roots, not biconsonantal roots.

---

1. JM, §80 says these are "generally called" ע"י verbs, but that they have two radical consonants joined by a "non-deletable vowel." See GKC, §72a.n1 as well. He calls them ע"וּ (*ayin shureq*) verbs that should be "rigidly distinguished" from true ע"ו (*ayin vav*) verbs that morph like the strong verb paradigm. See also Reymond, *Intermediate Biblical Hebrew Grammar*, §5.15, p. 200; Blau, *Phonology and Morphology of Biblical Hebrew*, §4.3.8.7.1, p. 252, who both mention how difficult the historical derivation is for II-ו/י verbs. Suchard comments that the *qal* perfect is a triphthong contraction that resulted in the long /a/ *qamets* thematic vowel (Suchard, *The Development of the Biblical Hebrew Vowels*, §4.2.6, p. 252). See GKC, §72 for ע"ו verbs and §73 for ע"י verbs or JM, §80 for ע"ו verbs and §81 for ע"י verbs.

If we set aside these triconsonantal forms with a consonantal II-ו, one indication that no strong forms exist for II-ו/י weak roots is that in the stems where we expect a *dagesh forte* in the R₂ position (*piel, pual, hithpael*), the stem normally (there are exceptions) shifts to a *polel, polal,* and *hithpolel,* respectively. Verbs with a ו as the true R₂ consonant remain strong in these stems.² Gesenius comments that the retention of a II-ו in the doubled stems is especially true with verbs that are also III-ה verbs.³ For II-ו/י weak verbs, we will address the morphological changes by verbal stem.

7.2 II-ו/י Verbs: *Qal*

In the *qal*, it is important to remember a couple of principles from our overview of the weak verb. First, remember that preformative vowels for weak verbs were originally a-class (§2.3.5). For II-ו/י verbs in the *qal*, the original a-class preformative vowel is retained (יָקוּם) whereas the strong form preformative vowel became *hireq* (יִקְטֹל).

Second, remember to think in terms of vowel classes rather than specific vowels when considering thematic vowels.⁴ With the *qal* imperfect, the thematic vowel may be /u/ (וּ) or sometimes it is /o/ (וֹ).⁵ But remember, these are the same vowel "class," and so when parsing, you can consider the thematic vowel as "o/u-class" and work from there.⁶

Finally, remember that when parsing, you will be looking at final forms. The morphological principles and changes we discuss in the chapter will help you "unravel" the final verbal form. As we have indicated before (§2.4), observe everything you can about the verb from what you know in the derived stems chart and the standard *qal* paradigms. Consider the key morphological principles addressed here, and then you should be very close to the right parsing.

---

2. GKC, §72gg. E.g., יְעַוֵּל *piel* impf 3ms of עוּל in Isa 26:10; הִתְעַוְּתוּ *hithpael* pf 3cp of עוּת in Eccl 12:3.

3. GKC, §72gg. E.g., צִוָּה "to command;" קִוָּה "to wait;" רִוָּה "to drink." See also Qimḥi, §37a.

4. For discussion on the vowel system with three vowel classes, see JM, §6e–f, §6i; GKC, §7a; §8a–c.

5. Gesenius designates the /u/ (וּ) thematic vowel to the *qal* active future and the /o/ (וֹ) thematic vowel to the *qal* stative future (GKC, §72b). Qimḥi on the other hand only points out that the two vowels "frequently interchange" (Qimḥi, §37p[b]).

6. When teaching vowels, many introductory grammars divide them into five vowel classes like English (a, e, i, o, u). However, Hebrew actually has three vowel classes, a, i/e, and o/u (GKC, §7a; JM, §6b). The combination of the i/e vowel class can be seen when a long *tsere* shortens to a *hireq*. Similarly, the combination of the o/u vowel class is observed when a long *holem* shortens to a *qibbuts*.

7.2.1 *Qal* Perfect and Participle [Compressed Forms][7]

In the *qal* perfect and participle, II-ו/י verbs will drop the middle ו or י. These forms show evidence of original biconsonantal roots because only two root letters remain in the final verbal form ($R_3R_2R_1 \rightarrow R_3R_1$). It may be helpful to remember the relationship of these forms by remembering that the "P" conjugations (**p**erfect and **p**articiple) dro**p** the II-ו/י. These forms do not retain any remnants of the original II-ו or II-י so these may be some of the more difficult verbal forms to identify. Only two root letters will be present. We will refer to these as "compressed" forms, again trying to play on the relationships of the "p" in all these words (**p**erfect and **p**articiple are com**p**ressed forms that dro**p** the middle ו/י).

7.2.1.1 *Qal* Perfect

In the *qal* perfect, the R_1 and R_3 remain and are united by the thematic vowel that is A-ā/ in standard verbs (e.g., קָם from קוּם), A-ē/ in some stative verbs (e.g., מֵת from מות), and Ô/ in other stative verbs (e.g., בוֹשׁ from בוש).[8] There is no need to memorize these thematic vowel changes. When you encounter these verbs in the Hebrew Bible, they will already be in their final form with their respective thematic vowels. However, knowing that the *qal* perfect can display a few different thematic vowel classes will help with recognition.

One thing to note is that the A-ā/ thematic vowel symbols now have the ā symbol. Previously, any "A" in the thematic vowel symbols (upper or lower case) represented a *pataḥ*. Now, the ā (with the macron) is used to represent a long *qamets*. Remember that the lower-case letters on the perfect side of the slash are for all third persons—A-ā/ (§1.3). Hence, the thematic vowel of the 3ms, 3fs, and 3cp for the *qal* perfect II-ו/י verbs will be a long *qamets*, whereas the other forms will have a *pataḥ*.[9] Here is a representative paradigm using קוּם.

---

7. The concept of a "compressed" form is a descriptive pedagogical name to help remember which forms will lose the middle ו. There is nothing about these forms that historically or morphologically triggers a "compression." The term is only descriptive.

8. Blau, *Phonology and Morphology of Biblical Hebrew*, §4.3.8.7.2.1, pp. 252–53. For בוש, see Blau, *Phonology and Morphology of Biblical Hebrew*, §4.3.8.7.2.4 and associated note, p. 254. With בוש, most forms are written defectively with a *holem* instead of *holem vav*.

9. Qimḥi comments that the long vowel *qamets* is due to a quiescent א into which the middle radical has changed (Qimḥi, §37b). This explanation is conjectural, but interesting in light of א/י interchanges in comparative Semitics (cf. GKC, §80k). Qimḥi's explanation also fails to explain the short *pataḥ* that remains in the rest of the paradigm.

Table 7.1: II-ו/י *Qal* Perfect of קוּם

3ms	קָם	A-ā/
3fs	קָ֫מָה	
2ms	קַ֫מְתָּ	
2fs	קַ֫מְתְּ	A-ā/
1cs	קַ֫מְתִּי	
3cp	קָ֫מוּ	A-ā/
2mp	קַמְתֶּם	
2fp	קַמְתֶּן	A-ā/
1cp	קַ֫מְנוּ	

Notice that all of the forms accent the first root letter with the exception of the heavy sufformatives of the 2mp and 2fp. With II-ו/י verbs, the *qal* perfect 3fs and the *qal* participle fs are distinguishable only by the accent.[10]

7.2.1.2 Qal Participle

For the *qal* participle, the inflected form again drops the II-ו/י and has a long *qamets* as the thematic vowel uniting R₁ and R₃. As such, the II-ו/י participle is the only *qal* active participle without the irreducible *holem* in the first root consonant position. The participle sufformatives are then added directly to the R₃.

Table 7.2: II-ו/י *Qal* Participles of קוּם

Participle of קוּם	
ms	קָם
fs	קָמָה
mp	קָמִים
fp	קָמוֹת

Notice here that the perfect 3ms and the participle ms are identical.[11] This similarity, however, should not cause significant difficulty in context. Similarly, the perfect 3fs and the participle fs look identical initially. However, notice that

---

10. Reymond, *Intermediate Biblical Hebrew Grammar*, §5.15, p. 200.

11. Suchard argues that the participle underwent the same contraction as the perfect (Suchard, *The Development of the Biblical Hebrew Vowels*, §4.2.6, p. 252).

the participle fs accents the final syllable (קָמָ֫ה) whereas the perfect 3fs accents the first syllable (קָ֫מָה). So, for fs forms, the accent is necessary to distinguish these forms.

7.2.1.3 *Qal Vav*-Consecutives (*Vayyiqtol*) and Jussive

Two additional forms should be considered as compressed forms: jussives and *vav*-consecutives (*vayyiqtol*).[12] In some discussions, the jussive is referred to as the "short *yiqtol*" or the "short imperfect."[13] This nomenclature can be helpful to remember these forms as what we are calling compressed forms ("short" *yiqtols*). For consistency in our discussion of II-ו/י verbs, we will continue to call these "compressed" forms since II-ו/י verbs display compressed ("short") forms (perfect and participle as we have already seen) other than the jussive and *vav*-consecutive. We include jussives and *vav*-consecutives here because the majority of forms do *not* display the middle ו or י and can therefore be considered "compressed" forms.

The table below lists representative forms of the *qal* jussives and *vav*-consecutives for II-ו/י verbs. While most jussives and *vav*-consecutives display compressed forms, the table below also lists standard forms with the fully written I-ו/י as the thematic vowel for comparison.[14]

Table 7.3: II-ו/י Jussive and *Vav*-Consecutive

Qal Jussive (Compressed)		*Qal* Jussive		*Qal Vav*-Consecutive (Compressed)		*Qal Vav*-Consecutive	
יָקֻ֫מוּ	Josh 18:4	יָק֫וּמוּ	Deut 32:38	וַיָּ֫קָם	Gen 22:3	וַיָּק֫וּמוּ	Gen 24:54
יָבֹא	2 Kgs 5:8	יָב֫וֹא	Judg 13:8	וַיָּבֹא	Exod 7:10	וַיָּב֫וֹא	1 Sam 4:13
יָשֵׂם	Num 6:26	יְשִׂימוּ	Zech 3:5	וַיָּ֫שֶׂם	Lev 8:8	וַיָּשִׂ֫ימוּ	Gen 9:23

---

12. GKC, §72t; JM, §80b.

13. Reymond, *Intermediate Biblical Hebrew Grammar*, §5.15, p. 202; H. H. Hardy II and Matthew McAffee, *Going Deeper with Biblical Hebrew: An Intermediate Study of the Grammar and Syntax of the Old Testament* (Brentwood, TN: B&H Academic, 2024), 198; Jan Joosten, *The Verbal System of Biblical Hebrew: A New Synthesis Elaborated on the Basis of Classical Prose*, Jerusalem Biblical Studies 10 (Jerusalem: Simor, 2012), 13–15.

14. If we consider our representative form קום, the SESE and WIVU morphology databases in the BHS modules of Logos Bible Software produce 168 occurrences of the *qal vav*-consecutive (*vayyiqtol*) form. Only fifteen of those are standard forms (~9%). The historical relationship between the jussive and *vav*-consecutive would suggest that these forms should both be understood as compressed forms with some exceptional standard forms (see Reymond, *Intermediate Biblical Hebrew Grammar*, §5.15, p. 202).

If we consider שׁוב, the most frequent II-ו verb after בוא (which inflects slightly differently, cf. JM, §80r), there are 25 *qal* jussives in *The Lexham Hebrew Bible* morphology database with only 6 of them as

One thing to highlight is the retraction of the accent to the preformative in the *qal vav*-consecutive compressed forms.[15] When the accent retracts, the final syllable is left closed and unaccented, requiring a short vowel (§1.7). In Table 7.3, this phenomenon is noticeable in קוּם and שִׂים. For בוֹא, the final א likely causes the vowel to remain a long *holem*.[16] Also, בוא very often, if not exclusively, fails to retract the accent to the preformative.

7.2.2 *Qal* Imperfect, Imperative, and Infinitives

Earlier we aligned the "P's" (perfect and participle) of the conjugation names for the compressed forms. We can now align the "I's" for the standard forms (imperfect, imperative, and infinitive). By "standard" forms, we mean forms that retain the original II-ו/י as a contracted thematic vowel.

The standard forms are similar to the infinitive construct of each respective II-ו/י verb. In fact, the lexical form of II-ו/י verbs *is* the infinitive construct since the typical lexical form, *qal* perfect 3ms, drops the middle ו or י in II-ו/י roots. The II-ו/י standard forms appear in three vowel classes. The following table displays each of the three vowel classes for II-ו/י verbs. Notice in each of these that the II-ו/י remains present as the thematic vowel.

Table 7.4: II-ו/י Imperfect, Imperative, and Infinitive

	Qal Infinitive Construct	*Qal* Imperfect (3ms)	*Qal* Imperative (2ms)
u-class[17]	קוּם	יָקוּם	קוּם
o-class	בּוֹא	יָבוֹא	בּוֹא
i-class[18]	שִׂים	יָשִׂים	שִׂים

---

standard forms (~25 %). There are 157 *qal vav*-consecutive forms with 17 as standard forms (~11 %). Most of those may be considered late Biblical Hebrew in the books of Zechariah, Nehemiah, or Chronicles. The statistics show that the compressed forms are more common for II-ו/י jussives and *vav*-consecutives.

15. Reymond points out that the short-*yiqtol* (jussive) and the *vayyiqtol* are distinguishable by this accent shift (Reymond, *Intermediate Biblical Hebrew Grammar*, §5.15, p. 202). Compare this to the accent retraction in I-ו/י verbs with *vav*-consecutive (§4.2.4).

16. See JM, §80r (cf. §47b) for more on the morphology of בוא.

17. These representative forms entail the vast majority of forms, but there are exceptions. According to the SESE morphology in Logos Bible Software, there is one compressed form of קוּם out of 45 *qal* infinitives construct. There are nine compressed forms out of 90 *qal* imperfects of קוּם. There are four compressed forms out of 94 *qal* imperatives of קוּם. In this case, the compressed forms are a result of the historically long vowel begin written defectively, without the *matres lectionis* (e.g., יָקָם *qal* impf 3ms, Gen 27:31). These forms are distinguishable from the perfect and participle compressed forms because of the preformatives of the prefixed conjugation (i.e., imperfect).

18. For i-class II-ו/י verbs, we would technically consider them II-י verbs and hence the thematic vowel in this form is the *hireq yod*.

7.2.2.1 *Qal* Imperfect

In the *qal* imperfect the preformative vowel is a-class, usually the long *qamets* (ָ).[19] The original a-class vowel of the preformative would have been a *pataḥ*. However, when the II-ו/י contracts to the thematic vowel, the preformative syllable becomes an open pretonic syllable that lengthens the vowel to *qamets*. The theoretical paradigms are listed in the table below. Not all of these forms appear in the Hebrew Bible.

Table 7.5: II-ו/י Imperfect Representative Paradigms

	U-Class	O-Class	I-Class
3ms	יָקוּם	יָבוֹא	יָשִׂים
3fs	תָּקוּם	תָּבוֹא	תָּשִׂים
2ms	תָּקוּם	תָּבוֹא	תָּשִׂים
2fs	תָּקוּמִי	תָּבוֹאִי	תָּשִׂימִי
1cs	אָקוּם	אָבוֹא	אָשִׂים
3mp	יָקוּמוּ	יָבוֹאוּ	יָשִׂימוּ
3fp	תְּקוּמֶינָה	תָּבוֹאנָה	תָּשֵׂמְנָה
2mp	תָּקוּמוּ	תָּבוֹאוּ	תָּשִׂימוּ
2fp	תְּקוּמֶינָה	תָּבוֹאנָה	תָּשֵׂמְנָה
1cp	נָקוּם	נָבוֹא	נָשִׂים

Notice that across the paradigms the distinctive preformatives and sufformatives of each conjugated form are the same as the strong verb (e.g., imperfect 2fs shell is still תּ○○◌ִי).

Next, notice that the imperfect 2fp, in the u-class forms, takes a helping vowel (◌ֶי) before the sufformative.[20] The standard form having all the lexical consonants and the shell (תּ○○◌ֶינָה) should direct you to the 2/3fp imperfect without the need to consider the helping vowel directly when parsing.

Finally, notice also that in the i-class imperfect 2/3fp the thematic vowel

---

19. GKC, §72d.
20. This helping vowel occurs somewhat inconsistently. See Reymond, *Intermediate Biblical Hebrew Grammar*, §5.15, p. 203 where he lists Ezek 16:55 with שׁוּב having a normal ending (תָּשֹׁבְןָ) in one form and the helping vowel (תְּשֻׁבֶינָה) in the other. He also lists תָּבֹאנָה (Isa 47:9) and תְּבֹאֶינָה (Ps 45:16), again without and with the helping vowel, respectively.

shifts to the *tsere*. This phenomenon is unattested for the root שִׂים and only occurs here for the purposes of a representative paradigm. The i-class imperfect 2/3fp only occurs twice in the Hebrew Bible with the verbal root גִיל (תָּגֵלְנָה, Ps 48:12; 51:10). This form need not be memorized since it is so rare.

7.2.2.2 *Qal* Imperative

The *qal* imperative 2ms is identical to the standard forms of the infinitive construct.[21] This phenomenon is the same as the standard verb *qal* paradigm as well (impv—קְטֹל; inf cstr—קְטֹל). If you compare the table below with the imperfect table above, you will also notice that the imperative, once again, can be formed by removing the preformative of the imperfect.

Table 7.6: II-ו/י Imperative Representative Paradigms

	U-Class	O-Class	I-Class
2ms	קוּם	בּוֹא	שִׂים
2fs	קוּמִי	בּוֹאִי	שִׂימִי
2mp	קוּמוּ	בּוֹאוּ	שִׂימוּ
2fp	קֹמְנָה[22]	בֹּאנָה	גֵּלְנָה[23]

While we expect to see standard forms in the *qal* imperative based on their relationship to the imperfect, one should note that compressed forms occur as well.[24] These imperative forms may have the middle vowel written

---

21. GKC, §72q; JM, §80c.

22. The *qal* imperative 2fp of קוּם only occurs one time in the Hebrew Bible (Isa 32:9) and it is a compressed form with the *holem vav* written defectively (קֹמְנָה). With an accented R₁, the long *holem* is expected versus a short *qamets ḥatuf* or *qibbuts*. Since Hebrew does not have a nonhistorically long /ū/ vowel, then the o-class *holem* was the necessary vowel point. Hence, קוּם can still be considered a u-class II-ו/י verb even though the form in Isa 32:9 requires a *holem*.

23. This form is hypothetical based on the *qal* imperfect of גִיל in Ps 48:12; 51:10 (תָּגֵלְנָה). From the 180 biconsonantal roots listed in Gary Pratico and Miles Van Pelt's *Vocabulary Guide to Biblical Hebrew and Aramaic*, 2nd ed. (Grand Rapids: Zondervan, 2019), fourteen have a lexical form with a II-י. Assuming these fourteen roots represent the i-class II-י verbs, none of them attest to a *qal* imperative 2fp in the Hebrew Bible. Since תָּגֵלְנָה is the only attested imperfect fp, we must assume that the *tsere* thematic vowel is normal even for the imperative. This may reflect thematic vowel symbols for impf/impv of II-י verbs that are /î-ē.

24. For example, the SESE morphology produces nine feminine singular imperative forms of בּוֹא. Only two of those are standard forms with the *holem vav* written fully. Similarly, of fifty-eight masculine *qal* imperatives of בּוֹא, only four are standard forms. Alternatively, of seventy-nine masculine *qal* imperatives of קוּם, only three are compressed forms.

defectively, without the full *mater lectionis* (e.g., שִׂמִי impv 2fs שִׂים, Jer 31:21; שִׂמוּ impv 2mp שִׂים, Jer 40:10).

7.2.2.3 *Qal* Infinitive

As previously mentioned, the *qal* infinitive construct is the lexical form for II-ו/י verbs.[25] In one sense, the more vocabulary you learn for II-ו/י verbs, the more easily you will recognize the infinitive construct forms. You should not embark on a project to learn all of the II-ו/י vocabulary but be encouraged that as you progress in learning vocabulary, you will also be improving your parsing of weak verbs.

7.2.2.3.1 *Qal* Infinitive Construct

The infinitive construct follows the lexical forms of the respective vowel classes.

Table 7.7: II-ו/י Infinitive Construct

U-Class	O-Class	I-Class
קוּם	בּוֹא	שִׂים

These are, once again, what we are calling standard forms since the lexical roots retain the II-ו/י. However, there are some minor exceptions.[26]

7.2.2.3.2 *Qal* Infinitive Absolute

For the infinitives absolute, the thematic vowel follows the original *qal* paradigm (קָטוֹל) with a *holem vav* thematic vowel across all vowel classes.[27]

---

25. GKC, §72a.
26. Of the twenty-five *qal* infinitive construct forms of קוּם, one is a compressed form—וּבְקֻמָהּ (Gen 19:35). However, this form can still easily be recognized as an infinitive construct with the בְּ preposition and the pronominal suffix. The infinitive construct of בּוֹא occurs 286 times in the Hebrew Bible. Several of these are compressed forms without the middle ו or י. Most of these compressed forms have pronominal suffixes typical of the noun, and so these will also not be problematic to parse as infinitives construct.
27. In the Groves-Wheeler Westminster Hebrew Morphology in Accordance Bible Software, II-י verbs occur twenty-six times as infinitives absolute. Some thematic vowels are written defectively as a *holem*, but only two of those forms have an original II-י—רִיב in Jer 50:34 and בִּין in Prov 23:1. The infinitive absolute בֹּז occurs two other times. For II-ו verbs, Accordance Bible Software produces eighty-nine forms, and all of them have the /o/ thematic vowel with variations of fully written *holem vav* and defectively written *holem*.
  According to *The Lexham Hebrew Bible* morphology database, there are seventy-one *qal* infinitives absolute of II-ו verbs and ten occurrences of II-י verbs (five of those are היה). All have the *holem vav* thematic vowel for the infinitives absolute (though some are written defectively—e.g., שֹׁ *qal* inf abs שִׁית, Isa 22:7).

In that sense, the *qal* infinitive absolute is a "strong" form. Granted, the middle ו/י is no longer a root consonant but is now a vowel. However, that it becomes a *holem vav* is representative of the strong form in the original *qal* paradigm.

Table 7.8: II-ו/י Infinitive Absolute

U-Class	O-Class	I-Class
קוֹם	בוֹא	שׂוֹם

7.3 II-ו/י Verbs: *Niphal*

For *niphal* II-ו/י verbs, the perfect and participle (the P's) can once again be considered together.[28] They are not "compressed forms" in the *niphal*, but they are morphologically related to one another. Remember that in the derived stems chart, both the *niphal* perfect and participle shell is נָOOO, so it makes sense that they would morph similarly in II-ו/י verbs as well.

The thematic vowel for *niphal* II-ו/י verbs is o/u-class. Most often, it will be written as a *holem vav* (וֹ), although sometimes, the *holem vav* may be written defectively in the o/u vowel class (נָמֹגוּ *niphal* pf 3cp מוג, Exod 15:15; נְבָכִים *niphal* ptc mp בוּךְ, Exod 14:3). The thematic vowel may shift to a *shureq* (וּ), allowing for dissimilation of sound with syllabic sufformatives in the perfect (נְסוּגֹתִי, Isa 50:5). Even when the vowel is reduced or changes to the *shureq*, the thematic vowel will remain in the o/u vowel class.

Syllabic sufformatives in the *niphal* perfect use a helping vowel (*holem vav*) to connect the sufformative to the root (נְפוּגוֹתִי *niphal* pf 1cs פוג, Ps 38:9).[29] When the *niphal* perfect takes a syllabic sufformative (1cs, 2ms, 2fs, 1cp, 2mp, 2fp), the thematic vowel will shift to a *shureq* (נְקוּמֹתִי). Gesenius argues this shift to the /u/ thematic vowel is a result of the accent shift.[30] It could also be a dissimilation of sound as it is somewhat easier to pronounce "$ô \rightarrow û$" than "$ô \rightarrow ô$."[31] No matter how you explain the thematic vowel shift, when parsing a final form, the remnants of the middle ו of the root will still be present, albeit a vowel instead of a root consonant. The syllabic sufformative remains the same as the standard *qal* paradigm only with the helping vowel between the R_3 and the sufformative.

---

28. GKC, §72v; JM, §80f; §81c; Qimḥi, §37h–k.
29. Reymond, *Intermediate Biblical Hebrew Grammar*, §5.15, pp. 200–01, highlights that the second- and first-person forms attest the /o/ connecting vowel, but not the third person forms. This explanation aligns with what we are calling forms with syllabic sufformatives in the perfect conjugation.
30. GKC, §72i; Suchard, *The Development of the Biblical Hebrew Vowels*, §4.2.6, p. 251.
31. Blau, *Phonology and Morphology of Biblical Hebrew*, §4.3.8.7.3.2, p. 255; Qimḥi, §37i.

7.3.1 *Niphal* Perfect and Participle

In the *niphal* perfect and participle, the preformative vowel follows the historical /a/ vowel as is the tendency in other weak verbs.[32] Because the middle ו or י contracts to become the thematic vowel, the preformative syllable is most often left in an open pretonic syllable and therefore the *pataḥ* lengthens to a *qamets* (נָדוֹשׁ *niphal* pf 3ms דושׁ, Isa 25:10). When sufformatives shift the accent further down the word such that the preformative syllable is left open propretonic, the original *pataḥ* will reduce to a vocal *shewa* (נְסוּגֹתִי *niphal* pf 1cs סוג, Isa 50:5). The following forms provide some examples from the Hebrew Bible. Notice that in some cases, the thematic vowel may be written defectively.

Perfect

נָפֹצוּ	*niphal* pf 3cp פוץ	Gen 10:18	*thematic vowel written defectively*
נָמוֹג	*niphal* pf 3ms מוג	1 Sam 14:16	
נָכוֹנָה	*niphal* pf 3fs כון	1 Kgs 2:46	
נְפֹצוֹתֶם	*niphal* pf 2mp פוץ	Ezek 11:17	*thematic vowel written defectively*

Participle

נָכוֹן	*niphal* ptc ms כון	Gen 41:32
נְכוֹנָה	*niphal* ptc fs כון	Ps 5:10
נְפוֹצִים	*niphal* ptc mp פוץ	2 Chr 18:16

7.3.2 *Niphal* Imperfect, Imperative, and Infinitive

The imperfect, imperative, and infinitive of the *niphal* II-ו/י verbs will generally be recognizable due to the distinctive *dagesh forte* in the R₁.[33] On the representative root קום, the normal shell for the *niphal* imperfect 3ms is *יִקּוֹם. Similarly, the infinitive absolute, infinitive construct, and imperative display the same shell, but with the ה preformative—*הִקּוֹם. Again, the distinctive *dagesh forte* in the R₁ will help with parsing these *niphal* forms.

The thematic vowel for these *niphal* conjugations is still a *holem vav* (וֹ).[34] This is analogous to the *aw* → *ô* contraction, though we do not technically

---

32. Joüon calls this the "primitive *na*" of the *niphal* (JM, §80f). One exception is מול that inflects in the *niphal* perfect and participle with a *dagesh forte* in the R₁ (נִמֹּל pf 3ms, Gen 17:26; נִמֹּלִים ptc mp, Gen 34:22). This is analogous to the *niphal* imperfect and imperative that also have a *dagesh forte* in the R₁. The *dagesh forte* in the R₁ requires the retention of the short *hireq* preformative vowel.

33. GKC, §72ee. The distinctive *dagesh forte* in the R₁ of the *niphal* will not be present when the II-ו/י verb is doubly weak with a I-guttural as well (e.g., יֵעוֹר *niphal* impf 3ms עור, Jer 6:22). Cf. §3.3 in this book.

34. Some forms are written defectively without the *mater lectionis* (לְהִמֹּל *niphal* inf cstr מול, Gen 34:15). One exception is the *niphal* infinitive construct, הִדּוֹשׁ, in Isa 25:10, with a *shureq*.

have a middle ו with a silent *shewa*. Additionally, continue to remember that we will be parsing final forms that have already shifted the II-ו/י to a *holem vav* and so explaining its origin will be unnecessary for parsing. The following table provides the representative paradigms using קוּם. Not all forms are attested in the Hebrew Bible.

Table 7.9: II-ו/י Niphal Imperfect, Imperative, and Infinitive

	Imperfect	Imperative		Infinitive	
3ms	יִקּוֹם			הִקּוֹם	absolute
3fs	תִּקּוֹם			נָמוֹג³⁵	(Isa 14:31)
2ms	תִּקּוֹם	הִקּוֹם			
2fs	תִּקּוֹמִי	הִקּוֹמִי			
1cs	אֶקּוֹם			הִקּוֹם	construct
3mp	יִקּוֹמוּ				
3fp	תִּקּוֹמְנָה				
2mp	תִּקּוֹמוּ	הִקּוֹמוּ			
2fp	תִּקּוֹמְנָה	הִקּוֹמְנָה			
1cp	נִקּוֹם				

7.4 II-ו/י Verbs: *Hiphil*

The perfect and participle can once again be considered together in the *hiphil* of II-ו/י verbs.[36] Both the perfect and the participle take *hireq* preformative vowels that follow vowel adjustment patterns we covered in the first chapter (cf. §1.7). Pretonic open syllables will lengthen the preformative vowel (הֵקִים) whereas open propretonic syllables will reduce the vowel to a vocal *shewa* when syllabic sufformatives pull the accent down the word (הֲקִימוֹתִי).[37] *Hiphil* participles change similarly, but with the מ preformative (מֵקִים) *hiphil* ptc ms קוּם,

---

35. This form is based on the *niphal* infinitive absolute shell, ○○○ַנ that shifts to an /a/ preformative like the *niphal* perfect and participle (cf. §7.3.1).

36. GKC, §72w.

37. See discussion in Blau, *Phonology and Morphology of Biblical Hebrew*, §4.3.8.7.4.1, p. 256.

Gen 9:9; מְשִׁיבִים *hiphil* ptc mp שׁוב, Judg 11:9). You will notice in Table 7.10 that the preformative vowels in every form are different from the strong verb paradigms. Knowing these two vowel adjustment patterns will provide the reason why each form is different rather than trying to memorize so many unique forms for the *hiphil* II-ו/י verbs.

The thematic vowel in the *hiphil* is mostly a *hireq yod*, as expected from the strong verb thematic vowel symbols.[38] The forms that do not have a *hireq yod* thematic vowel are the four *tsere* forms (J.I.I.V.E.; cf. §1.3).

The preformative vowel for the imperfect, imperative, and infinitive is *patah*, as expected from our derived stems chart. The preformative vowel in the imperfect, imperative, and infinitive also follows expected vowel lengthening rules. In the imperfect paradigm (and hence also the imperative and infinitive), the preformative vowel will be an open pretonic syllable, lengthening the *patah* from our derived stems chart (ΟΟַΟ) to the *qamets* we see in these final forms (יָקִים).[39]

The following table provides a representative paradigm in which not all forms are attested in the Hebrew Bible.

Table 7.10: II-ו/י *Hiphil* Representative Paradigms

	Perfect	Imperfect	Imperative	Participle	
3ms	הֵקִים	יָקִים		מֵקִים	ms
3fs	הֵקִימָה	תָּקִים		מְקִימָה	fs
2ms	הֲקִימֹוֹתָ	תָּקִים	הָקֵם[40]	מְקִימִים	mp
2fs	הֲקִימֹוֹת	תָּקִימִי	הָקִימִי	מְקִימוֹת	fp
1cs	הֲקִימֹוֹתִי	אָקִים			
3cp/3mp	הֵקִימוּ	יָקִימוּ			
3fp		תְּקִמֶנָה		**Infinitive**	
2mp	הֲקִימוֹתֶם	תָּקִימוּ	הָקִימוּ	הָקֵם	absolute
2fp	הֲקִימוֹתֶן	תְּקִמֶנָה	הֲקֵמְנָה	הָקִים	construct
1cp	הֲקִימֹונוּ	נָקִים			

---

38. GKC, §72f.

39. A few *hiphil* forms take a *dagesh forte* in the R₁ akin to transposition of gemination (see §8.3.1.2). In these cases, the final form will retain a short vowel in the preformative. For example, תַּסִּיג (impf 2ms סוג, Deut 19:14) and the jussive תַּסֵּג (Mic 6:14; Prov 22:28; 23:10). Blau comments that the *dagesh forte* may be akin to I-נ behavior in addition to the possibility of geminate behavior (Blau, *Phonology and Morphology of Biblical Hebrew*, §4.3.8.7.4.4, p. 256). Gesenius relates these forms to a "quasi-Aramaic formation" like geminate verbs (GKC, §72ee). Qimḥi also notes these forms (Qimḥi, §37p[a]).

40. Note the two *tsere* forms in this paradigm, the imperative 2ms and the infinitive absolute. These are two of the *hiphil* J.I.I.V.E. forms that take a *tsere* thematic vowel.

7.5 II-ו/י Verbs: *Hophal*

Thankfully, the *hophal* forms are relatively simple.[41] In the *hophal* of II-ו/י verbs, the middle ו flips places with the R_1 and becomes a *shureq*. The forms follow the *uw* → *û* contraction that we have seen before.

הוּקַם	←	הֻוְקַם	←	וְקַם	←	קוֹם
û		*uw*		ו Switches Places		Original II-ו Root

As with most historically long vowels in weak verbs, the *shureq* may be written defectively with a *qibbuts* (הֻקַם *hophal* pf 3ms קום, 2 Sam 23:1).

The thematic vowel for II-ו/י *hophal* verbs can be represented as A/A. The a-class thematic vowels vary between *pataḥ* and *qamets* depending on pausal forms and other factors.[42] *Hophal* participles have a long *qamets* thematic vowel as is expected from the strong verb (§1.3).

Hophal verbs are not extremely common compared to the active stems (396 occurrences out of 73,186 tagged verbs in *The Lexham Hebrew Bible*), but there are 129 *hophal* II-ו/י verbs tagged in *The Lexham Hebrew Bible*. Almost 33 percent of all *hophals* are II-ו/י *hophals*! So, while they are relatively few, they are worth knowing. Here are some examples from the Hebrew Bible.

יוּשַׁת	*hophal* impf 3ms שׁית	Exod 21:30 (2x)
תּוּרַק	*hophal* impf 3fs ריק	Song 1:3
מוּבָאִים	*hophal* ptc mp בוא	Gen 43:18
הוּנַף	*hophal* pf 3ms נוף	Exod 29:27
יוּמְתוּ	*hophal* impf 3mp מות	Deut 24:16 (2x)

7.6 II-ו/י Verbs: *Polel, Polal, Hithpolel* (*Piel, Pual,* and *Hithpael*)

At the beginning of the chapter, we mentioned that there are a few forms that retain the middle ו as a quasi-strong form. There are nine *piel* forms of קום with *piel* morphology (e.g., לְקַיֵּם [inf cstr]; קִיַּם [pf 3ms]; קִיְּמוּ [pf 3cp], all three in Esth 9:31). However, the more common morphology is to reduplicate

---

41. GKC, §72bb; JM, §80g; Qimḥi, §37o.
42. There is one debatable exception in Zech 5:11. הַנִּיחָה (*hophal* pf 3fs נוח) has a *hireq yod* thematic vowel. *HALOT* and BDB both list this form as a *hophal* but refer the reader to the *hiphil* entry. Gesenius comments that this form may be an isolated passive *hiphil* but should probably be read as a true *hiphil* as the LXX suggests with a future active indicative 3pl in Greek (GKC, §72ee).

the R₃ and contract the middle ו to a וֹ.⁴³ These forms essentially become additional stems commonly known as the *polel*, *polal*, and *hithpolel*.⁴⁴ These correspond in meaning to the *piel*, *pual*, and *hithpael*, respectively, but shift the stem morphology due to the weakness of the II-ו/י.

Polel

יְעוֹפֵף	*polel* impf 3ms עוף	Gen 1:20
מְמוֹתֵת	*polel* ptc ms מות	1 Sam 14:13
רוֹמַמְתִּי	*polel* pf 1cs רום	Isa 23:4

Polal

כּוֹנָנוּ	*polal* pf 3cp כון	Ps 37:23
תְּרוֹמַמְנָה	*polal* impf 3fp רום	Ps 75:11
חוֹלָלְתָּ	*polal* pf 2ms חיל	Job 15:7

Hithpolel

הִתְמוֹטְטָה	*hithpolel* pf 3fs מוט	Isa 24:19
מִתְבּוֹסֶסֶת	*hithpolel* ptc fs (t-form) בוס	Ezek 16:6
אֶתְבּוֹנֵן	*hithpolel* impf 1cs בון	Job 31:1

While the most common reduplication is of the single R₃, some II-ו/י verbs may reduplicate both consonants (R₁ and R₃). These forms result in any variety of stem names depending on the vowels: *pilpel*, *palpel*, etc. We will see this phenomenon more with geminate verbs as well, but for now, it is sufficient to know reduplication of both consonants is possible.

Pilpel/Palpel

| כִּלְכַּלְתִּי | *pilpel* pf 1cs כול | Gen 45:11 |
| יְסַכְסֵךְ | *palpel* impf 3ms סוך | Isa 9:10 |

Polpal

| כָּלְכְּלוּ | *polpal* pf 3cp כול | 1 Kgs 20:27 |

Apart from the reduplication of the R₃ (or the R₁ and R₃), the other preformatives and sufformatives of the standard paradigm will distinguish these

---

43. Blau, *Phonology and Morphology of Biblical Hebrew*, §4.3.8.7.5.1, pp.256–57; Reymond, *Intermediate Biblical Hebrew Grammar*, §5.15, p. 203; GKC, §72m.

44. For summaries of these rare stems, see JM, §59 and GKC, §55.

forms regarding conjugation and PGN as can be seen from the representative forms above.

7.7 Conclusion

II-ו/י verbs can certainly feel overwhelming when you consider all the details of this chapter. However, as with most ו/י verbs, the basic concepts boil down to (1) ו and י may contract into historically long vowels or (2) ו and י may drop out (cf. §2.3.3). As in most cases, the *qal* is the most complicated stem since it is the most common stem. Generally in languages, the most common words and conjugations are the ones prone to the most phonological (and hence morphological) abuse. When we encountered rare forms, my professors used to say, "Because that's how Hebrew mommas taught Hebrew babies." We should therefore expect the *qal* to show the most anomalies, but even there, the basic principles of the II-ו/י contracting or dropping out can help us "unravel" the final form back to an original shell.

CHAPTER 8

Geminate Verbs

8.1 Introduction

Geminate verbs are verbs with identical second and third root consonants (e.g., קלל, ארר, סבב). If you remember from our general discussion of weak verb traits, Hebrew tends not to write the same two consonants consecutively (§2.3.4). For geminate verbs this means they will often display a "collapsed" form such that only the R_1 and R_2 remain and the R_3 may or may not appear as a *dagesh forte*.[1] In many ways, geminate verbs are analogous to II-ו/י verbs.[2] Final forms may only have two of the original consonants remaining and so some scholars consider these biconsonantal roots as well, or at least derived from them.[3] Eric Reymond comments that geminate verbs "are the most complex of the root types."[4] However, with knowledge of some general characteristics and a few specific characteristics of individual conjugations, even geminate verbs can become manageable. Once you identify the root, the preformatives and sufformatives of the strong verb shells will guide you to the correct parsing.

8.2 Strong Forms of Geminate Verbs

In some cases, geminate verbs may be written as a strong form. Since these will be easily recognizable, only a few representative examples are provided below. The strong forms are largely limited to the *qal* perfect third persons (3ms, 3fs, 3cp), *qal* participle, and *qal* infinitives.[5] The following list includes

---

1. GKC, §67a.1; JM, §82a. For geminate verbs, we will use the terminology "collapsed" forms rather than "compressed" forms that we used with II-ו/י verbs. This is essentially a way to separate the pedagogical terminology for the two different weak verb types.
2. Joüon calls this "contamination" (JM, §82o).
3. E.g., Blau, *Phonology and Morphology of Biblical Hebrew*, §4.3.8.8, pp. 258–60. Francis Anderson argues geminates may have byforms that follow triconsonantal paradigms in some cases and biconsonantal paradigms in other places without predictability (Francis I. Anderson, "Biconsonantal Byforms of Weak Hebrew Roots," *Zeitschrift für die alttestamentliche Wissenschaft* 82/2 [1970]: 271).
4. Reymond, *Intermediate Biblical Hebrew Grammar*, §5.17, p. 208.
5. In the active participles, the R_1 *holem* may be written fully (סוֹרֵר *qal* ptc ms סרר, Deut 21:18, 20). Alternatively, the passive participles may write the *shureq* thematic vowel defectively (צְרֻרֹת *qal* pass ptc

examples of each. Notice in each of these examples that the *qal* paradigm shells are represented exactly.

סָבַב	*qal* pf 3ms סבב	Ezek 42:19	
נָדְדָה	*qal* pf 3fs נדד	Isa 10:31	
סָבְבוּ	*qal* pf 3cp סבב	Josh 6:15	
חֹבֵב	*qal* ptc ms חבב	Deut 33:3	
סֹכְכִים	*qal* ptc mp סכך	Exod 25:20	
שֹׁגֶגֶת	*qal* ptc fs (t-form) שגג	Num 15:28	*t-form ptc retains a strong form*
אָרוּר	*qal* pass ptc ms ארר	Gen 3:14	
פָּתוֹת	*qal* inf abs פתת	Lev 2:6	
מְשׁוֹשׁ	*qal* inf cstr משׁשׁ	Isa 8:6	

8.3 General Characteristics of Geminate Verbs

In this section, we will consider the characteristics of geminate verbs that occur in most forms. These are not absolute rules, but they are the general tendencies for geminate verbs that will help you decipher and "unravel" the final form and "see" the distinguishing marks of the stem and conjugation for parsing purposes.

8.3.1 Collapsed Forms with Sufformatives Often Get a *Dagesh Forte*

In forms that have sufformatives, the presence of a *dagesh forte* will be your biggest ally in determining the root as a geminate root.

8.3.1.1 Doubling Usually Happens with R₂/R₃

Geminate verbal roots frequently represent the two geminate consonants as a single consonant with *dagesh forte* (e.g., חַתּוּ *qal* pf 3cp חתת, 2 Kgs 19:26).[6] When the final form does not display three original consonants, a *dagesh forte* may indicate the doubled R₂ and R₃. This phenomenon occurs when sufformatives are added such that the remaining geminate consonant does not end the word (e.g., תָּבֹסּוּ *qal* impf 2mp בסס, Exod 12:4).[7] This *dagesh forte* will be a helpful indicator that you are parsing a geminate verb.[8] We should also note

---

fp צרר, Exod 12:34). Furthermore, the infinitive absolute may also be written defectively but should still be considered a strong form (טָפֹף *qal* inf abs טפף, Isa 3:16).

6. Blau, *Phonology and Morphology of Biblical Hebrew*, §4.3.8.8.1(a), p. 258; Reymond, *Intermediate Biblical Hebrew Grammar*, §5.17, p. 209; GKC, §67a.

7. GKC, §67c.

8. At times, *qal* geminate verbs may look like *piel* forms of other roots. For example, the first representative form listed in this section (גַּלּוֹתִי) could be parsed as a *piel* infinitive construct of גלה with a 1cs

that with syllabic sufformatives, geminate verbs use a helping vowel between the root and the sufformative (see §8.3.5 below).

The following list provides a few representative examples that display the *dagesh forte*.

גַּלּוֹתִי	*qal* pf 1cs גלל	Josh 5:9
חַקּוֹתָ	*qal* pf 2ms חקק	Ezek 4:1
בַּזּוֹנוּ	*qal* pf 1cp בזז	Deut 3:7
קַלּוּ	*qal* pf 3cp קלל	Gen 8:11
יָלֹקּוּ	*qal* impf 3mp לקק	1 Kgs 21:19
תְּסֻבֶּינָה	*qal* impf 3fp סבב	Gen 37:7
סֹבִּי	*qal* impv 2fs סבב	Isa 23:16
סֹבּוּ	*qal* impv 2mp סבב	Josh 6:7

8.3.1.2 Doubling May Happen with R₁: Transposition of Gemination

While most geminate verbs double the R₂/R₃, occasionally these verbs may double the R₁. This phenomenon may be called *transposition of gemination* in which the doubling "switches places" (סבב → *סס*ב).[9] Historically, it is probable that this phenomenon is an influence of Aramaic, but for pedagogical purposes, we will speak of it as transposition of gemination.[10] Note that this is not an actual change in the root. Notice the asterisk that indicates a hypothetical form (*סס*ב). This is simply a way to represent transposition of gemination where the word inflects as if the R₁ has doubled (יִדְּמוּ *qal* impf 3mp דמם, Exod 15:16).

8.3.1.3 Doubling May Happen in R₁ and R₂/R₃

On occasion, geminate verbs will double both the R₁ and the R₃ leaving both remaining root consonants with a *dagesh forte*.[11] The following representative forms show this phenomenon.

יֻכַּתּוּ	*hophal* impf 3mp כתת	Jer 46:5
יִתַּמּוּ	*qal* impf 3mp תמם	Num 14:35

---

pronominal suffix. You will have to rely on contextual clues and pay close attention to other features of the morphology in order to distinguish some *qal* geminate forms from other *piel* forms.

9. Fuller and Choi, *Invitation to Biblical Hebrew*, 280–81.

10. Blau, *Phonology and Morphology of Biblical Hebrew*, §4.3.8.8.1(b), p. 258; Reymond, *Intermediate Biblical Hebrew Grammar*, §5.17, pp. 209–10; Suchard, *The Development of the Biblical Hebrew Vowels*, §4.2.5, p. 251; GKC, §67g; JM, §82h.

11. Blau, *Phonology and Morphology of Biblical Hebrew*, §4.3.8.8.1(d), p. 258. Reymond comments that this may be a result of confusion with the *niphal* stem, citing the *niphal* of סבב in Ezek 1:12—יִסַּבּוּ (Reymond, *Intermediate Biblical Hebrew Grammar*, §5.17, p. 210). Gesenius includes these with the Aramaizing forms that double the R₁ (GKC, §67g).

8.3.2 Hebrew Does Not Double Final Consonants

Hebrew will not double the final consonant of a word when that consonant ends the word.[12] Therefore, it is possible for a geminate verb to be a "collapsed" form and not get a *dagesh forte* in either of the two remaining consonants.[13] This phenomenon occurs when there are no imperfect sufformatives, leaving what would have been the "doubled" consonant at the end of the word (יָסֹב, *qal* impf 3ms סבב, 1 Kgs 7:15). The final consonant in this situation will not display the *dagesh forte*.

יָלֹק	*qal* impf 3ms לקק	Judg 7:5
יִמָּס	*niphal* impf 3ms מסס	Isa 13:7
תָּעֹז	*qal* impf 3fs עזז	Eccl 7:19

8.3.3 Thematic Vowel Shifts Between R₁ and R₂

When geminate verbs collapse, the thematic vowel shifts so that it is now between the R₁ and R₂. This is a similar concept to the II-ו/י verbs when the middle ו dropped out and an a-class vowel occurred between R₁ and R₃ (in the pf and ptc) or when the middle ו or י contracted to become the historically long thematic vowel (in the impf, impv, and inf).[14]

qal imperfect 3ms סבב

יָסֹב ← יִסְבֹּב*

Collapsed Form   Hypothetical Strong Form

In the form presented here, the *holem* that was the thematic vowel on the R₂ (ב) in the hypothetical form shifts so that it now occurs between the R₁ and R₂ in the final collapsed form.

We will discuss the specific thematic vowels for geminate verbs when we cover the individual stems below, but the general characteristic here is that the thematic vowel shifts between R₁ and R₂.

8.3.4 Gutturals Do Not Double

The next general characteristic of geminate verbs is related to the principle that gutturals to not admit a *dagesh forte* (cf. §2.3.1.1). Certain gutturals (primarily א, ע, and ר) reject a *dagesh forte* and lengthen the preceding vowel

---

12. GKC, §67c, §20l.3(a); JM, §18l.
13. Blau, *Phonology and Morphology of Biblical Hebrew*, §3.5.11.3, p. 139; §4.3.8.8.5, p. 259; Reymond, *Intermediate Biblical Hebrew Grammar*, §5.17, p. 209.
14. GKC, §67b.

by compensation while other gutturals (primarily ה and ח) imply the *dagesh forte* (virtual doubling), but do not lengthen the preceding vowel (§2.3.1).[15] Both of these principles occur in geminate verbs with gutturals. If the R_2/R_3 is a guttural (and so doubly weak), then the R_2 will not admit a *dagesh forte* in the collapsed form. For these examples, it is helpful to see the progression. The first example shows rejection of the *dagesh forte* in the ע while the second demonstrates the implied *dagesh* in the ח.

| רָעָה | *qal* pf 3fs | רעע | 2 Sam 19:8 | רָעָ֫ה ← *רָעֲעָה |
| שַׁח֫וֹתִי | *qal* pf 1cs | שחח | Ps 35:14 | שַׁח֫וֹתִי ← *שַׁחַ֫חְתִּי |

8.3.5 Syllabic Sufformatives Use Helping Vowels

The final general characteristic for geminate verbs is that they use helping vowels before syllabic sufformatives.[16] In the perfect, geminate verbs use a *holem vav* (וֹ) helping vowel and the imperfect often uses a *segol yod* (ֶי) as the helping vowel.[17] Fairly often, the *holem vav* helping vowel will be written defectively as just a *holem*.

קַלּ֫וֹתָ	*qal* pf 2ms	קלל	Nah 1:14	
דַּלּ֫וֹנוּ	*qal* pf 1cp	דלל	Ps 79:8	
חַנֹּ֫תִי	*qal* pf 1cs	חנן	Exod 33:19	*helping vowel written defectively*
תְּסֻבֶּ֫ינָה	*qal* impf 3fp	סבב	Gen 37:7	

8.4 Specific Characteristics of Geminate Verbs

In this section, we will note some of the specific characteristics of geminate verbs across the stems. Most of these characteristics are specific applications of the principles given already. The following lists are intended to be representative, but extensive in order to provide examples of the various characteristics for geminate verbs. Where forms are missing (e.g., *qal* pf 2fs), those forms are unattested in the Hebrew Bible.

There are some forms that display anomalies, and so do not align with the general characteristics of geminate verbs. So for this section, it is best to observe the specific characteristics from final forms in the Hebrew Bible rather than attempt to reproduce historical derivations for these forms.

---

15. GKC, §22b–c.
16. Blau, *Phonology and Morphology of Biblical Hebrew*, §4.3.8.8.6n, 259; GKC, §67d; JM, §82f.
17. Suchard, *The Development of the Biblical Hebrew Vowels*, §4.2.5, p. 251.

8.4.1 Qal

In the *qal*, stative verbs will nearly always take the *dagesh forte* of a collapsed form when possible (רַבָּה *qal* pf 3fs רבב, Exod 23:29).[18] *Qal* transitive verbs, on the other hand, may display strong forms or collapsed forms. When geminate verbs double the R₂ with *dagesh forte*, the syllable will follow the characteristics of the rules for vowel adjustment, leaving a short vowel in the closed syllable (§1.7).[19] When the accent remains on the middle syllable, the vowel will remain long (תָּבֹסּוּ *qal* impf 2mp בסס, Exod 12:4).[20] When the accent shifts down the word, the thematic vowel syllable will be closed and unaccented and so the vowel will become short (תְּסֻבֶּינָה *qal* impf 3fp סבב, Gen 37:7). The *qal* jussive and *vav*-consecutive forms may retract the accent, leaving the final syllable with a short vowel in a closed syllable, analogous to III-ה (see §9.4.2) and II-ו/י verbs (see §7.2.1.3).[21] The following lists are not exhaustive, but should provide a representative sample of the general characteristics of geminate verb morphology.[22]

Qal Perfect

3ms	בָּלַל	בלל	Gen 11:9	*strong form*
	דַּק	דקק	Deut 9:21	*collapsed form/no dagesh in final consonant*
3fs	נָדְדָה	נדד	Esth 6:1	*strong form*
	רַבָּה	רבב	Isa 6:12	*collapsed form*
2ms	קַלּוֹתָ	קלל	Nah 1:14	*collapsed form/helping vowel (וֹ) with syllabic sufformative*
1cs	זָמַמְתִּי	זמם	Zech 8:14	*strong form*
	גַּלּוֹתִי	גלל	Josh 5:9	*collapsed form/helping vowel (וֹ) with syllabic sufformative*
3cp	מָדְדוּ	מדד	Deut 21:2	*strong form*
	יַדּוּ	ידד	Joel 4:3	*collapsed form*
1cp	בַּזַּזְנוּ	בזז	Deut 2:35	*strong form*
	בַּזּוֹנוּ	בזז	Deut 3:7	*collapsed form/helping vowel (וֹ) with syllabic sufformatives*
2mp	עֲסוֹתֶם	עסס	Mal 3:21	*collapsed form/helping vowel (וֹ) with syllabic sufformatives*

---

18. Blau, *Phonology and Morphology of Biblical Hebrew*, §4.3.8.8.4, p. 259; Reymond, *Intermediate Biblical Hebrew Grammar*, §5.17, pp. 208–9.
19. GKC, §67k; JM, §82g.
20. Blau, *Phonology and Morphology of Biblical Hebrew*, §4.3.8.8.6, p. 259.
21. Reymond, *Intermediate Biblical Hebrew Grammar*, §5.17, pp. 210–11. For stative verbs and Aramaized forms (transposition of gemination), the jussive and *vav*-consecutive forms are identical to the imperfect (Aramaized form—וַיִּקֹּד *qal* impf 3ms קדד + *vav*-cons, Exod 34:8; stative verb—וָאֵקַל *qal* impf 1cs קלל + *vav*-cons, Gen 16:5).
22. For full representative paradigms of geminate verbs, see Qimḥi, §38, pp. 150–51.

Qal Imperfect

3ms	יָסֹב	סבב	2 Sam 14:24	*doubled R₁—transposition of gemination*
	יָסֹב	סבב	1 Kgs 7:15	*no dagesh allowed in a final consonant*
3fs	תָּסֹב	סבב	Num 36:7	*doubled R₁—transposition of gemination*
	תִּכְהֶה	כהה	Zech 11:17	*strong form with III-ה impf basic ending*
2ms	תָּסֹב	סבב	Ps 114:5	*doubled R₁—transposition of gemination*
	תָּחֹג	חגג	Deut 16:15	*no dagesh allowed in a final consonant*
2fs	תִּדֹּמִּי²³	דמם	Jer 48:2	*doubled gemination*
1cs	אָקֹב	קבב	Num 23:8	*doubled R₁—transposition of gemination*
	אָאֹר	ארר	Gen 12:3	*no dagesh allowed in a final consonant*
3mp	יָחֹגּוּ	חגג	Exod 5:1	*doubled R₂ with sufformative*
	יִתַּמּוּ	תמם	Ps 104:35	*doubled gemination*
	יִדְּמוּ	דמם	Lam 2:10	*doubled R₁—transposition of gemination*
3fp	תְּסֻבֶּינָה	סבב	Gen 37:7	*doubled R₂; י֯ helping vowel before syllabic sufformative*
	תְּצִלֶּינָה	צלל	1 Sam 3:11	*doubled R₂; י֯ helping vowel before syllabic sufformative*
	תִּצַּלְנָה	צלל	Jer 19:3	*doubled R₁—transposition of gemination*
	תִּקְהֶינָה	קהה	Jer 31:29	*likely doubled R₁ (קּ) without the dagesh forte due to the SQNMLVY rule.²⁴*
2mp	תָּבֹסּוּ	כסס	Exod 12:4	*doubled R₂ with sufformative*
1cp	נָסֹב	סבב	1 Sam 16:11	*no dagesh allowed in a final consonant*
	נִדְּמָה	דמם	Jer 8:14	*cohortative; doubled R₁—transposition of gemination*

Qal Jussive and *Vav*-Consecutive Short Forms

	יֵצֶר	צרר	Job 20:22	*qal jussive 3ms*
	יָרְדְּ	רדד	Isa 41:2	*qal jussive 3ms*
	וַיָּגֶל	גלל	Gen 29:10	*qal impf 3ms + vav-consecutive*
	וַנִּסָּב	סבב	Deut 2:1	*qal impf 1cp + vav-consecutive*
	וַתָּעָז	עזז	Judg 3:10	*qal impf 3fs + vav-consecutive*

---

23. This example is a pausal form with a *zaqeph qaton* in the Hebrew prosody. Hence, it retains the long /o/ vowel rather than reducing it to a vocal *shewa* as would be expected from the vocalic sufformative (י֯).

24. For SQNMLVY, recall §5.4, n. 163. These consonants with a *dagesh forte* and a vocal shewa will sometimes lose the *dagesh forte*.

With pronominal suffixes, the thematic vowel may shift to /u/.

| 2ms + 1cs | תְּסֻכֵּנִי | סכך | Ps 139:13 |
| 3ms + 1cs | יְמֻשֵּׁנִי | משש | Gen 27:12 |

Qal Imperative

2ms	נְהֵה	נהה	Ezek 32:18	*strong form; III-ה sufformative (see §9.3)*
	גֹּל	גלל	Ps 22:9	*no dagesh allowed in a final consonant*
	חָנֵּנִי	חנן	Ps 31:10	*doubled R₂ with pronominal suffix (1cs)*
2fs	רָנִּי	רנן	Isa 12:6	*all 2fs in the HB have double R₂ with the sufformative*
2mp	סֹבּוּ	סבב	Josh 6:7	*doubled R₂ with sufformative*
	רֹעוּ	רעע	Isa 8:9	*no doubling since R₂/R₃ is a guttural*
2fp	עֹרָה	ערר	Isa 32:11	*debated form*[25]

Qal Infinitive Construct

	סְבֹב	סבב	Num 21:4	*strong form*
	רֹב	רבב	Hos 10:1	*no dagesh allowed in a final consonant*
	תֻּמּוֹ	תמם	1 Kgs 14:10	*doubled R₂ with pronominal suffix (3ms)*

Qal Infinitive Absolute

	פָּתוֹת	פתת	Lev 2:6	*strong form*
	שֹׁל	שלל	Ruth 2:16	*collapsed form written defectively; no dagesh allowed in final consonant*
	פּוֹר	פרר	Isa 24:19	*collapsed form written fully; no dagesh allowed in final consonant*

Qal Participle

ms	סוֹרֵר	סרר	Deut 21:18	*strong form; sometimes written defectively*
fs	שׁוֹמֵמָה	שמם	Isa 54:1	*strong form; sometimes written defectively*[26]
	נוֹדֶדֶת	נדד	Prov 27:8	*strong form; t-form participle*
mp	סוֹרְרִים	סרר	Isa 1:23	*strong form; most often written defectively*
fp	רֹצְצוֹת	רצץ	Amos 4:1	*strong form; most often written defectively*

---

25. The parsing databases divide on this form. WIVU/ETCBC and SESE parse this form as a long form 2ms imperative (cf. קָטְלָה with the *qamets ḥatuf* in the R₁). The Westminster Hebrew Morphology v. 4.20 and *The Lexham Hebrew Bible* by Logos Bible Software parse the form as a 2fp imperative. The feminine plural parsing is likely based on the context of Isa 32:11 being explicitly feminine plural. However, the forms of the imperatives in the second half of the verse all appear to be long form masculine singular imperatives.

26. While these examples are intended to be representative, it must also be noted that the *qal* fs participles in geminate verbs do not reduce the R₂ as in other *qal* participles. There are thirteen forms in the Hebrew Bible, and between t-forms (הַשֹּׁגֶגֶת, Num 15:28), pausal forms (שֹׁקֵקָה, Ps 107:9), and standard forms (סֹרְרָה, Hos 4:16), none reduce the R₂ vowel.

Table 8.1: Geminate Verb Representative Paradigm (סבב)

	Perfect	Imperfect	Imperative	Participle	
3ms	סַב/סָבַב	יָסֹב/יִסֹּב		סֹבֵב	ms
3fs	סַבָּה/סָבְבָה	תָּסֹב/תִּסֹּב		סֹבֵבָה	fs
2ms	סַבּוֹתָ	תָּסֹב/תִּסֹּב	סֹב	סֹבְבִים	mp
2fs	סַבּוֹת	תָּסֹבִּי/תִּסְבִּי	סֹבִּי	סֹבְבוֹת	fp
1cs	סַבּוֹתִי	אָסֹב/אֶסֹּב			
3cp/3mp	סַבּוּ/סָבְבוּ	יָסֹבּוּ/יִסֹּבּוּ		**Infinitive**	
3fp		תְּסֻבֶּינָה/תִּסֹּבֶּינָה			
2mp	סַבּוֹתֶם	תָּסֹבּוּ/תִּסֹּבּוּ	סֹבּוּ	סֹב	absolute
2fp	סַבּוֹתֶן	תְּסֻבֶּינָה/תִּסֹּבֶּינָה	סֻבֶּינָה	סֹב	construct
1cp	סַבּוֹנוּ	נָסֹב/נִסֹּב			

Table 8.1 provides a representative paradigm using סבב as the root so that the patterns can be observed more consistently. The table shows alternate forms where those are possible.

8.4.2 Niphal

For the *niphal* geminates, the preformative vowel in the perfect and participle is *pataḥ* and will either lengthen in open pretonic syllables (נָסַבּוּ *niphal* pf 3cp סבב, Josh 7:9) or reduce to a vocal *shewa* in open propretonic syllables (נְמַלְתֶּם *niphal* pf 2mp מלל, Gen 17:11).[27]

The preformative vowel for the imperfect, imperative, and infinitive is i-class (*ḥireq* or *segol*) that will remain a short vowel because of the R₁ *dagesh forte* of the original shell. In the *niphal*, the R₁ *dagesh* is *not* an instance of transposition of gemination although these shells may appear to be the *qal* stem with transposition of gemination (יִמַּס *niphal* impf 3ms מסס, Deut 20:8; יִמַּקּוּ *niphal* impf 3mp מקק, Lev 26:39). When the R₁ is a guttural letter, these forms will reject the *dagesh forte* of the *niphal* shell and lengthen the preformative vowel by compensation (e.g., יֵחַתּוּ *niphal* impf 3mp חתת, 1 Sam 2:10; see Chapter 3 for I-guttural verbs). Otherwise, the preformative vowel will remain short in a closed and unaccented syllable (יִנָּהוּ *niphal* impf 3mp נהה, 1 Sam 7:2).

The thematic vowel symbols for *niphal* geminate verbs are A/A.[28]

---

27. Suchard, *The Development of the Biblical Hebrew Vowels*, §4.2.5, p. 251.
28. Blau, *Phonology and Morphology of Biblical Hebrew*, §4.3.8.8.7, p. 260. In the imperfect, a few forms have a *holem vav* as the thematic vowel (GKC, §67t), which may attest to the close association of geminate verbs with II-ו/י verbs. In Isa 24:3, תִּבּוֹק and תִּבּוֹז, two imperfects, mirror their respective

Some third person forms in the *niphal* perfect have a *tsere* as the thematic vowel (e.g., [קלל] נָקֵל in 1 Kgs 16:31; [מסס] נָמֵס in Ezek 21:12, Nah 2:11, and Ps 22:15; [סבב] נָסֵבָּה in Ezek 26:2).[29] In the case of קלל, this may reflect a stative verb pattern. However, קלל appears in 2 Kgs 3:18 as וְנָקַל with the /a/ thematic vowel as expected. For נָסֵבָּה in Ezek 26:2, the thematic vowel fails to reduce to a vocal *shewa* because the syllable is closed and accented, retaining the long vowel it prefers. The same form in Ezek 41:7 (נָסֵבָה) reduces the thematic vowel due to the accent shift to the final syllable without the *dagesh forte*.

Like the *qal*, the *niphal* perfect uses helping vowels before syllabic sufformatives (נְקַלֹּתִי pf 1cs קלל in 2 Sam 6:22).[30] In the Hebrew Bible, these helping vowels are regularly, if not always, written defectively (נְמַקֹּתֶם [מקק], Ezek 24:23; נְקַלֹּתִי [קלל], 2 Sam 6:22). There is only one imperfect feminine plural in the Hebrew Bible, and it does not take a helping vowel (תִּמַּקְנָה [מקק], Zech 14:12).

It will not be helpful at this point to produce a full theoretical paradigm for the *niphal*. Most of the forms are unattested, and the ones we do find follow the patterns just described.

8.4.3 *Poel, Poal, Hithpoel (Piel, Pual, Hithpael)*

In II-ו/י verbs, we discussed the *polel, polal,* and *hithpolel* as the more common morphological stems for the *piel, pual,* and *hithpael*, respectively. In II-ו/י verbs, these stems reduplicated the R_2 to form the new stem name. Since geminate verbs already have a doubled R_2, these unique stems in geminate verbs are often called *poel, poal,* and *hithpoel*, respectively.[31] If the root reduplicates both the R_1 and R_2, then we may encounter of a variety of stem names such as *pilpel, pulpal,* and *hithpalpel*.[32] These stems demonstrate the close analogy of geminate verbs with II-ו/י verbs.

Geminate verbs may also occur as strong forms, mainly in the *piel*.[33] When the forms are strong, they will match the shells and thematic vowels and parsing will be easy. Here are examples of the various "extra" stems along with a *piel* strong form.

---

infinitives absolute with a *holem vav* thematic vowel (הָבוֹק and הָבוֹז). It is possible that these forms are stylistic to match the sound of the imperfects with the intensity of the infinitives absolute and should not be considered exceptions to the A/A thematic vowel symbols.

29. GKC, §67t; JM, §82c, m.
30. Reymond, *Intermediate Biblical Hebrew Grammar*, §5.17, p. 212.
31. Blau, *Phonology and Morphology of Biblical Hebrew*, §4.3.8.7.5.3, p. 257.
32. GKC, §55f, g; JM, §59c.
33. Reymond, *Intermediate Biblical Hebrew Grammar*, §5.17, p. 213.

strong form	חִלַּלְתָּ	*piel* pf 2ms חלל	Gen 49:4
poel	מְחֹקֵק	*poel* ptc ms חקק	Gen 49:10
poal	עוֹלָל	*poal* pf 3ms עלל	Lam 1:12
hithpoel	מִסְתּוֹלֵל	*hithpoel* ptc ms סלל	Exod 9:17[34]
hithpalpel	לְהִתְמַהְמֵהַּ	*hithpalpel* inf cstr ל + מהה	Exod 12:39[35]

8.4.4 *Hiphil*

In the *hiphil*,[36] preformative vowels for geminate verbs are I (*hireq*) in the perfect and participle and A (*patah*) in the imperfect, imperative and infinitive.[37] The preformative vowels lengthen (pf 3ms הֵסֵב) or reduce (pf 1cs הֲסִבֹּתִי) based on the vowel adjustment rules (§1.7).[38]

The thematic vowel for the *hiphil* in geminate verbs is mainly *tsere* (הֵחֵלּוּ pf 3cp חלל, 1 Sam 3:2) although it can occasionally be *patah* (הֵסַבּוּ pf 3cp סבב, 1 Sam 5:9).[39] When the verbal form displays doubling in the R₂ and also has a syllabic sufformative the accent moves off of the middle syllable and the form will reduce the *tsere* to a short *hireq* in a closed unaccented syllable (הֲשִׁמֹּתִי pf 1cs שמם, Lev 26:31). Otherwise, when the middle syllable is closed and accented, it will prefer the long *tsere* (הֵחֵלּוּ pf 3cp חלל, 1 Sam 3:2).

With the thematic vowel as *tsere*, there is no distinction between the infinitive construct and the infinitive absolute in *hiphil* geminates. For example, הָחֵל (inf abs חלל, 1 Sam 3:12) is identical to הָחֵל (inf cstr חלל, Deut 16:9). For these forms, their syntactical context will have to help with parsing.

None of the *hiphil* participles of geminate verbs display the *dagesh forte* and so the thematic vowels are *tsere* throughout with very few exceptions.[40]

---

34. As in the *hithpael* of the strong verb, when the ת of the *hithpael* is adjacent to a sibilant, the two consonants will switch places (metathesis; GKC, §54b; JM, §53e).

35. Notice the *mappiq* in the final ה to indicate that it is one of the original root consonants. Because the final original consonant is a guttural, and because this form is a nonfinite verb (infinitive), it retains the *tsere* thematic vowel and gets the furtive *patah* for the /a/ sound that gutturals prefer (see III-gutturals in Chapter 10). Proverbs 26:18 has an infinitive construct of להה that also reduplicates and takes a furtive *patah* under the original final ה (כְּמִתְלַהְלֵהַּ). In finite verbal forms of III-guttural verbs, the thematic vowel will shift to an /a/ vowel. In Gen 19:16, the imperfect 3ms of מהה appears with an /a/ thematic vowel (וַיִּתְמַהְמָהּ) and the *mappiq* since the final ה was part of the original root.

36. See Qimḥi, §380-r for comments on *hiphil* geminate verbs.

37. Occasionally, the *hiphil* perfect has an /a/ preformative vowel, but this seems to be limited to cases in which the suffixed conjugation pulled the accent down the word with the helping vowel and the reduced *hatef patah* (ֲ) under the preformative gave way to a full *patah* vowel before a guttural in the root (e.g., הַחֲלוֹת in Esth 6:13 where the preformative ה should have a *hatef patah*, but before the guttural ח becomes a full vowel [GKC, §67w; JM, §82n]). This only happens with the verbal roots חלל and חתת, both of which begin with a ח.

38. Reymond, *Intermediate Biblical Hebrew Grammar*, §5.17, p. 211.

39. Blau, *Phonology and Morphology of Biblical Hebrew*, §4.3.8.8.8, p. 260.

40. Judg 3:24 has the form מֵסִיךְ (ptc ms סכך) with the *hireq yod*, perhaps an influence from II-ו/י verbs. מֵרַע in Isa 9:16 and Prov 17:4 retains a *patah* thematic vowel perhaps due to the ע preferring the /a/ sound, and yet מֵצַל gets a *patah* thematic vowel in Ezek 31:3 without a III-guttural.

8.4.5 *Hophal*

The major consideration with the *hophal* is that the preformative takes a u-class vowel in geminate verbs.[41] This means that the preformative vowel for the *hophal* in geminate verbs is a *shureq* (וּ) that can be written defectively as a *qibbuts* (מֻסַבָּת *hophal* ptc fp סבב, Exod 28:11; cf. מוּסַבֹּת written fully, Exod 39:13 and Num 32:38). With שׁמם, the preformative becomes *qamets hatuf* either as a full vowel (הָשַׁמָּה in Lev 26:35 and 2 Chr 36:21) or as a *hatef shewa* (הֳשַׁמָּה in Lev 26:34; בְּהֳשַׁמָּה in Lev 26:43).[42] Gesenius points out that these forms are more "Aramaïzing forms" with *o* in the preformative, but he does not comment on their development or why שׁמם is the only geminate verb that gets the *qamets hatuf* as the *hophal* preformative.[43]

Thematic vowels in the *hophal* are A/A. These are quite consistent in the *hophal* with variations in pausal forms lengthening to a *qamets* (מוּפָז ptc ms פזז, 1 Kgs 10:18; יוּסָב impf 3ms סבב, Isa 28:27). One form reduces the thematic vowel to a *shewa*, likely due to the transposition of gemination in the R₁ (הֻמְּכוּ pf 3cp מכך, Job 24:24). The vocalic ending of the perfect 3cp would warrant the R₂ vowel reduction, but forms in which the *dagesh* remains in the R₂ do not reduce the thematic vowel since it is in a closed syllable (יֻכַּתּוּ impf 3mp כתת, Jer 46:5; Mic 1:7; Job 4:20). *Hophal* participles do not reduce the thematic vowel with sufformatives as in the *qal* (מוּסַבּוֹת ptc fp סבב, Ezek 41:24).[44]

8.5 Conclusion

Geminate verbs display many of the same characteristics that we have seen with II-ו/י verbs. The presence of a *dagesh forte* in the R₂ may indicate that you are parsing a geminate verb. With some variation, the R₁ may double, or the R₁ and R₂ both may double. The presence of *dagesh forte* in many of these forms may indicate that you are encountering a geminate root. Once you recognize the geminate root, the preformatives and sufformatives of the strong verb shells remain the same. Thankfully, the variety of detailed vowel changes that happen in the middle of the word should not distract from the final parsing, especially with the knowledge of a few of these specific characteristics under your belt.

---

41. Blau, *Phonology and Morphology of Biblical Hebrew*, §4.3.8.8.9, p. 260. Cf. with I-ו/י and II-ו/י verbs (§4.2.1.3 and §5.5, respectively).

42. This last form in Lev 26:43 would have had a *hatef qamets* before the addition of the בְּ preposition that produced the *qamets hatuf* followed by the silent *shewa* under the ה.

43. GKC, §67y.

44. Out of seven geminate *hophal* participles (based on the Groves-Wheeler Westminster Morphology), five are fp participles of סבב that have the typical geminate *dagesh* in the R₂, securing the thematic vowel in a closed syllable (e.g., מוּסַבֹּת, Exod 39:6, 13).

CHAPTER 9

III-ה Verbs (III-י Verbs)

9.1 Introduction

III-ה verbs should technically be considered III-י verbs. The development of the lexical form with a III-ה appears to be the result of a triphthong contraction with an original *yod*.[1] Because these verbs occur in the lexicon as III-ה verbs, we will use that terminology here. Where we need to specify that the morphological changes are related to a *yod*, we will consider them as III-י.

9.2 General Principles

Speaking generally about III-ה verbs, there are a few things to keep in mind. First, the morphological changes to III-ה verbs only affect the end of the verb. No preformatives are affected by changes in III-ה verbs.

Additionally, the morphological features of III-ה verbs are consistent across all verbal stems. The changes in the *qal* occur also in all the derived stems.[2] This means that the morphological features we will address are specific to each of the various conjugations, and so we will discuss these changes based on each of the conjugations (e.g., perfect, imperfect, imperative, infinitive, and participle) rather than the various stems.

Next, III-ה verbs contract with syllabic sufformatives (e.g., *qal* pf 1cs גָּלִיתִי). Contraction will happen most often in the perfect conjugation since that is the suffixed conjugation and has the most syllabic sufformatives (תָ-, תְ-, נוּ-, etc.). These contractions will nearly always be with the III-י making it seem as though the III-י "replaces" the III-ה in the verbal form.[3]

---

1. Reymond, *Intermediate Biblical Hebrew Grammar*, §5.16, pp. 203–4; Suchard, *The Development of the Biblical Hebrew Vowels*, §4.2.7.

2. JM, §79b. Joüon says, "The conjugation of ל"ה verbs in Hebrew is characterized by *considerable uniformity*" (italics original). Joshua Blau says, "The most conspicuous feature of this verbal class is the almost complete homogeneity of all verbal patterns regarding their endings;..." (Blau, *Phonology and Morphology of Biblical Hebrew*, §4.3.8.6.4, p. 249).

3. Qimḥi, §40a.

To further illustrate this contraction with syllabic suffixes, we will use the *qal* perfect 1cs (קָטַלְתִּי) and 2ms (קָטַלְתָּ) as examples. In these forms, the original III-י of the root contracts to become the thematic vowel under the R₂ consonant. The vowel that is produced by this contraction is largely unimportant for III-י verbs. The identifying characteristic to look for is that the original III-י consonant has reappeared as the *hireq yod* in the perfect conjugation of this type.

qal perfect 1cs
גָּלִ֫הְתִּי* ← גָּלַ֫יְתִּי* ← גָּלִ֫יתִי

The first two forms here are just hypothetical, but they show the original י taking the place of the III-ה of the lexical root.

The perfect 2ms, being another example of a syllabic sufformative, behaves similarly.

qal perfect 2ms
גָּלִ֫הְתָ* ← גָּלַ֫יְתָ* ← גָּלִ֫יתָ

Because the sufformative is itself an entire syllable, the original III-י contracts to form the thematic vowel under the R₂ consonant. A distinguishing mark of contraction in a III-ה verb is the י where we would expect to see the ה of the lexical root. Knowing these were originally III-ו/י verbs will help you recognize the verbal root even if the final ה of the lexical form is replaced by a III-י.[4]

Finally, III-ה verbs will drop the original III-ו or י with vocalic sufformatives (leaving only the sufformative, e.g., *qal* pf 3cp גָּלוּ). We will speak about the original III-ו or III-י dropping out, but the loss of the original third root consonant is more likely the product of contraction.[5] The concept of "dropping" is a pedagogical help. In summary, the primary changes that will affect the end of the III-ה verbal forms are limited to (1) contraction of the original root consonant with syllabic sufformatives or (2) the dropping out of the original root consonant with vocalic sufformatives.

---

4. JM, §79c.
5. Reymond argues that the loss of the final ו or י is the result of various contractions (Reymond, *Intermediate Biblical Hebrew Grammar*, §5.16, pp. 203–8) whereas Blau states that the final י was "elided" or dropped (Blau, *Phonology and Morphology of Biblical Hebrew*, §4.3.8.6.4.1, p. 249). Suchard calls this the "regular occurrence of this contraction" and then proceeds through the forms that attach the vocalic sufformative directly to the R₂ of the root (Suchard, *The Development of the Biblical Hebrew Vowels*, §4.2.7, pp. 252–53). Gesenius says that the original י or ו was dropped (GKC, §75c [1]).

9.3 Basic Endings

Because of the consistency of III-ה endings across all conjugations, it is a bit easier to learn what the final form of the sufformative should be rather than recreating the detailed contractions.

The table below provides the basic endings for III-ה verbs. By "basic endings," we mean those endings that mark the verbal forms when there are no other sufformatives on the form. These endings are unique to III-ה verbs and will direct you to the correct parsing even when there are no other distinguishing sufformatives. Note that the perfect 3fs inserts a feminine ת as part of the basic ending.[6]

Table 9.1: III-ה Basic Endings

Conjugation	Basic Ending	
perfect	◌ָה (3ms) ◌ְתָה (3fs)	גָּלָה (3ms) גָּלְתָה (3fs)
imperfect	◌ֶה	יִגְלֶה
imperative	◌ֵה	גְּלֵה
infinitive absolute	◌ֹה	גָּלֹה
infinitive construct	◌וֹת	גְּלוֹת
participle	◌ֶה	גֹּלֶה

9.4 Specific Principles

Since the morphological phenomena for III-ה verbs are consistent across conjugations, we will address the specific principles by conjugation, beginning with the perfect.

9.4.1 Perfect

The perfect conjugation primarily displays a contraction of the original III-י with syllabic sufformatives because it is the "suffixed conjugation."[7]

---

6. Reymond points to the Siloam Tunnel inscription, which has the form הית for היה in line 3. Additionally, some biblical Hebrew forms display this feminine ת in the pf 3fs (וְעָשָׂת, Lev 25:21; וְהָיָת, 2 Kgs 9:37; וְהִרְצָת, Lev 26:34). He comments that by the late first millennium BC, the 3fs form had two feminine morphemes, namely, the feminine ת and the final ◌ָה (Reymond, *Intermediate Biblical Hebrew Grammar*, §5.16, p. 205). Cf. Blau, *Phonology and Morphology of Biblical Hebrew*, §4.3.8.6.4.2, p. 250; Suchard, *The Development of the Biblical Hebrew Vowels*, §4.2.7, p. 253; GKC, §75i; Qimḥi, §40.b.

7. GKC, §75f.

The following examples illustrate both the basic endings as well as the III-י contractions with syllabic sufformatives. These examples are from different derived stems to show the consistency of the endings regardless of stem.

Perfect

3ms	הִשְׁקָה	*hiphil* pf 3ms שקה	Gen 2:6	*basic ending (3ms)*
3fs	גָּלְתָה	*pual* pf 3fs גלה	Nah 2:8	*basic ending (3fs)*
2ms	עָשִׂיתָ	*qal* pf 2ms עשה	Gen 3:14	*III-י contracts to hireq yod*
2fs	הִתְגָּרִית	*hithpael* pf 2fs גרה	Jer 50:24	*III-י contracts to hireq yod*
1cs	פָּנִיתִי	*piel* pf 1cs פנה	Gen 24:31	*III-י contracts to hireq yod*
3cp	נִגְלוּ	*niphal* pf 3cp גלה	Gen 35:7	*III-י drops; sufformative attaches directly to R₂*
1cp	נִפְלֵינוּ	*niphal* pf 1cp פלה	Exod 33:16	*III-י contracts to tsere yod*
2mp	כִּלִּיתֶם	*piel* pf 2mp כלה	Exod 5:14	*III-י contracts to hireq yod*
2fp	רְאִיתֶן	*qal* pf 2fp ראה	Exod 1:16	*III-י contracts to hireq yod*

In these forms, we find a sampling of III-ה verbs in the perfect.[8] Notice that the 3ms and 3fs are the only forms in the perfect conjugation with basic endings. All other forms have a sufformative and therefore contract the III-י.[9]

The III-י may contract to either a *hireq yod* or a *tsere yod*. However, the contractions are consistent within the verbal stems. The *qal, piel, hithpael* and *hiphil* all contract the III-י as a *hireq yod*. Alternatively, the *niphal, pual,* and *hophal* contract the thematic vowel to a *tsere yod*.[10] If we recognize the *hishtaphel* as a separate stem, it consistently contracts the III-י to a *hireq yod* (הִשְׁתַּחֲוִיתָ *hishtaphel* pf 2ms חוה, Deut 8:19).[11]

When parsing III-ה verbs, it is not entirely necessary to memorize these contractions. The key indicator that you are looking at a III-ה verb is the presence of the י (גָּלִיתִי), not the vowel into which it contracted. Hence, when you see the י in the R₃ position, you can recognize a III-ה verb if you know the original י "replaces" the ה of the lexical form.

Also for parsing, since the III-ה verb morphology only changes at the end

---

8. JM, §79d, q.

9. Blau covers these verbs as III-י verbs only and does not include any sections labeled "III-ה Verbs" or "III-ו Verbs." Blau comments that III-ו verbs were "absorbed" into III-י verbs due to similar sound shifts between the two (Blau, *Phonology and Morphology of Biblical Hebrew*, §4.3.8.6.1, p. 248; cf. §3.4.7.1, p. 102). Forms that seem to display an original III-ו must be considered historically late according to Blau (e.g., שָׁלַוְתִּי Job 3:26).

10. For *pual* examples, see חֻלֵּיתָ (*pual* pf 2ms חלה, Isa 14:10) or עֻנֵּיתִי (*pual* pf 1cs ענה, Ps 119:71). For a *hophal* example, see הָרְאֵיתָ (*hophal* pf 2ms ראה, Exod 26:30). GKC, §75g, x, z.

11. JM, §79t.

of the word, the stem preformatives will remain unchanged. In the examples above, all the non-*qal* stems retain their distinctive preformative morphology in the shells. Therefore, after learning the strong verb paradigm to perfection and also accounting for these changes to the end of III-ה verbs, parsing these weak verbs will become routine.

9.4.2 Imperfect

In the imperfect conjugation, the morphological changes again occur at the end of the word.[12] The preformatives and shells across all stems will remain the same as the strong verb. The changes we see at the end of the imperfect are, once again, either (1) dropping the original י or (2) contracting the original י with syllabic sufformatives.

The following table provides a summary of the morphological changes using *qal* forms as representative examples. Specific examples from the Hebrew Bible are provided at the end of this section.

Table 9.2: III-ה Imperfect Specific Principles

		Imperfect		Notes
Without Sufformatives	ֶה	*qal* impf 3ms	יִגְלֶה	ֶה is the basic ending for the imperfect without sufformatives
		qal impf 2ms	תִּגְלֶה	
Vocalic Sufformatives		*qal* impf 2fs	תִּגְלִי	Vocalic sufformatives attach directly to the R₂ with the loss of the final root letter/vowel letter.
		qal impf 2mp	תִּגְלוּ	
		qal impf 3mp	יִגְלוּ	
Syllabic Sufformative	ֶיׄ	*qal* impf 2/3fp	תִּגְלֶינָה	In the imperfect, the only syllabic sufformative is the 2/3fp. In the imperfect, the III-י contracts to a *segol yod*.
Short Forms		*qal* jussives	יִגֶל, יֶגֶל, יִגְל, יֶגְל	Drop final ה and employ a variety of short-form consonant clusters or segolized vowel patterns.
		qal vav-cons	וַיִּגֶל	
		hiphil jussive	יֶגֶל	

---

12. GKC, §75c.

For the imperfect conjugation, the basic ending is הֶ‍ for imperfect forms that do not take sufformatives.[13] The preformatives remain the same throughout the paradigm across all stems.[14]

Vocalic sufformatives (2fs, 2mp, 3mp) attach directly to the R_2.[15] Since we already know the imperfect sufformatives from the strong verb paradigm, it is again simplest here to think of the III-י dropping and the vocalic sufformatives attaching directly to the R_2.

The original III-י will contract with syllabic sufformatives, but in the imperfect, the only syllabic sufformatives are in the 2/3fp. In the imperfect, the III-י contracts to a *segol yod* (יֶ‍).[16] It is not important to memorize this as there will be other indicators of the full parsing besides the thematic vowel contraction. Like the perfect paradigm, if you notice the י in the R_3 position, and you know that III-ה verbs were originally III-י verbs, then the contracted י with syllabic sufformatives will guide you to the correct verbal root (e.g., גלי = גלה).

Finally, this representative table shows apocopated ("shortened") forms. These forms are limited to the jussives and *vav*-consecutive forms.[17] When these forms drop the final III-י, they are left with a consonant cluster (יִגְל), or they take an epenthetic vowel (יִגֶל).[18] All of the examples in the chart are possible forms. The lone *hiphil* apocopated form (יֶגֶל) is in the chart to show that preformative vowels are not affected by the III-י morphology across the various stems.

Rather than thinking only theoretically about these forms, here are some examples from the Hebrew Bible.

---

13. Reymond proposes that these are triphthong contractions of *iyu > -ɛ, *-ayu > -ɛ, or *-uyu > -ɛ depending on the verbal root. However, it is simplest to know they all end in הֶ‍. (Reymond, *Intermediate Biblical Hebrew Grammar*, §5.16, pp. 203–4.; Suchard, *The Development of the Biblical Hebrew Vowels*, §4.2.7, p. 252). Cf. Blau who suggests a simple elision of the III-י in various, but not all, Semitic languages (Blau, *Phonology and Morphology of Biblical Hebrew*, §4.3.8.6.2, p. 249). See also GKC, §75e; JM §79e, i.

14. E.g., תִּרְבֶּה (*hiphil* impf 2ms רבה, Lev 25:16) retains the *patah* preformative vowel as expected.

15. Reymond attributes this to triphthong contractions, whereas Blau argues the final י was elided "when preceded by a(n originally) short vowel" (Reymond, *Intermediate Biblical Hebrew Grammar*, §5.16, p. 204; Blau, *Phonology and Morphology of Biblical Hebrew*, §4.3.8.6.4.1, p. 249).

16. GKC, §75g; JM, §79c.

17. Reymond, *Intermediate Biblical Hebrew Grammar*, §5.16, pp. 205–7; Blau, *Phonology and Morphology of Biblical Hebrew*, §4.3.8.6.7, p. 251; GKC, §75o–r, y, gg; JM, §79i; Qimḥi, §40j.

18. See discussion in Lutz Edzard, "Phonology, Optimality Theory: Biblical Hebrew," *EHLL* 3:135–36, §2 on epenthetic vowels of III-ה apocopated forms. An epenthetic vowel is a vowel sound that is added between two consonants for ease or efficiency of pronunciation. For יִגֶל, the *segol* is essentially the fully written sound resulting from the pronunciation of יִגְל. A ג and a ל cannot be pronounced side-by-side without a slight vowel sound. That epenthetic ("added") vowel sound is the *segol* in יִגֶל.

Imperfect

3ms	יִמָּנֶה	niphal impf 3ms מנה	Gen 13:16	basic endings
3fs	תְּאֻנֶּה	pual impf 3fs אנה	Ps 91:10	
2ms	תְּצַפֶּה	piel impf 2ms צפה	Exod 26:29	
2fs	תְּדַמִּי	piel impf 2fs דמה	Esth 4:13	vocalic sufformative attaches directly to R2
1cs	אַרְבֶּה	hiphil impf 1cs רבה	Gen 3:16	basic endings
3mp	יַשְׁקוּ	hiphil impf 3mp שקה	Gen 29:2	vocalic sufformative attaches directly to R2
3fp	תִּרְפֶּינָה	qal impf 3fp רפה	Isa 13:7	III-י contracts to יִ
2mp	תִּתְרָאוּ	hithpael impf 2mp ראה	Gen 42:1	vocalic sufformative attaches directly to R2
2fp	תְּחַיֶּינָה	qal impf 2fp חיה	Ezek 13:18	III-י contracts to יִ
1cp	נִבְנֶה	qal impf 1cp בנה	Gen 11:4	basic endings

Short Form Jussives and *Vav*-Consecutives (*Vayyiqtol*)

qal	וַיִּבֶן	vav-cons 3ms בנה	Gen 2:22
	יִבֶן	jussive 3ms בנה	Ezra 1:3
	וַתֵּשְׁתְּ	vav-cons 3fs שתה	Num 20:11
	תֵּשְׁתְּ	jussive 3fs שתה	Judg 13:14
piel	וַיְכַל	vav-cons 3ms כלה	Gen 2:2
	תְּכַל	jussive 3fs כלה	Num 17:25
hiphil	וַיַּעַל	vav-cons 3ms עלה	Exod 40:25
	יַעַל	jussive 3ms עלה	2 Sam 24:22
hithpael	וַיִּתְאָו	vav-cons 3ms אוה	1 Chr 11:17
	תִּתְאָו	jussive 2ms אוה	Prov 23:3
niphal	וַיֵּרָא	vav-cons 3ms ראה	Gen 12:7
	יֵרָא	jussive 3ms ראה	Exod 34:3

9.4.3 Imperative

The 2ms basic ending for the imperative is הֵ◌. In the imperative, III-ה verbs drop the original III-י with vocalic sufformatives or contract the III-י with syllabic sufformatives like the imperfect.[19] The imperative may also have short forms (צַו *piel* impv 2ms צוה, Lev 6:2; הַעַל *hiphil* impv 2ms עלה, Exod 8:1). Below are some representative examples from a variety of stems to show the consistency of the endings across all stems.

---

19. GKC, §75c, g, cc, hh, mm.

Imperative

2ms	רְאֵה	*qal* impv 2ms ראה	Gen 13:14	*basic ending*
	צַוֵּה	*piel* impv 2ms צוה	Josh 4:16	*basic ending*
	נַס	*piel* impv 2ms נסה	Dan 1:12	*short form*
	הֶרֶב	*hiphil* impv 2ms רבה	Judg 20:38	*short form*
2fs	הִתְעַנִּי	*hithpael* impv 2fs ענה	Gen 16:9	*vocalic sufformative attaches directly to R₂*
	הִנָּקִי	*niphal* impv 2fs נקה	Num 5:19	*vocalic sufformative attaches directly to R₂*
2mp	הַשְׁקוּ	*hiphil* impv 2mp שקה	Gen 29:7	*vocalic sufformative attaches directly to R₂*
	פְּנוּ	*piel* impv 2mp פנה	Isa 40:3	*vocalic sufformative attaches directly to R₂*
2fp	בְּכֶינָה	*qal* impv 2fp בכה	2 Sam 1:24	*III-י contracts to* יָ
	רְאֶינָה	*qal* impv 2fp ראה	Song 3:11	*III-י contracts to* יָ

9.4.4 Infinitive
9.4.4.1 Infinitive Absolute

In the infinitive absolute, we will only address basic endings since this form does not have any vocalic or syllabic sufformatives. The basic endings may be either a הֹ or a הֹ.²⁰ The infinitive absolute is one conjugation in which the ending varies depending on the derived stem, but the changes still only affect the endings. The *qal* and *niphal* generally get הֹ in the III-ה infinitive absolute.²¹ The *hiphil* and *piel* generally get הֹ in the III-ה infinitive absolute.²² Whether this phenomenon is a result of dropping the original III-י or the result of contraction, we cannot be sure. Since the III-ה verb morphology only affects the end of the word, all preformatives and derived stem shells will remain the same in their respective stems.

Infinitive Absolute

הֹ	גָּאֹה	*qal* inf abs גאה	Exod 15:21	*basic endings*
	נִדְמֹה	*niphal* inf abs דמה	Hos 10:15	
	בָּכֹה	*qal* inf abs בכה	Jer 22:10	*some forms may drop the final* ה
הֵה	נַקֵּה	*piel* inf abs נקה	Num 14:18	*basic endings*
	הַזְנֵה	*hiphil* inf abs זנה	Hos 4:18	
	הַעֲוֵה	*hiphil* inf abs עוה	Jer 9:4	

---

20. GKC, §75n; JM, §79f.
21. One exception is הַנָּקֹה (*niphal* inf abs נקה, Jer 25:29) with a הֵה, but the form clearly functions syntactically as an infinitive absolute.
22. An exception here is הַרְבָּה (*hiphil* inf abs רבה, Gen 3:16; 16:10; 22:17).

9.4.4.2 Infinitive Construct

The infinitive construct forms of III-ה verbs are unique.²³ These forms drop the original III-י and then add וֹת directly to the R₂.²⁴ The key to remember is that the infinitive construct forms of III-ה verbs end with וֹת. As usual, no preformatives of the various stems will be affected.

Table 9.3: III-ה Infinitive Construct Specific Principles

	Infinitive Construct		
וֹת	All forms contract the original III-י to a *holem vav* and add ת.	*qal* inf cstr	גְּלוֹת (גלה) עֲשׂוֹת (עשׂה)

Infinitive Construct

רְאוֹת	*qal* inf cstr ראה	Gen 8:8	
הַרְבּוֹת	*hiphil* inf cstr רבה	Deut 17:16	
הִתְעוֹת	*niphal* inf cstr תעה	Isa 19:14	
עֻנּוֹת	*pual* inf cstr ענה	Ps 132:1	
הִתְחַלּוֹת	*hithpael* inf cstr חלה	2 Sam 13:2	
צַוֹּת	*piel* inf cstr צוה	2 Sam 6:21	*many forms write the holem vav defectively as holem*
לִרְאֹת	*qal* inf cstr ל + ראה	Gen 11:5	*holem vav written defectively as holem*
הַעֲלֹת	*hiphil* inf cstr עלה	Exod 27:20	*holem vav written defectively as holem*

9.4.5 Participles

The ms basic ending for III-ה participles is ֶה. While this is the same as the imperfect 3ms, any preformatives on participles will be distinct from the preformatives of the imperfect. All other forms of the active participle *drop* the original III-י and add the normal participle sufformatives directly to

---

23. JM, §79f. Joüon says that the infinitive construct form is one whose "origin is not clear." Blau includes the III-ה infinitive construct in a discussion on the Canaanite shift. He does not attribute the /o/ vowel to the Canaanite shift, but says that "as a rule," the infinitive construct ends with וֹת (Blau, *Phonology and Morphology of Biblical Hebrew*, §4.3.8.6.4.2, p. 250).

24. Reymond comments that the infinitive construct resembles feminine plural nouns. He notes that the infinitive construct of weak roots often takes on a "feminine morphological feature" (Reymond, *Intermediate Biblical Hebrew Grammar*, §5.16, p. 208, n. 105). Qimḥi also comments that "The Infinitive and the noun, being kindred in meaning, sometimes share the characteristics of each other. Thus, the Infinitive occurs with plural endings... while nouns sometime occur in the sense of the Infinitive" (Qimḥi, §40.e).

the R₂ consonant.²⁵ Some forms retain the original III-י when a *dagesh forte* is present (פִּרְיָה *qal* ptc fs פרה, Isa 17:6; הֹמִיָּה *qal* ptc fs המה, Prov 7:11).²⁶

For the passive participle, the original III-י is retained in all forms as a true consonant.²⁷ The *shureq* thematic vowel is typical of the passive participle (cf. the *qal* pass ptc קָטוּל), and in each form, the original III-י follows the *shureq* before adding the participle endings. The mp passive participle does not write both the original III-י and the י of יםִ◌. The following table provides a summary of forms using גלה as the representative root.

Table 9.4: III-ה Participle Specific Principles

		Participle		
Active	◌ֶה	Drop the original III-י and add the participle ending directly to the R₂.	*qal* ptc ms	גֹּלֶה
	◌ִים		*qal* ptc mp	גֹּלִים
	◌ָה		*qal* ptc fs	גֹּלָה
	◌וֹת		*qal* ptc fp	גֹּלוֹת
Passive		Retain the original III-י as a consonant.	*qal* pass ptc ms	גָּלוּי
			qal pass ptc mp	גְּלוּיִם
			qal pass ptc fs	גְּלוּיָה
			qal pass ptc fp	גְּלוּיוֹת

Below are forms found in the Hebrew Bible. Notice the consistency of the endings across all verbal stems.

Active Participles

ms	מְכַסֶּה	*piel* ptc ms כסה	Gen 18:17	
fs	נִלְאָה	*niphal* ptc fs לאה	Ps 68:10	
mp	מַרְבִּים	*hiphil* ptc mp רבה	Exod 36:5	
fp	עֹלֹת	*qal* ptc fp עלה	Gen 41:18	*many forms write the holem vav defectively as holem*

---

25. Qimḥi points to a couple of exceptions where "the feminine occurs with distinct Yod as third radical," e.g. עֹטִיָּה, Song 1:7; הוֹמִיָּה, Isa 22:2 (Qimḥi, §40.n).

26. These forms are likely analogous to III-א verbs. With פרה, for example, *HALOT* begins the entry with "by-form of פרא."

27. GKC, §75c; JM, §79c.

Passive Participles

ms	קָלוּי	*qal* pass ptc ms קלה	Lev 2:14
fs	נְטוּיָה	*qal* pass ptc fs נטה	Exod 6:6
mp	תְּלוּיִם	*qal* pass ptc mp תלה	Josh 10:26
fp	רְאֻיוֹת	*qal* pass ptc fp ראה	Esth 2:9

Some forms write the shureq defectively as a qibbuts.

9.5 Conclusion

According to the ETCBC/WIVU parsing database, there are a little over 15,300 III-ה verbs in the Hebrew Bible. This is about 21 percent of all the verbs in the Hebrew Bible. Thankfully, III-ה morphology displays significant consistency across all verbal stems and conjugations. Three things will help with parsing III-ה verbs. First, learn the basic endings for each conjugation (Table 9.1) so that if you see a form without identifying sufformatives, you will have direction for what conjugation you are looking at. Second, remember that vocalic sufformatives will drop the original III-י and add the vocalic sufformative directly to the R_2. Third, syllabic sufformatives will most often contract the original III-י with the thematic vowel to become part of the thematic vowel. There are, of course, nuances to each of these principles as we have discussed in the chapter. However, these applications of the morphological principles of weak verbs will greatly improve your confidence in parsing III-ה (III-י) verbs.

CHAPTER 10

III-ח, III-ע, and III-ה Verbs

10.1 Introduction

In this chapter, we will address III-guttural verbs. However, notice that when we say III-guttural, we are not referring to *all* roots with a guttural in the R₃. We have already said that lexical III-ה verbs were originally III-ו/י verbs. In Chapter 11, we will address III-א verbs since they inflect differently in the perfect conjugation. The semi-guttural ר does not cause any changes when in the R₃ position. So, when we speak of III-gutturals in this chapter, we are referring specifically to III-ח, III-ע, and III-ה verbs.[1] For ease, we will call the verbs we cover in this chapter "III-gutturals."

The primary characteristic of gutturals to keep in mind for this chapter is that gutturals prefer /a/ sounds under and before them (§2.3.1.3). This phenomenon occurs primarily when the III-guttural pushes the thematic vowel to an /a/ even when the thematic vowel symbols indicate something else. Likewise, III-gutturals will prefer /a/ sounds even when the verbal form retains an /e/ or /i/ thematic vowel. In those cases, the III-guttural gets a furtive *pataḥ* to "glide" into that preferred /a/ sound. With these verbs, we will not normally encounter the rejection of a *dagesh forte* or the change to a *ḥatef shewa*.[2]

Since gutturals prefer a-class vowels, any stem or conjugation that already has an a-class thematic vowel will retain strong forms (e.g., הָטְבְּעוּ *hophal* pf 3cp [pausal form], Prov 8:25).

---

1. Notice that III-ה verbs have a *mappiq*. There are a few verbs that have a true consonantal ה (גבה, תמה, כמה) as the R₃ and these will morph like III-guttural verbs.
2. III-gutturals are prone to retain the silent *shewa* when it falls in the R₃ position though some situations will result in the *ḥatef shewa* (see §10.3.3).

10.2 III-Gutturals Prefer A-Class Vowels Under and Before Them

When learning the changes to III-guttural verbs, it is useful to categorize the conjugations into *finite* and *nonfinite* verbal forms. Therefore, the perfect, imperfect, and imperative (finite verb forms) are grouped together in this discussion, and infinitives and participles (nonfinite verb forms) are grouped together. These distinctions will display similar morphology patterns, namely III-guttural verbs prefer a-class vowels under and before them (cf. §2.3.1.3).

10.2.1 Perfect, Imperfect, Imperative (Finite Verbs)

For the finite verbal forms, *tsere* thematic vowels will shift to *pataḥ* in most forms. However, if the thematic vowel is a historically long vowel (e.g., *hiphil hireq yod*) or if the verbal form is a pausal form, then the original thematic vowel is retained, and the III-guttural will take a furtive *pataḥ*.[3]

10.2.1.1 *Tsere* Becomes *Pataḥ*

In nonpausal forms, any *tsere* (◌) thematic vowel will become *pataḥ* (◌) with III-gutturals.[4] Notice particularly the *hiphil vav*-consecutive that will shift the thematic vowel from a *tsere* of the J.I.I.V.E. form to a *pataḥ*.[5] The following examples have the strong form with קטל in order to see the vowel shift from *tsere* to *pataḥ* as a result of the III-guttural.

III-Guttural Form	Strong Form		
יִשְׁמַע	יִקְטֵל	*niphal* impf 3ms שמע	Exod 23:13
שָׂמַח	קָטֵל	*piel* pf 3ms שמח	Deut 24:5
הִתְגַּלַּע	הִתְקַטֵּל	*hithpael* pf 3ms גלע	Prov 17:14
וַיַּצְמַח	וַיַּקְטֵל	*hiphil* impf 3ms צמח + *vav*-cons	Gen 2:9

10.2.1.2 III-Gutturals Retain Thematic Vowel but with Furtive *Pataḥ*

With finite verbs, historically long vowels and pausal forms will withstand the pressure of the III-guttural and retain the expected thematic vowel.[6]

---

3. Blau, *Phonology and Morphology of Biblical Hebrew*, §4.3.7.3.4, p. 239 and associated note (§4.3.7.3.4n, pp. 239–40); GKC, §65a; JM §70a–b.
4. GKC, §65c–e.
5. The *hiphil* thematic vowel is usually a *hireq yod* in the *hiphil* imperfect 3ms (A-i/I-e). However, remember that the *hiphil vav*-consecutive is one of the J.I.I.V.E. *tsere* forms. The *hiphil* does not often adjust the thematic vowel because it is usually the historically long *hireq yod*. The J.I.I.V.E. forms, however, will be affected by the III-guttural preference for /a/ sounds. GKC, §65f.
6. This historically long vowel principle applies mainly to the *hiphil* perfect and imperfect since

However, when this happens, the guttural still prefers the /a/ sound and so it takes a furtive *pataḥ*.

We will use the *hiphil* as the example of a finite verbal form that retains the original *hireq yod* thematic vowel.

Hiphil

תַּזְרִיעַ	impf 3fs זרע	Lev 12:2	
יַקְצֵעַ	impf 3ms קצע	Lev 14:41	*theme vowel may be written defectively*
הִצְלִיחַ	pf 3ms צלח	Gen 24:56	
הִזְנִיחַ	pf 3ms זנח	2 Chr 29:19	

Not only do III-guttural verbs retain historically long vowels, but they also retain original *tsere* thematic vowels when the verb is a pausal form.[7] In order to designate pausal forms, we will use either an *athnaḥ* (֑) or a *silluq/sof pasuq* (׃֑) to show that the form has a heavy disjunctive accent and thus retains the original *tsere* thematic vowel with the furtive *pataḥ*.

אֶשָּׁבֵעַ׃	*niphal* impf 1cs שבע	Gen 21:24
בִּקֵּעַ׃	*piel* pf 3ms בקע	2 Kgs 15:16
יִפָּתֵחַ	*niphal* impf 3ms פתח	Job 32:19
תִּתְיַפֵּחַ[8]	*hithpael* impf 3fs יפח	Jer 4:31

10.2.2 Infinitive and Participle (Nonfinite Verbs)

Nonfinite forms (infinitives and participles) retain the original thematic vowels and take a furtive *pataḥ* (with a few rare exceptions). Below are some representative forms for the nonfinite III-guttural verbs. Notice in all of these, the III-guttural takes a furtive *pataḥ* whether or not the thematic vowel is historically long or a pausal form. These nonfinite forms retain the original thematic vowel and get the furtive *pataḥ*.

---

those forms have a historically long thematic vowel (*hireq yod*). The *hiphil* imperative 2ms is a *tsere* form and will shift to *pataḥ* (הוֹקַע) *hiphil* impv 2ms יקע, Num 25:4). Other *hiphil* imperatives (2fs and 2mp) have sufformatives blocking the need for a furtive *pataḥ* (הַשְׁמִיעִנִי *hiphil* impv 2fs שמע + 1cs suffix, Song 2:14; הַצְלִיחוּ *hiphil* impv 2mp צלח, 2 Chr 18:14).

7. For discussion on pausal forms, see Blau, *Phonology and Morphology of Biblical Hebrew*, §3.5.13, pp. 154–55; Reymond, *Intermediate Biblical Hebrew Grammar*, §3.17, pp. 111–12; Steven E. Fassberg, "Pausal Forms," *EHLL*, 3:54–55.

8. The disjunctive *tifḥa* does not often produce a pausal form. However, in this verse (and some others), the morphology displays a pausal form even with the *tifḥa*. One primary indicator that this is a pausal form is that the finite verb (imperfect) retains the *tsere* thematic vowel and takes the furtive *pataḥ*.

הַשֹּׁמֵעַ	*qal* ptc ms שמע + הַ	Gen 21:6
כִּשְׁמֹעַ	*qal* inf cstr שמע + כ	Gen 27:34
רָבוּעַ	*qal* pass ptc ms רבע	Exod 30:2
שָׁמוֹעַ	*qal* inf abs שמע	Deut 15:5
לְשַׁלַּח	*piel* inf cstr שלח + ל	Exod 7:27
מְשַׁלֵּחַ	*piel* ptc ms שלח	Exod 8:17
מִשְׁתַּגֵּעַ [9]	*hithpael* ptc ms (pausal) שגע	1 Sam 21:15
מַבְרִחַ [10]	*hiphil* ptc ms ברח	Exod 26:28

10.3 Miscellaneous Issues

While most of the III-guttural characteristics follow the patterns discussed above, there are some areas that need consideration. As expected, not everything is as neat and clean as we would like it to be.

10.3.1 III-Gutturals in the *Qal* Imperfect and Imperative

As with II-gutturals, the thematic vowel for III-gutturals in the *qal* imperfect and imperative becomes /A. What was previously an /O thematic vowel in standard *qal* imperfects and imperatives becomes /A due to the influence of the III-guttural.[11] The following examples are all *qal* imperfects and imperatives that would have had an /O thematic vowel in the original strong verb shells.

יִשְׁלַח	*qal* impf 3ms שלח	Gen 3:22
נִזְבַּח	*qal* impf 1cp זבח	Exod 8:22
תִּמְשַׁח	*qal* impf 2ms משח	1 Kgs 19:16
בְּרַח	*qal* impv 2ms ברח	Gen 27:43
שְׁמַע	*qal* impv 2ms שמע	Gen 21:12
פְּגַע	*qal* impv 2ms פגע	Judg 8:21

---

9. Note first that this form is a *hithpael* with a verbal root that has a sibilant consonant in the R₁. This is the situation for *hithpael* metathesis (GKC, §54b; JM, §53e). Notice with metathesis, that the vowel pattern of the *hithpael* remains the same; only the ת and שׁ switch places. Note secondly that this is a form in which the *zaqef qaton* (◌֔) is "heavy" enough to warrant a pausal form. It is important to remember that the furtive *patah* in this form is a result of the participle being a nonfinite form rather than a pausal form. Nonfinite III-guttural verbs will get the furtive *patah* regardless of whether the form is in pause.

10. In this form the *hireq yod* is written defectively (without the *yod* consonant), and yet it still withstands the pressure of the III-ח. The form takes the furtive *patah* to achieve the /a/ sound gutturals prefer.

11. GKC, §65b.

Also, as with II-gutturals, this shift to the /A thematic vowel means that the imperative 2ms and infinitive construct forms are distinguishable (cf. §6.4.2).

| שְׁמַע | *qal* impv 2ms שמע | Deut 6:4 |
| שְׁמֹעַ | *qal* inf cstr שמע | Num 30:9 |

| שְׁלַח | *qal* impv 2ms שלח | Exod 4:4 |
| שְׁלֹחַ | *qal* inf cstr שלח | Josh 14:11 |

10.3.2 Segolate Patterns with Gutturals

One "exception" to the discussion of nonfinite forms above is the t-form participle. While most participles retain the thematic vowel and take a furtive *pataḥ*, the t-form participles will take the a-class vowel, *pataḥ*. The reason for this is that when the t-form participle applies the segolization pattern to a III-guttural verb, the III-guttural is in the position to prefer *pataḥs* under and before it. Even though this is an "exception" to the broader rule that nonfinite forms take the furtive *pataḥ*, this morphology of segolization with gutturals is a common principle in Hebrew.

| שֹׁלַחַת | ← | שֹׁלַחְתְּ* | ← | שֹׁלְחְתְּ* | ← | שֹׁלֵחַ* |
| Segolization | | Shift to /a/ Vowel | | Addition of ת | | "Strong" form |

10.3.3 III-Gutturals and *Shewas*

While *shewas* are not a major problem for III-gutturals, there are a few principles to consider.

10.3.3.1 III-Gutturals Often Retain Silent *Shewas*

III-gutturals are often able to retain a silent *shewa* with syllabic sufformatives.[12] They do not "flip" the silent *shewa* like I-gutturals. Blau suggests this retention of the silent *shewa* is related to the accent of the word.[13] He lists the form בִּלְעָנוּהוּ (*piel* pf 1cp + 3ms בלע, Ps 35:25) to show that when the accent shifts to the 1cp sufformative, the III-guttural indeed gets the *ḥatef pataḥ*.[14] However, the heavy sufformatives of the perfect conjugation (2mp, 2fp) pull

---

12. GKC, §65g.
13. Blau, *Phonology and Morphology of Biblical Hebrew*, §4.3.7.3.2, p. 239.
14. See also JM, §70b(3).

the accent to the sufformative and yet still retain the silent *shewa* under the III-guttural (e.g., יְדַעְתֶּן pf 2fp ידע, Gen 31:6; זְרַעְתֶּם pf 2mp זרע, Lev 25:22).[15] It seems that the shift to a *ḥatef shewa* is more related to the presence of a pronominal suffix rather than to the accent shift.[16] The following examples all retain the R₃ silent *shewa* with syllabic sufformatives.

שָׁמַעְתִּי	*qal* pf 1cs שמע		Gen 3:10
מָשַׁחְתָּ	*qal* pf 2ms משח		Gen 31:13
נִשְׁבַּעְתִּי	*niphal* pf 1cs שבע		Gen 22:16
יְדַעְתֶּם	*qal* pf 2mp ידע		Gen 29:5
שִׁלַּחְנוּ	*piel* pf 1cp שלח		Exod 14:5
תִּפָּקַחְנָה	*niphal* impf 3fp פקח		Isa 35:5

10.3.3.2 Perfect 2fs Forms

Secondly, we must account for an interesting change in the perfect 2fs forms. In all stems, the perfect 2fs of III-guttural verbs follows the segolate spelling pattern with a-class vowels (*pataḥ*) in each of the final two syllables of the verb.[17] These verbs then take a segolate vowel and accent pattern with *pataḥ*s. The following examples show the progression from the strong form shell to the final form in the Hebrew Bible.

שָׁמַעַתְּ	*qal* perfect 2fs שמע	1 Kgs 1:11	שָׁמַעַתְּ ← *שָׁמַעְתְּ ← ◌ָ◌ַ◌ְתְּ
הָמְלַחַתְּ	*hophal* perfect 2fs מלח	Ezek 16:4	הָמְלַחַתְּ ← *הָמְלַחְתְּ ← ◌ָ◌ְ◌ַתְּ
הִשְׁבַּעַתְּ	*hiphil* perfect 2fs שבע	Ezek 27:33	הִשְׁבַּעַתְּ ← *הִשְׁבַּעְתְּ ← ◌ִ◌ְ◌ַתְּ

In all these forms, notice that the III-guttural takes the *pataḥ* with a segolized vowel pattern beginning with the R₂ of the verbal root. However, notice also that the ת sufformative still takes the *dagesh lene*! This is a rare exception when the *dagesh lene* is preceded by vowel sound.[18]

---

15. Blau attributes this to the influence of the other forms of the perfect conjugation that accent the preceding syllable (e.g., שָׁלַחְתִּי) and to the preservation of the "occlusive pronunciation of the *t*" (Blau, *Phonology and Morphology of Biblical Hebrew*, §4.3.7.3.2n, p. 239).

16. Gesenius comments that the composite *shewa* only occurs in the perfect 1cp with suffixes and before the 2ms suffix (GKC, §65h; cf. §10.3.3.3 below).

17. Blau, *Phonology and Morphology of Biblical Hebrew*, §4.3.7.3, p. 239; GKC, §65g; JM, §70f.

18. Joüon says that the *pataḥ* under the III-guttural is an auxiliary *pataḥ* and "does not lead to the spirantization of the ת" (JM, §70f). Gesenius comments that the *dagesh* remains to show that the "helping *Pathaḥ*" is not a full vowel (GKC, §28e, n. 2).

10.3.3.3 Addition of "Heavy" Pronominal Suffixes

Finally, the addition of the "heavy" pronominal suffixes push the accent to the pronominal suffix.[19] These suffixes have a medial *shewa* preceding the suffix (ךָ֯; כֶם֯; כֶן֯).[20] When this suffix attaches to a III-guttural, a vocal *shewa* would occur under the III-guttural consonant. This is a situation in which the vocal *shewa* will become a composite *shewa* because gutturals prefer composite *shewas* (see §2.3.1.2).

אַשְׁבִּיעֲךָ	*hiphil* impf 1cs שׁבע + 2ms	Gen 24:3
נְשַׁלְּחֲךָ	*piel* impf 1cp שׁלח + 2ms	Gen 26:29
בָּרְחֲךָ	*qal* inf cstr ברח + 2ms	Gen 35:1
מְנָעֲךָ	*qal* pf 3ms מנע + 2ms	Num 24:11
כְּשָׁמְעֲכֶם	*qal* inf cstr שׁמע + 2mp + בְּ	Deut 5:23
יֹשִׁיעֲכֶם	*hiphil* impf 3ms ישׁע + 2mp	Isa 35:4

10.4 Conclusion

With finite forms, the R_3 guttural will normally cause a shift of the expected thematic vowel to the a-class. When the thematic vowel is a historically long vowel or the verb is a pausal form, the original thematic vowel is retained, and the III-guttural takes a furtive *pataḥ* in order to preserve the desired /a/ sound. The nonfinite verbal forms retain the original thematic vowel, and the III-guttural takes a furtive *pataḥ*. Remember that the III-guttural verbs that exhibit these morphological principles are technically limited to III-ע, III-ח, and III-ה verbs.

---

19. Blau, *Phonology and Morphology of Biblical Hebrew*, §4.3.7.3.2, p. 239.

20. "Medial" *shewa* is a way to describe a *shewa* that in some situations is considered vocal while in other situations is considered silent. These *shewas* must be considered medial because of forms like this. The 2ms suffix nearly always behaves like the *shewa* is a vocal *shewa*. Vowels before it lengthen in an open pretonic syllable, suggesting that the *shewa* of the suffix begins the suffixed syllable (נְשַׁלְּחֲךָ *piel* impf 1cp שׁלח + 2ms, Gen 26:29). Typically, the second person plural suffixes (2mp, 2fp) treat the *shewa* as a silent *shewa*, closing the syllable and not allowing for the pretonic open vowel to lengthen. However, we do not see a *dagesh lene* in the כּ of the suffix. Hence, the *shewa* is medial, behaving somewhat like a silent *shewa* and somewhat like a vocal *shewa*. In the 2mp examples listed in this section, the *shewa* of the second plural suffix is vocal enough to warrant the composite *shewa* under a III-guttural, but not vocal enough to lengthen the pretonic vowel (כְּשָׁמְעֲכֶם).

CHAPTER 11

III-א Verbs

11.1 Introduction

Although III-א verbs could technically be considered III-guttural verbs, we will examine them separately. Some grammars that may not consider III-guttural verbs as "weak" verbs will still consider III-א verbs alongside other weak verbs because of the analogous forms with III-י verbs.[1] III-א verbs are not "weak" in the sense that they lose the R_3, but they do obscure the thematic vowel of the original shell. For our purposes, we will focus on the most common morphological phenomena for III-א verbs.[2]

---

1. Blau, *Phonology and Morphology of Biblical Hebrew*, §4.3.8.5, p. 248; Suchard, *The Development of the Biblical Hebrew Vowels*, §4.2.8, p. 253; GKC, §74; JM, §78; Qimḥi, §39a. Blau argues that there is a historical analogy between III-א verbs and III-י verbs. He comments that the quiescent ending on a form without suffformatives is analogous to the similar III-י forms (e.g., מָצָא and גָּלָה) (Blau, *Phonology and Morphology of Biblical Hebrew*, §4.3.8.5.1, p. 248; cf. Reymond, *Intermediate Biblical Hebrew Grammar*, §5.13, p. 197; JM, §78g; Qimḥi, §39h). This may be true insofar as ה or א could be used as *matres lectionis*. However, it is debatable that א served as a *mater lectionis* in exactly the same way as ה, ו, and י (See JM, §7b, particularly the discussion of א near the end of that section and §78e, g; cf. GKC, §7b, e; Blau, *Phonology and Morphology of Biblical Hebrew*, §3.3.4.1.1, p. 86). Therefore, it is more helpful to describe these morphological phenomena separately from III-י verbs. We will talk about III-א verbs "quiescing, resulting in compensatory lengthening" rather than displaying diphthong and triphthong contractions as we did in III-י (III-ה) verbs (cf. Chapter 3).

2. As with all the weak verb types, there are unique forms to consider. Forms like נְשׂוּא־ (*qal* pass ptc ms cstr נשׂא, Ps 32:1), which is clearly analogous to III-י verbs and וַתִּשֶּׂנָה (*qal* impf 3fp נשׂא + *vav*-cons, Ruth 1:14; Jer 9:17) where the III-א has dropped. A few verses earlier in Ruth (1:9), the III-א in וַתִּשֶּׂאנָה is preserved, but without the compensatory lengthening of the thematic vowel. This evidence seems to support the argument that III-א is analogous to III-י verbs in which a III-י that has contracted could be written defectively (e.g., תִּכְלֶנָה *qal* impf 3fp כלה, Job 17:5; cf. תִּכְלֶינָה with the vocalic *yod* in Job 11:20) (See GKC, §74k; JM, §78f; and Qimḥi, §39i on the א being omitted in spelling). Similarly, הִתְנַבִּיתָ (*hithpael* pf 2ms נבא) in 1 Sam 10:6 inflects with a III-י rather than a III-א. Likewise, הִתְנַבּוֹת (*hithpael* inf cstr נבא) in 1 Sam 10:13 inflects like a III-ה with the וֹת ending in the infinitive construct. And yet, in Zech 13:4, the *niphal* infinitive construct retains the III-א *and* takes the וֹת suffformative analogous to the III-ה infinitive construct (הִנָּבְאֹת). Other forms of נבא morph like III-ה verbs. E.g., נִבֵּיתָ (*niphal* pf 2ms נבא, Jer 26:9). However, compare Jer 28:6 and Ezek 4:7 where the same form retains the III-א (נִבֵּאתָ *niphal* pf 2ms נבא). *HALOT* comments that a few forms of נבא occur as ל"ה verbs but does not give an explanation. Gesenius comments that "frequently an א that quiesces is omitted in writing" (GKC, §23f; §74k; cf. JM, §78e–f). Finally, Ps 4:7 has the form נְסָה (*qal* impv 2ms נשׂא) where the ה seems to be serving as the vowel marker in place of a III-א. The point is that even though we will distinguish the exact morphological principles between III-י verbs and III-א verbs, there is indeed some historical analogy between the two weak verb types.

The two main characteristics to keep in mind with III-א verbs are (1) א likes to quiesce, often resulting in compensatory lengthening of the thematic vowel (R₂ vowel) and (2) III-א verbs tend to shift the thematic vowel to Ē/ (*tsere*) in the perfect conjugation of the derived stems and *qal* stative. This is not a wholesale shift to *tsere* thematic vowels, but it is rather consistent in the perfect conjugation.

11.2 III-א Often Quiesces with a Silent *Shewa*

The first characteristic of III-א verbs involves the quiescent א (§2.3.1.5).[3] Visually, the א looks as if it has no vowel pointing at all (קָרָאתִי). When the א quiesces, the preceding vowel often lengthens by compensation (קָרָאתִי).[4] The morphological progression may be represented like this:

qal perfect 1cs קרא

קָרָאתִי	←	קָרְאתִי*	←	קָרַאְתִי*
Compensatory Lengthening		Quiescent א		"Strong" Form

Another place that an א will quiesce is at the end of the verb with no suffformatives. This is also a quiescent א since the א closes the final syllable. All final CVC syllables imply a silent *shewa* since the word ends with the consonant and no further vowel sounds. The Masoretes did not write this final silent *shewa* since the word simply ended with the consonant sound. Without suffformatives, III-א verbs will quiesce and display compensatory lengthening.

qal perfect 3ms קרא (Gen 1:5)

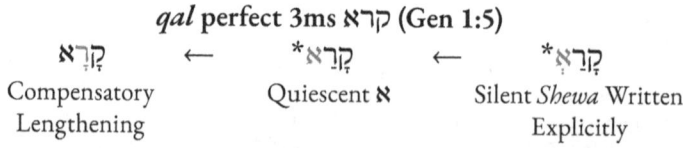

קָרָא	←	קָרְא*	←	קָרַאְ*
Compensatory Lengthening		Quiescent א		Silent *Shewa* Written Explicitly

---

3. Reymond, *Intermediate Biblical Hebrew Grammar*, §5.13, p. 197; Blau, *Phonology and Morphology of Biblical Hebrew*, §4.3.8.5.2, p. 248; GKC, §74a.

4. To say that the vowel lengthens "by compensation" is the consistent way that we have talked about vowel changes when a consonant quiesces. In this case, when the א loses its consonantal value, it no longer closes the syllable and so in an open syllable, the vowel lengthens (GKC, §27g).

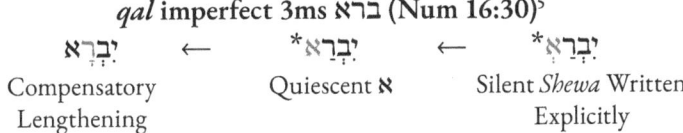

qal imperfect 3ms ברא (Num 16:30)[5]

יִבְרָא	←	*יִבְרָא	←	*יִבְרְאָ
Compensatory Lengthening		Quiescent א		Silent *Shewa* Written Explicitly

This phenomenon will not negatively impact our ability to parse III-א verbs. First, in the perfect conjugation, the only form without a suffixformative is the perfect 3ms, which is also the lexical form. Therefore, when you see the lengthened R_2 vowel, you will not be concerned about it since the verb form looks identical to the lexical form. Secondly, outside the perfect, the thematic vowel classes remain the same for their respective stems and conjugations, they simply lengthen.

11.3 III-א Verbs Display a Tendency Toward *Tsere* Thematic Vowels in the Perfect Conjugation

The second trend with III-א verbs that needs attention is that they tend to show an A/ → Ē/ shift in the thematic vowels of the perfect conjugation of the derived stems and *qal* stative.[6] The words "tend" and "perfect" are important to remember. Notice in Table 11.1 below there is not a wholesale shift to *tsere* thematic vowels. Some stems end up with *tsere* or *pataḥ* thematic vowels depending on their conjugation and form (e.g., *niphal* and *pual*). Also, this "less-than-wholesale" shift only occurs in the perfect conjugation. So, while this is a distinguishing mark of the III-א morphology, it is limited to the perfect conjugation. The key phrase to help you anticipate what vowel change will occur is, *Mixed stems become pure Ē/ and pure stems become mixed Ē/*.[7] The following table illustrates this phenomenon.

---

5. We will see shortly that like II- and III-guttural verbs, III-א thematic vowels in the *qal* imperfect and imperative become /A. Hence, in this form, the compensatory lengthening is from a *pataḥ* (◌ַ) to a *qamets* (◌ָ).

6. GKC, §74c. For the derived stems, Joüon comments that the *tsere* thematic vowel comes from ל״ה verbs or from an analogy to *qal* stative verbs (JM, §78c). Joüon is not commenting on the explanation given here, but simply states his observation of the *tsere* thematic vowel.

7. Fuller and Choi, *Invitation to Biblical Hebrew*, 223–24.

Table 11.1[8]

		Normal	III-א Effect
"Mixed"	*qal* stative[9]	A-ē/	Ē/
	piel	A-ē/	Ē/
	hithpael	A-ē/	Ē/
	hiphil	A-î/	Ē-î/
"Pure"	*niphal*	A/	Ē-ā/
	pual	A/	Ē-ā/

If we further explain the key phrase in the previous paragraph, when the "mixed" stems tend toward Ē/ thematic vowels, they become "pure" Ē/. Notice in the *qal* stative, the *piel*, and the *hithpael*, what was previously "mixed" (A-ē/) becomes "pure" (Ē/) as a result of the III-א. The *hiphil* is a bit of an anomaly in the chart since it does not become "pure" Ē/. The historically long *hireq yod* withstands the pressure of the III-א, and so the *hiphil* perfect third persons retain the *hireq yod*.[10]

Alternatively, when the "pure" stems tend toward Ē/ thematic vowels, they become "mixed" Ē/. This is the inverse of the previous paragraph. Those stems that normally have the same vowel throughout the entire perfect conjugation ("pure"), will now display a "mixed" set of thematic vowels but with Ē/ in all forms except the third persons that retain that "mixed" -ā/ thematic vowel.

This "tendency" is general. There are several exceptions, including entire lexemes that do not follow these patterns. However, this discussion should provide a good basis for why III-א verbs have a *tsere* thematic vowel in verbal stems where we expect a *patah*.

11.4 Miscellaneous Issues

As with most weak verbs, there are always some issues requiring a little extra attention.

---

8. Table 11.1 is adapted from Fuller and Choi, *Invitation to Biblical Hebrew*, 226.

9. *Qal* perfect "standard" verbs are a pure stem (A/), but they are not affected by the trend toward Ē/ thematic vowels. Again, this is why we say III-א verbs "tend" toward Ē/ and that it is not a wholesale shift.

10. Remember that the lower-case letter on the left side of the slash in the thematic vowel symbols stands for third person forms only (§1.3).

11.4.1 *Qal* Imperfect and Imperative Take *Pataḥ* Thematic Vowel

Like II- and III-guttural verbs, III-א verbs take *pataḥ* thematic vowels in the *qal* imperfect and imperative.[11] The *pataḥ* will lengthen to *qamets* when the final א quiesces. Other forms of the imperfect and imperative (impf 2fs, 2mp, 3mp; impv 2fs, 2mp) have vocalic sufformatives that reduce the thematic vowel and thus obscure the /a/ vowel. The following forms all show the shift to *pataḥ* that then lengthened to *qamets* because the III-א quiesces at the end of the word.

יִקְרָא	*qal* impf 3ms	קרא	Gen 2:19 (2x)
תִּמְצָא	*qal* impf 3fs	מצא	Deut 24:1
קְרָא	*qal* impv 2ms	קרא	Deut 31:14
אֶרְפָּא	*qal* impf 1cs	רפא	Deut 32:39
בְּרָא	*qal* impv 2ms	ברא	Ps 51:12

11.4.2 Imperfect and Imperative 2/3fp Forms Take *Segol* Thematic Vowel

One caveat with III-א verbs is that the 2/3fp forms in the imperfect and imperative do not lengthen the thematic vowel by compensation. The III-א will still quiesce, but the thematic vowel becomes a *segol* (ֶ).[12] It does not lengthen to a *tsere* in the 2/3fp imperfect and imperative of all stems. Herein lies another analogy to III-י verbs but with א as the vowel marker.[13] Some forms retain the III-א and add a *yod* by way of analogy with III-י verbs (תִּמְצֶאןָה *niphal* impf 3fp מצא, Jer 50:20; תִּשֶּׁאינָה *qal* impf 2fp נשא, Ezek 23:49).

תִּקְרֶאןָה	*qal* impf 3fp	קרא	Exod 1:10
תְּמַלֶּאןָה	*piel* impf 3fp	מלא	Exod 2:16
מְצֶאןָ	*qal* impv 2fp	מצא	Ruth 1:9

---

11. GKC, §74b; JM, §78b.

12. בוא is doubly weak verb with a II-ו, and the II-ו takes precedence over the III-א. Hence, בוא retains the *holem* or *holem vav* thematic vowel in the *qal* (תָּבֹאנָה *qal* impf 3fp, Isa 44:7) and the *hireq yod* thematic vowel in the *hiphil* impf or impv 2/3fp (תְּבִיאֶינָה *hiphil* impf 3fp, Lev 7:30).

13. GKC, §74d; JM, §78b. Blau argues the *segol* is a result of "assimilation" to the *qamets* of the sufformative in these forms (Blau, *Phonology and Morphology of Biblical Hebrew*, §4.3.8.5.2n, p. 248; §3.5.10.4, p. 137). To call this "assimilation," one must review Blau's discussion of vowel pronunciation (Blau, *Phonology and Morphology of Biblical Hebrew*, §2.4.10, pp. 65–66). *Segol* is certainly an e-class vowel, but in his trapezoid of vowels (Blau, *Phonology and Morphology of Biblical Hebrew*, §2.4.12, p. 66), the *segol* (a front, half-high vowel) leans more toward the *pataḥ* (a front low vowel). The point here is that there may be legitimate phonological principles that warrant the *segol* in these forms. It is not a random vowel assignment; rather, it demonstrates the meticulous way that the Masoretes preserved the nuances of pronunciation.

11.4.3 T-Form Participles Have a Quiescent א and *Tsere* Thematic Vowel

The last miscellaneous issue for III-א verbs is that the t-form participles will have a quiescent א and the preceding *segol* (from the segolization of the t-form) will lengthen to a *tsere*.[14] This leaves both the III-א and the final ת without any vowel pointing. The following example shows the progression.

hiphil participle (t-form) fs יצא (2 Sam 18:22)[15]

מֹצֵאת ← מֹצֶאת* ← מֹצֶאְת* ← קֹטֶלֶת
Compensatory   Quiescent א   "Strong" Form   Paradigm T-Form
Lengthening   Participle

In order to make sense of an א quiescing with a *segol*, we must consider a historical form analogous to segolate nouns. This phenomenon may be compared to noun formation in which the original form has one short vowel and two silent *shewas* (cf. מֶלֶךְ ← *מַלְךְ).[16] According to this explanation, III-א verbs would have a silent *shewa* that would quiesce and lengthen the preceding *segol* to *tsere* (מֹצֵאת ← *מֹצֶאְת). This explanation then is consistent with a quiescent א. Fuller and Choi compare this phenomenon to the ל preposition on אֱלֹהִים (לֵאלֹהִים), a phenomenon that Joüon describes as the א occasioning a contraction (לֵא ← לֶא).[17] Neither Fuller and Choi nor Joüon connect this phenomenon specifically to III-א verbs, but by analogy with segolate noun formation, we can observe that the explanation may be related. Regardless of how we derive the quiescent א and *tsere* vowel in the fs (t-form) participle, this is indeed the form we see in the Hebrew Bible.

Here are some additional representative forms from the Hebrew Bible.

יֹצֵאת	*qal* ptc fs יצא	Gen 24:45
יוֹצֵת[18]	*qal* ptc fs יצא	Deut 28:57
מֹצֵאת	*qal* ptc fs מצא	2 Sam 18:22
נְשֵׂאת	*niphal* ptc fs נשא	2 Sam 19:43
חֹטֵאת	*qal* ptc fs חטא	Ezek 18:4, 20

---

14. GKC, §74i.

15. The *holem* vowel here is from the contraction *aw* → *ô* with the *hiphil* preformative and the root יצא.

16. The second *segol* in these segolized forms is an epenthetic vowel to represent the actual pronunciation of the consonant cluster as the end of the historical form with only one vowel (*מַלְךְ). Therefore, to consider the derivation of the *tsere* in these forms, it is reasonable to restore the historical form with only one vowel, leaving the III-א with a silent *shewa* (*מֹצֶאְת).

17. Fuller and Choi, *Invitation to Biblical Hebrew*, 225; JM, §24e.

18. The *BHS* apparatus includes a note for this form that multiple manuscripts, including the SP have יֹצֵאת(ו) with the III-א preserved. *HALOT* and BDB mark the participle form as יוֹצֵאת/יֹצֵאת but

11.5 Conclusion

For III-א verbs, the thematic vowel is a *tsere* in the derived stems and *qal* stative where we expect *pataḥ* in the perfect conjugation. This is not a wholesale shift to *tsere*; rather, the "pure" stems generally become "mixed" Ē/ and the "mixed" stems generally become "pure" Ē/. For the *qal* imperfect and imperative, we can expect to see a shift toward a-class thematic vowels, usually a long *qamets* when the III-א quiesces and the *pataḥ* lengthens to a *qamets*. This shift to a-class thematic vowels is analogous to III-guttural verbs, and is once again, not a new morphological anomaly. It is the application of the characteristic that gutturals prefer /a/ sounds around them.

I hope that you have begun to see that weak verbs are not a random assortment of exceptions to the strong verb. Rather, they display the application of slightly more specific morphological principles that represent various phonological principles associated with each of the different categories of weak verb consonants. We will certainly encounter exceptions, but with all of these morphological principles now in our mental file cabinet, we can observe the consistency with which weak verbs inflect.

Remember that this methodology requires that you know the strong verb paradigms inside and out, backwards and forwards, with precision. If you know that the *hiphil* imperfect shell for a 2fs is תַּ◌ֹ◌ִי, then you may be shocked at how often you can parse an unknown verb based on that information alone. Furthermore, now that you know some specific weak verb characteristics, you will be able to recognize, for example, the *hiphil* imperfect 2fs of a I-ו verb that has contracted the original I-ו to a *holem vav* (תּוֹסִיפִי *hiphil* impf 2fs יסף, Isa 23:12). The shift from *תַּוְסִיפִי to תּוֹסִיפִי is now no longer a problem for you and it is certainly not an exception to the strong verb paradigms. You know the imperfect shell has a תּ preformative with a *hireq yod* sufformative. You also now know the *aw → ô* contraction. With these tools now in your Hebrew tool belt, you are equipped to handle weak verbs with confidence. I admit that there are some exceptions and that the task of solidifying these weak verb principles will be challenging for some. But hopefully this methodology provides you with a set of principles that will help you down what many students see as the most challenging aspect of their Hebrew journey.

---

include this exceptional form in Deut 28:57 without comment. *DCH* does not comment on the form. If we accept Joüon's explanation that the א occasions a contraction this could be an instance of the א serving as a vowel marker written defectively, without the consonant.

Finally, it is important to note that our ultimate goal is to read God's Word in Hebrew more fluently and effectively. I hope that the principles provided in these chapters will allow you to enjoy the Hebrew Bible more fully. It is indeed hard work to retain all of these morphological principles, but to know God more richly in the Hebrew Bible is always worth the effort. To be equipped and motivated to quarry "the depth of the riches and wisdom and knowledge of God" (Rom 11:33 ESV) revealed to us in the Hebrew Bible will prove to enhance your walk with the Lord Jesus Christ. I pray that these chapters will help you make progress in that direction.

PART 3

Weak Verbs in Context

CHAPTER 12

Weak Verbs in Context

12.1 Introduction

This final chapter of the book is what we may think of as the exercises for weak verb morphology. As we have indicated throughout, the goal of learning morphology is to better understand and identify weak verbs. In the following exercises, there are approximately 470 weak verbs in 70 different verses for practicing in context.

Some of you may recognize this concept from Van Pelt and Pratico's, *Biblical Hebrew Vocabulary in Context: Building Competency with Words Occurring 50 Times or More*. In that book, the authors identified 195 verses that contain all of the vocabulary words that occur 50 times or more. Once students translate those 195 verses, they will have encountered (in context) the most common vocabulary in the Hebrew Bible.

With the help of Joe Harrod, my colleague at Southern Seminary, we initially zeroed in on 48 verses that provide examples of each type of weak verb. Those initial verses were a great start. However, even with at least fifteen examples of each weak verb type, I noticed that not every weakness of every weak verb type was represented. For example, those initial verses may have contained several III-guttural verbs, but they did not contain an example of a III-guttural verb that retained the thematic vowel as a pausal form (§10.2.1.2). And so, I searched for and hand-picked 23 more verses to reach the new total of 70 verses. The goal was to find the minimum number of verses that would provide maximum practice with parsing weak verbs in context rather than in isolated lists.

The verses provided in §12.2 will provide the reader with a preliminary and basic exposure to the exercises associated with the book's content. The weak verbs are in a grey font so that they are easily recognized. Translations are available for a quick reference for rare vocabulary or sentence structure. The goal of these exercises is to practice parsing the weak verbs, but feel free to cover up the English translations and translate each verse on your own. That would be an added bonus of these exercises.

The English translations provided are intentionally not formal. The goal is not a wooden translation that preserves strict Hebrew word order but rather a readable English translation that addresses various nuances of the forms. If English words are added to the translation that do not formally appear in the Hebrew, those words are in brackets. If an idiom or a verbal nuance should be simplified, those translations are in parentheses. For example, a *hiphil* may be expressed using the causative notion, "I caused you to go out" (הוֹצֵאתִיךָ Gen 15:7). However, that is better expressed in English as, "I brought you out." We have attempted in the English translations to supply the "not formal" translation with the more idiomatic meaning in parentheses.

In addition to the verses and translations listed here, extended practice documents are available at Zondervan Academic's TextbookPlus. Visit https://zondervanacademic.com/products/weak-verb-morphology to access these resources. While the exercises in this book are a start, the documents available at TextbookPlus include more features that will aid the student's learning of weak verbs.

Three documents are provided at TextbookPlus for both students and instructors: Extended Exercises, Extended Exercises Without English Translations, and an Answer Key. Both of the exercises documents are set in landscape and provide extra space between each line of the Hebrew text so that students can write their own notes as they work through the weak verb parsings. This extra space will also allow users to more easily work on an independent translation before referring to the ones provided. The exercises without English translations are included for those who want an added challenge. In addition, the exercises documents include a parsing table with the weak verbs in each verse already listed so that users can fill in the parsings as they work through the verse. Also included in the first column of the parsing tables are the section number(s) in the book to which one can refer in order to see the discussions of the weak verb morphology for each particular verb (see Table 12.1 below). So, not only will students be able to dive deeply into the work of parsing, but they will also have section references available to reinforce the elements of this book.

Finally, a complete answer key for the parsings of the verbs in the exercises is provided. While the exercises here can provide an entry point into practicing the content of this book, the TextbookPlus files provide a more robust student experience with more opportunities for actively learning these weak verb principles.

Table 12.1

וַיֹּאמֶר אֵלָיו יִצְחָק אָבִיו גְּשָׁה־נָּא וּשְׁקָה־לִּי בְּנִי:
And then Isaac, his father, said to him, "Approach please, and kiss me, my son."
Genesis 27:26

	Section	Stem	Conjugation	PGN	Root	Affixes
וַיֹּאמֶר	§3.5.1					
גְּשָׁה	§5.3					
וּשְׁקָה	§5.3					

One thing that I often tell my students is that reading Hebrew regularly is the key to improvement; read, read, and read some more. As you read more and more text, even slowly and with help, you will encounter all these weak verbs in their natural habitat. Somehow, encountering them in context helps more with retention than seeing them in a paradigm or parsing list. Also, the more you read, the more often you encounter the same type of weakness, even if it is a really challenging one like the doubly weak I-נ/III-ה verb נכה. While these exercises are not formally "reading" as I encourage my students to do, I hope that it provides a set of verses that will help you practice in context each type of weakness we have discussed in the previous pages.

12.2 Exercises

(1) הֲלוֹא אִם־תֵּיטִיב שְׂאֵת וְאִם לֹא תֵיטִיב לַפֶּתַח חַטָּאת רֹבֵץ וְאֵלֶיךָ תְּשׁוּקָתוֹ וְאַתָּה תִּמְשָׁל־בּוֹ:

Is it not [that] if you do well, [you will be] one lifted up? But if you do not do well, at the door, sin is lurking. And its desire [is] toward (for) you, but you must rule over it.
Genesis 4:7

(2) וַיֹּאמֶר אֵלָיו אֲנִי יְהוָה אֲשֶׁר הוֹצֵאתִיךָ מֵאוּר כַּשְׂדִּים לָתֶת לְךָ אֶת־הָאָרֶץ הַזֹּאת לְרִשְׁתָּהּ:

And he said to him, "I [am] YHWH who caused you to go out (brought you out) from Ur of the Chaldeans, to give to you this land, to possess it."
Genesis 15:7

(3) וְהָיָ֣ה הַֽנַּעֲרָ֗ אֲשֶׁ֨ר אֹמַ֤ר אֵלֶ֙יהָ֙ הַטִּי־נָ֤א כַדֵּךְ֙ וְאֶשְׁתֶּ֔ה וְאָמְרָ֣ה שְׁתֵ֔ה וְגַם־גְּמַלֶּ֖יךָ אַשְׁקֶ֑ה אֹתָ֤הּ הֹכַ֙חְתָּ֙ לְעַבְדְּךָ֣ לְיִצְחָ֔ק וּבָ֣הּ אֵדַ֔ע כִּי־עָשִׂ֥יתָ חֶ֖סֶד עִם־אֲדֹנִֽי׃

And it shall come about, the young woman, who I will say to her, "Please send down your jar that I may drink," and she will say, "Drink, and moreover, [for] your camels I will provide drink." Her, you shall assign as your servant for Isaac. And [by] this (situation), I will know that you have done steadfast love with my lord. *Genesis 24:14*

(4) וַיֹּ֥אמֶר אֵלָ֖יו יִצְחָ֣ק אָבִ֑יו גְּשָׁה־נָּ֥א וּשְׁקָה־לִּ֖י בְּנִֽי׃

And then Isaac, his father, said to him, "Approach please, and kiss me, my son." *Genesis 27:26*

(5) וַיְהִ֣י כְשָׁמְע֔וֹ כִּֽי־הֲרִימֹ֥תִי קוֹלִ֖י וָאֶקְרָ֑א וַיַּעֲזֹ֤ב בִּגְדוֹ֙ אֶצְלִ֔י וַיָּ֖נָס וַיֵּצֵ֥א הַחֽוּצָה׃

And it came to pass as (when) he heard that I lifted my voice and cried out that he left his garment beside me. And he fled, and he went out to the outside. *Genesis 39:15*

(6) וְעַתָּ֣ה ׀ אַל־תֵּעָ֣צְב֗וּ וְאַל־יִ֙חַר֙ בְּעֵ֣ינֵיכֶ֔ם כִּֽי־מְכַרְתֶּ֥ם אֹתִ֖י הֵ֑נָּה כִּ֣י לְמִֽחְיָ֔ה שְׁלָחַ֥נִי אֱלֹהִ֖ים לִפְנֵיכֶֽם׃

And now, do not be grieved, and do not be angry in your eyes (with yourselves) that you sold me here. For God sent me before you to preserve life. *Genesis 45:5*

(7) וַתֹּאמַ֕רְןָ אִ֣ישׁ מִצְרִ֔י הִצִּילָ֖נוּ מִיַּ֣ד הָרֹעִ֑ים וְגַם־דָּלֹ֤ה דָלָה֙ לָ֔נוּ וַיַּ֖שְׁקְ אֶת־הַצֹּֽאן׃

And they said, "An Egyptian man delivered us from the hand of the shepherds. And moreover, he diligently drew water for us and caused the flock to drink." *Exodus 2:19*

(8) וַיִּקְרָ֨א פַרְעֹ֜ה אֶל־מֹשֶׁ֗ה וַיֹּ֙אמֶר֙ לְכוּ֙ עִבְד֣וּ אֶת־יְהֹוָ֔ה רַ֥ק צֹאנְכֶ֛ם וּבְקַרְכֶ֖ם יֻצָּ֑ג גַּֽם־טַפְּכֶ֖ם יֵלֵ֥ךְ עִמָּכֶֽם׃

And Pharaoh called out to Moses and said, "Go! Serve YHWH! Only, your flock and your cattle must be left behind, but your children may go with you." *Exodus 10:24*

(9) וַיַּשְׁכִּ֙ימוּ֙ מִֽמָּחֳרָ֔ת וַיַּעֲל֣וּ עֹלֹ֔ת וַיַּגִּ֖שׁוּ שְׁלָמִ֑ים וַיֵּ֤שֶׁב הָעָם֙ לֶֽאֱכֹ֣ל וְשָׁת֔וֹ וַיָּקֻ֖מוּ לְצַחֵֽק׃

And they arose early the next day. And they caused to ascend burnt offerings, and they brought near peace offerings. And the people sat to eat and drink, and they arose to play. *Exodus 32:6*

(10) צַ֤ו אֶֽת־אַהֲרֹן֙ וְאֶת־בָּנָ֣יו לֵאמֹ֔ר זֹ֥את תּוֹרַ֖ת הָעֹלָ֑ה הִ֣וא הָעֹלָ֡ה עַל֩ מוֹקְדָ֨ה עַל־הַמִּזְבֵּ֤חַ כָּל־הַלַּ֙יְלָה֙ עַד־הַבֹּ֔קֶר וְאֵ֥שׁ הַמִּזְבֵּ֖חַ תּ֥וּקַד בּֽוֹ׃

Command Aaron and his sons, saying, "This is the law of the burnt offering. It is the burnt offering on the hearth, on the altar, all night until the morning. And the fire of the altar shall be caused to burn (kindled) on it." *Leviticus 6:2*

(11) דַּבֵּ֞ר אֶל־בְּנֵ֤י יִשְׂרָאֵל֙ לֵאמֹ֔ר אִשָּׁה֙ כִּ֣י תַזְרִ֔יעַ וְיָלְדָ֖ה זָכָ֑ר וְטָֽמְאָה֙ שִׁבְעַ֣ת יָמִ֔ים כִּימֵ֛י נִדַּ֥ת דְּוֺתָ֖הּ תִּטְמָֽא׃

Speak to the sons of Israel, saying, "A woman, if she brings forth seed, and bears a male (son), then she will be unclean seven days, like the days of the impurity of her flow [when] she is unclean." *Leviticus 12:2*

(12) וּבְי֨וֹם הֵרָא֥וֹת בּ֛וֹ בָּשָׂ֥ר חַ֖י יִטְמָֽא׃

And the day [when] living flesh appears on him, he will be unclean. *Leviticus 13:14*

(13) וְהִתְוַדּ֗וּ אֶֽת־חַטָּאתָם֮ אֲשֶׁ֣ר עָשׂוּ֒ וְהֵשִׁ֤יב אֶת־אֲשָׁמוֹ֙ בְּרֹאשׁ֔וֹ וַחֲמִישִׁת֖וֹ יֹסֵ֣ף עָלָ֑יו וְנָתַ֕ן לַאֲשֶׁ֖ר אָשַׁ֥ם לֽוֹ׃

And they shall confess their sin which they had done, then he will cause to return his restitution on his head, adding its fifth on it, and he shall give [it] to whom he wronged. *Numbers 5:7*

(14) אֲנִי יְהוָה דִּבַּרְתִּי אִם־לֹא ׀ זֹאת אֶעֱשֶׂה לְכָל־הָעֵדָה הָרָעָה הַזֹּאת הַנּוֹעָדִים עָלָי בַּמִּדְבָּר הַזֶּה יִתַּמּוּ וְשָׁם יָמֻתוּ:

I YHWH, have spoken. Surely this I will do to all this evil congregation who gathered against me. In this wilderness, they shall be finished, and there they shall die. *Numbers 14:35*

(15) וְלֹא־נָתַן סִיחֹן אֶת־יִשְׂרָאֵל עֲבֹר בִּגְבֻלוֹ וַיֶּאֱסֹף סִיחֹן אֶת־כָּל־עַמּוֹ וַיֵּצֵא לִקְרַאת יִשְׂרָאֵל הַמִּדְבָּרָה וַיָּבֹא יָהְצָה וַיִּלָּחֶם בְּיִשְׂרָאֵל:

And Sihon did not give (allow) Israel to pass through his border. And Sihon gathered all his people and went out to meet Israel to (at) the wilderness. And he came to Yahaz and fought against Israel. *Numbers 21:23*

(16) וַיֹּאמֶר בִּלְעָם אֶל־מַלְאַךְ יְהוָה חָטָאתִי כִּי לֹא יָדַעְתִּי כִּי אַתָּה נִצָּב לִקְרָאתִי בַּדָּרֶךְ וְעַתָּה אִם־רַע בְּעֵינֶיךָ אָשׁוּבָה לִּי:

And Balaam said to the angel of YHWH, "I have sinned, for I did not know that you were standing opposite me on the road. And now, if (it is) evil in your eyes, I shall turn myself back (turn back)." *Numbers 22:34*

(17) וְעַתָּה בְּרַח־לְךָ אֶל־מְקוֹמֶךָ אָמַרְתִּי כַּבֵּד אֲכַבֶּדְךָ וְהִנֵּה מְנָעֲךָ יְהוָה מִכָּבוֹד:

And now, flee for yourself to your place! I have spoken. I shall surely honor you. But behold, YHWH has withheld you from honor. *Numbers 24:11*

(18) לֹא־תֹאבֶה לוֹ וְלֹא תִשְׁמַע אֵלָיו וְלֹא־תָחוֹס עֵינְךָ עָלָיו וְלֹא־תַחְמֹל וְלֹא־תְכַסֶּה עָלָיו:

You shall not consent to him, and you shall not listen to him. And your eye shall not have pity on him. And you shall not spare [him], and you shall not cover over him. *Deuteronomy 13:9*

(19) לֹא־תָלִין נִבְלָתוֹ עַל־הָעֵץ כִּי־קָבוֹר תִּקְבְּרֶנּוּ בַּיּוֹם הַהוּא כִּי־קִלְלַת אֱלֹהִים תָּלוּי וְלֹא תְטַמֵּא אֶת־אַדְמָתְךָ אֲשֶׁר יְהוָה אֱלֹהֶיךָ נֹתֵן לְךָ נַחֲלָה:

His corpse shall not lodge (remain) on the tree, for burying you shall bury it (you shall surely bury it) on that day, because the curse of God [is on] the one being hanged. And you shall not make unclean your land, which YHWH your God [is] giving to you [as] a possession. *Deuteronomy 21:23*

(20) לֹא־יוּכַ֣ל בַּעְלָ֣הּ הָרִאשׁ֣וֹן אֲשֶֽׁר־שִׁ֠לְּחָהּ לָשׁ֨וּב לְקַחְתָּ֜הּ לִהְי֧וֹת ל֣וֹ לְאִשָּׁ֗ה אַחֲרֵי֙ אֲשֶׁ֣ר הֻטַּמָּ֔אָה כִּֽי־תוֹעֵבָ֥ה הִ֖וא לִפְנֵ֣י יְהוָ֑ה וְלֹ֤א תַחֲטִיא֙ אֶת־הָאָ֔רֶץ אֲשֶׁר֙ יְהוָ֣ה אֱלֹהֶ֔יךָ נֹתֵ֥ן לְךָ֖ נַחֲלָֽה׃

Her former husband, who sent her away, is not able to turn [again] to take her to be for himself as a wife (to be his wife) after which (because) she has been defiled, for that is an abomination before YHWH, and you shall not cause the earth to sin (bring sin on the earth) which YHWH your God [is] giving to you [as] an inheritance. *Deuteronomy 24:4*

(21) כִּֽי־אֲבִיאֶ֣נּוּ אֶֽל־הָאֲדָמָ֣ה ׀ אֲשֶׁר־נִשְׁבַּ֣עְתִּי לַאֲבֹתָ֗יו זָבַ֤ת חָלָב֙ וּדְבַ֔שׁ וְאָכַ֥ל וְשָׂבַ֖ע וְדָשֵׁ֑ן וּפָנָ֞ה אֶל־אֱלֹהִ֤ים אֲחֵרִים֙ וַעֲבָד֔וּם וְנִ֣אֲצ֔וּנִי וְהֵפֵ֖ר אֶת־בְּרִיתִֽי׃

For (when) I have caused them[1] to enter (brought them) to the land which I swore to their fathers, flowing [with] milk and honey, and they have eaten, and they are full and become fat, and they turn to other gods and they serve them and they despise me and break my covenant. *Deuteronomy 31:20*

(22) וַיַּשְׁבַּ֣ע יְהוֹשֻׁ֔עַ בָּעֵ֥ת הַהִ֖יא לֵאמֹ֑ר אָר֨וּר הָאִ֜ישׁ לִפְנֵ֣י יְהוָ֗ה אֲשֶׁ֤ר יָקוּם֙ וּבָנָ֞ה אֶת־הָעִ֥יר הַזֹּ֛את אֶת־יְרִיח֖וֹ בִּבְכֹר֣וֹ יְיַסְּדֶ֔נָּה וּבִצְעִיר֖וֹ יַצִּ֥יב דְּלָתֶֽיהָ׃

Then Joshua caused them to swear (adjured) at that time, saying, "Cursed [is] the man before YHWH who rises up and builds this city, Jericho. With his firstborn he shall lay its foundation and with his young[est] he will install its doors (gates)." *Joshua 6:26*

(23) וַיֹּ֨אמֶר יְהוָ֜ה אֶל־יְהוֹשֻׁ֗עַ אַל־תִּירָ֣א וְאַל־תֵּחָת֒ קַ֣ח עִמְּךָ֗ אֵ֚ת כָּל־עַ֣ם הַמִּלְחָמָ֔ה וְק֖וּם עֲלֵ֣ה הָעָ֑י רְאֵ֣ה ׀ נָתַ֣תִּי בְיָדְךָ֗ אֶת־מֶ֤לֶךְ הָעַי֙ וְאֶת־עַמּ֔וֹ וְאֶת־עִיר֖וֹ וְאֶת־אַרְצֽוֹ׃

---

1. The 3ms verbs in Deut 31:20 refer to Israel as a collective singular. The English translation provides the plural pronouns even though most of the Hebrew verbs are 3ms.

And YHWH said to Joshua, "Do not fear and do not be dismayed. Take with you all the people of war and arise, go up [to] Ai. Look, I have given into your hand the king of Ai and his people and his city and his land."

Joshua 8:1

(24) וְהָיָ֞ה כְּתָפְשְׂכֶ֣ם אֶת־הָעִ֗יר תַּצִּ֤יתוּ אֶת־הָעִיר֙ בָּאֵ֔שׁ כִּדְבַ֥ר יְהוָ֖ה תַּעֲשׂ֑וּ רְא֖וּ צִוִּ֥יתִי אֶתְכֶֽם׃

And it will come about when you take the city, you will kindle the city with fire (you will set the city on fire). According to the word of YHWH you will do [it]. Look, I have commanded you.

Joshua 8:8

(25) וַיִּקַּ֣ח אֶת־הָעָ֗ם וַֽיֶּחֱצֵם֙ לִשְׁלֹשָׁ֣ה רָאשִׁ֔ים וַיֶּאֱרֹ֖ב בַּשָּׂדֶ֑ה וַיַּ֗רְא וְהִנֵּ֤ה הָעָם֙ יֹצֵ֣א מִן־הָעִ֔יר וַיָּ֥קָם עֲלֵיהֶ֖ם וַיַּכֵּֽם׃

And he took the people and divided them to (into) three heads (groups), and he laid an ambush in the field, and he looked and behold, the people [were] coming out from the city, and he arose against them and he struck them.

Judges 9:43

(26) וַיְהִ֣י כִרְאוֹת֣וֹ אוֹתָ֗הּ וַיִּקְרַ֣ע אֶת־בְּגָדָיו֮ וַיֹּאמֶר֒ אֲהָ֤הּ בִּתִּי֙ הַכְרֵ֣עַ הִכְרַעְתִּ֔נִי וְאַ֖תְּ הָיִ֣יתְ בְּעֹֽכְרָ֑י וְאָנֹכִ֗י פָּצִ֤יתִי־פִי֙ אֶל־יְהוָ֔ה וְלֹ֥א אוּכַ֖ל לָשֽׁוּב׃

And it came about when he saw her that he tore his clothes and he said, "Ah, my daughter! Bowing you have bowed me (You have brought me very low) and you exist [as] one who troubles me, but I myself have opened my mouth to YHWH, and I am not able to return [it]."

Judges 11:35

(27) וַיַּשְׁכִּ֗מוּ וַיְהִ֞י כַּעֲל֤וֹת הַשַּׁ֙חַר֙ וַיִּקְרָ֨א שְׁמוּאֵ֤ל אֶל־שָׁאוּל֙ הַגָּ֣ג לֵאמֹ֔ר ק֖וּמָה וַאֲשַׁלְּחֶ֑ךָּ וַיָּ֣קָם שָׁא֗וּל וַיֵּצְא֧וּ שְׁנֵיהֶ֛ם ה֥וּא וּשְׁמוּאֵ֖ל הַחֽוּצָה׃

And they arose early, and it came about as the morning was going up (as dawn broke) that Samuel called to Saul [on] the roof, saying, "Arise, that I may send you [away]." And Saul arose and the two of them went out, he and Samuel, to the street.

1 Samuel 9:26

(28) וַיַּ֣עַל יוֹנָתָ֗ן עַל־יָדָיו֙ וְעַל־רַגְלָ֔יו וְנֹשֵׂ֥א כֵלָ֖יו אַחֲרָ֑יו וַֽיִּפְּלוּ֙ לִפְנֵ֣י יוֹנָתָ֔ן וְנֹשֵׂ֥א כֵלָ֖יו מְמוֹתֵ֥ת אַחֲרָֽיו׃

And Jonathan went (climbed) up on his hands and on his feet and the one carrying his vessels (weapons) [went up] after him. And they fell before Jonathan, and the one carrying his vessels (weapons) slaying after him (killed some after him). *1 Samuel 14:13*

(29) וַיַּשְׁכֵּם שְׁמוּאֵל לִקְרַאת שָׁאוּל בַּבֹּקֶר וַיֻּגַּד לִשְׁמוּאֵל לֵאמֹר בָּא־שָׁאוּל הַכַּרְמֶלָה וְהִנֵּה מַצִּיב לוֹ יָד וַיִּסֹּב וַיַּעֲבֹר וַיֵּרֶד הַגִּלְגָּל:

And Samuel rose early to meet Saul in the morning, and it was told to Samuel saying, "Saul came to Carmel and behold, [he] set up for himself a monument and he has gone around and passed over and gone down [to] Gilgal." *1 Samuel 15:12*

(30) וַיֹּאמֶר הַמֶּלֶךְ לָרָצִים הַנִּצָּבִים עָלָיו סֹבּוּ וְהָמִיתוּ ׀ כֹּהֲנֵי יְהוָה כִּי גַם־יָדָם עִם־דָּוִד וְכִי יָדְעוּ כִּי־בֹרֵחַ הוּא וְלֹא גָלוּ אֶת־אָזְנִי וְלֹא־אָבוּ עַבְדֵי הַמֶּלֶךְ לִשְׁלֹחַ אֶת־יָדָם לִפְגֹעַ בְּכֹהֲנֵי יְהוָה:

And the king said to the runners (messengers) stationed to him, "Turn and put to death the priests of YHWH, because even their hand [was] with David and because they knew that he [was] fleeing, and they did not uncover my ear (tell me)." But the servants of the king did not want to stretch out their hand to fall upon (kill) the priests of YHWH. *1 Samuel 22:17*

(31) וַיָּקָם דָּוִד אַחֲרֵי־כֵן וַיֵּצֵא מִן־הַמְּעָרָה וַיִּקְרָא אַחֲרֵי־שָׁאוּל לֵאמֹר אֲדֹנִי הַמֶּלֶךְ וַיַּבֵּט שָׁאוּל אַחֲרָיו וַיִּקֹּד דָּוִד אַפַּיִם אַרְצָה וַיִּשְׁתָּחוּ:

And David arose after this and he went out from the cave, and he called out after Saul, saying, "My lord, the king." And Saul looked after him and David knelt down [with] nose to the ground and he paid homage. *1 Samuel 24:9*

(32) וַיֹּאמֶר שְׁמוּאֵל אֶל־שָׁאוּל לָמָּה הִרְגַּזְתַּנִי לְהַעֲלוֹת אֹתִי וַיֹּאמֶר שָׁאוּל צַר־לִי מְאֹד וּפְלִשְׁתִּים ׀ נִלְחָמִים בִּי וֵאלֹהִים סָר מֵעָלַי וְלֹא־עָנָנִי עוֹד גַּם בְּיַד־הַנְּבִיאִם גַּם־בַּחֲלֹמוֹת וָאֶקְרָאֶה לְךָ לְהוֹדִיעֵנִי מָה אֶעֱשֶׂה:

And Samuel said to Saul, "Why have you caused me to be disquieted [by] bringing me up?" And Saul said, "It [is] distressed to me mightily (I am exceedingly distressed) and the Philistines war against me and God has turned aside from me and he does not answer me anymore, either by the hand of the prophets or by dreams, and so I called to you to cause me to know what I will (should) do." *1 Samuel 28:15*

(33) וַיָּבֹא כָל־הָעָם לְהַבְרוֹת אֶת־דָּוִד לֶחֶם בְּעוֹד הַיּוֹם וַיִּשָּׁבַע דָּוִד לֵאמֹר כֹּה יַעֲשֶׂה־לִּי אֱלֹהִים וְכֹה יֹסִיף כִּי אִם־לִפְנֵי בוֹא־הַשֶּׁמֶשׁ אֶטְעַם־לֶחֶם אוֹ כָל־מְאוּמָה:

And all the people came to cause David to eat bread while it was yet day, but David swore, saying, "Thus may God do to me and thus may he increase, if before the sun sets, I taste bread or anything." *2 Samuel 3:35*

(34) וַיְהִי בַּיּוֹם הַשְּׁבִיעִי וַיָּמָת הַיָּלֶד וַיִּרְאוּ עַבְדֵי דָוִד לְהַגִּיד לוֹ כִּי־מֵת הַיֶּלֶד כִּי אָמְרוּ הִנֵּה בִהְיוֹת הַיֶּלֶד חַי דִּבַּרְנוּ אֵלָיו וְלֹא־שָׁמַע בְּקוֹלֵנוּ וְאֵיךְ נֹאמַר אֵלָיו מֵת הַיֶּלֶד וְעָשָׂה רָעָה:

And it came about on the seventh day that the child died, and the servants of David feared to declare to him that the child was dead, for they said "Behold, when the child was yet alive we spoke to him and he did not listen to our voice. And how will we say to him, 'The child is dead?' And he may do evil (harm himself)?" *2 Samuel 12:18*

(35) וַיְצַו אַבְשָׁלוֹם אֶת־נְעָרָיו לֵאמֹר רְאוּ נָא כְּטוֹב לֵב־אַמְנוֹן בַּיַּיִן וְאָמַרְתִּי אֲלֵיכֶם הַכּוּ אֶת־אַמְנוֹן וַהֲמִתֶּם אֹתוֹ אַל־תִּירָאוּ הֲלוֹא כִּי אָנֹכִי צִוִּיתִי אֶתְכֶם חִזְקוּ וִהְיוּ לִבְנֵי־חָיִל:

And Absalom commanded his servants, saying, "Look now, when the heart of Amnon is good (merry) with wine and I say to you all, 'Strike Amnon, and kill him,' do not fear. Have not I not commanded you myself, be strong and exist [as] sons of valor?" *2 Samuel 13:28*

(36) וַיֹּסֶף עוֹד אֲחִימַעַץ בֶּן־צָדוֹק וַיֹּאמֶר אֶל־יוֹאָב וִיהִי מָה אָרֻצָה־נָּא גַם־אָנִי אַחֲרֵי הַכּוּשִׁי וַיֹּאמֶר יוֹאָב לָמָּה־זֶּה אַתָּה רָץ בְּנִי וּלְכָה אֵין־בְּשׂוֹרָה מֹצֵאת:

And again, Ahimaaz the son of Zadok spoke to Joab, "Let what may exist [be]. Let me run now, even me, after the Cushite." And Joab said, "Why would you run, my son, and (since) to you there is no messenger's reward found?" *2 Samuel 18:22*

(37) וַיַּֽעֲזָר־לוֹ֙ אֲבִישַׁ֣י בֶּן־צְרוּיָ֔ה וַיַּ֥ךְ אֶת־הַפְּלִשְׁתִּ֖י וַיְמִיתֵ֑הוּ אָ֣ז נִשְׁבְּע֣וּ אַנְשֵׁי־דָוִ֣ד ל֗וֹ לֵאמֹר֙ לֹא־תֵצֵ֨א ע֤וֹד אִתָּ֙נוּ֙ לַמִּלְחָמָ֔ה וְלֹ֥א תְכַבֶּ֖ה אֶת־נֵ֥ר יִשְׂרָאֵֽל׃

And Abishai son of Zeruiah helped him, and he smote the Philistine, and he killed him. Then the men of David swore to him saying, "Do not go out still with us for war, and do not extinguish the lamp of Israel."

2 Samuel 21:17

(38) וַיָּבֹא־גָ֥ד אֶל־דָּוִ֖ד וַיַּגֶּד־ל֑וֹ וַיֹּ֣אמֶר ל֡וֹ הֲתָב֣וֹא לְךָ֣ שֶֽׁבַע שָׁנִ֣ים ׀ רָעָ֣ב בְּאַרְצֶ֡ךָ אִם־שְׁלֹשָׁה֩ חֳדָשִׁ֨ים נֻסְךָ֤ לִפְנֵֽי־צָרֶ֙יךָ֙ וְה֣וּא רֹדְפֶ֔ךָ וְאִם־הֱי֣וֹת שְׁלֹ֣שֶׁת יָמִ֥ים דֶּ֖בֶר בְּאַרְצֶ֑ךָ עַתָּה֙ דַּ֣ע וּרְאֵ֔ה מָה־אָשִׁ֥יב שֹׁלְחִ֖י דָּבָֽר׃

And Gad came to David, and he declared to him, and he said to him, "What will come to you, seven years of famine in your land, or three months of your fleeing from before your enemies and he is pursuing you, or be three days of pestilence in your land? Now, know and see what word I shall return [to] the one sending me."

2 Samuel 24:13

(39) וְהָיָ֗ה אִם־תִּשְׁמַע֙ אֶת־כָּל־אֲשֶׁ֣ר אֲצַוֶּ֔ךָ וְהָלַכְתָּ֣ בִדְרָכַ֗י וְעָשִׂ֨יתָ הַיָּשָׁ֣ר בְּעֵינַ֔י לִשְׁמ֥וֹר חֻקּוֹתַ֖י וּמִצְוֺתַ֑י כַּאֲשֶׁ֥ר עָשָׂ֖ה דָּוִ֣ד עַבְדִּ֑י וְהָיִ֣יתִי עִמָּ֔ךְ וּבָנִ֨יתִי לְךָ֤ בַֽיִת־נֶאֱמָן֙ כַּאֲשֶׁ֣ר בָּנִ֣יתִי לְדָוִ֔ד וְנָתַתִּ֥י לְךָ֖ אֶת־יִשְׂרָאֵֽל׃

And it shall come about if you listen to all that I have commanded you and you walk in my ways and you do the upright [thing] in my eyes by keeping my statutes and my commandments just as David my servant did. And I will be with you, and I will build for you a house of faithfulness just as I built for David and I will give to you Israel.

1 Kings 11:38

(40) וְאִשָּׁ֣ה אַחַ֣ת מִנְּשֵׁ֣י בְנֵֽי־הַ֠נְּבִיאִים צָעֲקָ֨ה אֶל־אֱלִישָׁ֜ע לֵאמֹ֗ר עַבְדְּךָ֤ אִישִׁי֙ מֵ֔ת וְאַתָּ֣ה יָדַ֔עְתָּ כִּ֣י עַבְדְּךָ֗ הָיָ֥ה יָרֵ֖א אֶת־יְהוָ֑ה וְהַ֨נֹּשֶׁ֔ה בָּ֗א לָקַ֜חַת אֶת־שְׁנֵ֧י יְלָדַ֛י ל֖וֹ לַעֲבָדִֽים׃

And a wife, one from the women of the sons of the prophets, cried out to Elisha saying, "Your servant, my husband is dead and you yourself know that your servant existed [as] one fearing YHWH. And the one lending [money] (the creditor) came to take two of my children for himself as servants."

2 Kings 4:1

(41) וַיְהִי כִּקְרֹא מֶלֶךְ־יִשְׂרָאֵל אֶת־הַסֵּפֶר וַיִּקְרַע בְּגָדָיו וַיֹּאמֶר הַאֱלֹהִים אָנִי לְהָמִית וּלְהַחֲיוֹת כִּי־זֶה שֹׁלֵחַ אֵלַי לֶאֱסֹף אִישׁ מִצָּרַעְתּוֹ כִּי אַךְ־דְּעוּ־נָא וּרְאוּ כִּי־מִתְאַנֶּה הוּא לִי:

And it came about as the king of Israel was reading the letter that he tore his garments, and he said, "[Am] I God to kill and to let live that this [one] send to me to remove a man from his leprosy (to cure a man's leprosy)? Only know and see that he is seeking an opportunity [for a quarrel] with me." *2 Kings 5:7*

(42) וַיָּשָׁב יוֹרָם הַמֶּלֶךְ לְהִתְרַפֵּא בְיִזְרְעֶאל מִן־הַמַּכִּים אֲשֶׁר יַכֻּהוּ אֲרַמִּים בָּרָמָה בְּהִלָּחֲמוֹ אֶת־חֲזָאֵל מֶלֶךְ אֲרָם וַאֲחַזְיָהוּ בֶן־יְהוֹרָם מֶלֶךְ יְהוּדָה יָרַד לִרְאוֹת אֶת־יוֹרָם בֶּן־אַחְאָב בְּיִזְרְעֶאל כִּי־חֹלֶה הוּא:

And Joram the king returned to be healed in Jezreel from the wounds which the Arameans smote him in Ramah in (during) his fight with Hazael king of Aram. And Ahaziah, son of Jehoram, king of Judah, went down to see Joram son of Ahab in Jezreel for sick [was] he. *2 Kings 8:29*

(43) וַיְהִי כְּכַלֹּתוֹ לַעֲשׂוֹת הָעֹלָה וַיֹּאמֶר יֵהוּא לָרָצִים וְלַשָּׁלִשִׁים בֹּאוּ הַכּוּם אִישׁ אַל־יֵצֵא וַיַּכּוּם לְפִי־חָרֶב וַיַּשְׁלִכוּ הָרָצִים וְהַשָּׁלִשִׁים וַיֵּלְכוּ עַד־עִיר בֵּית־הַבָּעַל:

And it came about as he finished doing (offering) the burnt offering that Jehu said to the runners and the officers, "Come, smite them, do not let a man go out." And they smote them with the mouth (edge) of the sword and they threw [the bodies] out, the runners and the officers, and they went until a city, the house of Baal. *2 Kings 10:25*

(44) הִנֵּה יְהוָה מְטַלְטֶלְךָ טַלְטֵלָה גָּבֶר וְעֹטְךָ עָטֹה:

Behold, YHWH [will] hurl you away [as] a violent ejection (hurl you away violently), O strong man. And he will seize you a seizing (he will seize you firmly). *Isaiah 22:17*

(45) כִּי כֹה אָמַר־יְהוָה ׀ אֵלַי כַּאֲשֶׁר יֶהְגֶּה הָאַרְיֵה וְהַכְּפִיר עַל־טַרְפּוֹ אֲשֶׁר יִקָּרֵא עָלָיו מְלֹא רֹעִים מִקּוֹלָם לֹא יֵחָת וּמֵהֲמוֹנָם לֹא יַעֲנֶה כֵּן יֵרֵד יְהוָה צְבָאוֹת לִצְבֹּא עַל־הַר־צִיּוֹן וְעַל־גִּבְעָתָהּ:

For thus says YHWH to me, "Just as the lion growls and the young lion [growls] over his prey, that the full [group] of shepherds is called against him, from their voice he is not dismayed, and from their roar he is not afflicted. So, YHWH of hosts descends to wage war on mount Zion and on her hill."

Isaiah 31:4

(46) הֲלוֹא־שָׁמַעְתָּ לְמֵרָחוֹק אוֹתָהּ עָשִׂיתִי מִימֵי קֶדֶם וִיצַרְתִּיהָ עַתָּה הֲבֵיאתִיהָ וּתְהִי לְהַשְׁאוֹת גַּלִּים נִצִּים עָרִים בְּצֻרוֹת׃

Have you not heard from distance (long ago) her I made? From days of old I formed her. Now, have I brought [it] to pass that you will exist as bringing to ruin a pile of rocks, fallen in ruins fortified cities.

Isaiah 37:26

(47) וְהוּא עַם־בָּזוּז וְשָׁסוּי הָפֵחַ בַּחוּרִים כֻּלָּם וּבְבָתֵּי כְלָאִים הָחְבָּאוּ הָיוּ לָבַז וְאֵין מַצִּיל מְשִׁסָּה וְאֵין־אֹמֵר הָשַׁב׃

And it [is] a people having been plundered and plundered (looted), trapped in holes [are] all of them, and in houses of imprisonment they are hidden. They have become like plunder and there is no rescuer, [like] booty but there does not exist one saying, "Return."

Isaiah 42:22

(48) שְׂאוּ לַשָּׁמַיִם עֵינֵיכֶם וְהַבִּיטוּ אֶל־הָאָרֶץ מִתַּחַת כִּי־שָׁמַיִם כֶּעָשָׁן נִמְלָחוּ וְהָאָרֶץ כַּבֶּגֶד תִּבְלֶה וְיֹשְׁבֶיהָ כְּמוֹ־כֵן יְמוּתוּן וִישׁוּעָתִי לְעוֹלָם תִּהְיֶה וְצִדְקָתִי לֹא תֵחָת׃

Lift up to the heavens your eyes and look to the earth from under (below), for heavens [are] like smoke [which is] dispersed and the earth [is] like a garment worn out and the one who dwells [in] it [is] like dying gnats. And my salvation forever will exist, and my righteousness will not be shattered.

Isaiah 51:6

(49) לְמַעַן תִּינְקוּ וּשְׂבַעְתֶּם מִשֹּׁד תַּנְחֻמֶיהָ לְמַעַן תָּמֹצּוּ וְהִתְעַנַּגְתֶּם מִזִּיז כְּבוֹדָהּ׃

So that you may nurse and be satisfied from the breast of her consolations; so that you may drain out [by drinking deeply] and refresh yourself from the abundance of her glory.

Isaiah 66:11

(50) אֵיךְ תֹּאמְרִי לֹא נִטְמֵאתִי אַחֲרֵי הַבְּעָלִים לֹא הָלַכְתִּי רְאִי דַרְכֵּךְ בַּגַּיְא דְּעִי מֶה עָשִׂית בִּכְרָה קַלָּה מְשָׂרֶכֶת דְּרָכֶיהָ׃

How can you say, "I have not been defiled after the Baals, I have not gone after [them]?" Look, your way [is] in the valley; know what you have done, a swift young camel running about senselessly in her way. *Jeremiah 2:23*

(51) וְאָמַרְתִּי לֹא־אֶזְכְּרֶנּוּ וְלֹא־אֲדַבֵּר עוֹד בִּשְׁמוֹ וְהָיָה בְלִבִּי כְּאֵשׁ בֹּעֶרֶת עָצֻר בְּעַצְמֹתָי וְנִלְאֵיתִי כַּלְכֵל וְלֹא אוּכָל׃

And I said, "I will not remember him, and I will not speak again in his name and it is in my heart like a fire burning restrained in my bones. And I am wearied to contain [it] and I [am] not able." *Jeremiah 20:9*

(52) בֵּית דָּוִד כֹּה אָמַר יְהוָה דִּינוּ לַבֹּקֶר מִשְׁפָּט וְהַצִּילוּ גָזוּל מִיַּד עוֹשֵׁק פֶּן־תֵּצֵא כָאֵשׁ חֲמָתִי וּבָעֲרָה וְאֵין מְכַבֶּה מִפְּנֵי רֹעַ מַעַלְלֵיהֶם׃

House of David, thus says YHWH, "Execute in the morning justice, and deliver the seized from the hand of the oppressor, lest my wrath go forth like a fire and burn and there is no one extinguishing from the face of (on account of) their evil deeds." *Jeremiah 21:12*

(53) וּבִנְבִאֵי יְרוּשָׁלַם רָאִיתִי שַׁעֲרוּרָה נָאוֹף וְהָלֹךְ בַּשֶּׁקֶר וְחִזְּקוּ יְדֵי מְרֵעִים לְבִלְתִּי־שָׁבוּ אִישׁ מֵרָעָתוֹ הָיוּ־לִי כֻלָּם כִּסְדֹם וְיֹשְׁבֶיהָ כַּעֲמֹרָה׃

And among the prophets of Jerusalem, I have seen horror. Committing adultery and walking in deception and strengthening the hands of the evildoers. [so that] each one does not turn back from his evil. They are to me all of them as Sodom and those dwelling in her like Gomorrah. *Jeremiah 23:14*

(54) וּבַיִת לֹא־תִבְנוּ וְזֶרַע לֹא־תִזְרָעוּ וְכֶרֶם לֹא־תִטָּעוּ וְלֹא יִהְיֶה לָכֶם כִּי בָּאֳהָלִים תֵּשְׁבוּ כָּל־יְמֵיכֶם לְמַעַן תִּחְיוּ יָמִים רַבִּים עַל־פְּנֵי הָאֲדָמָה אֲשֶׁר אַתֶּם גָּרִים שָׁם׃

And a house you shall not build and seed you shall not sow and a vineyard you shall not plant; [these things] shall not exist to you, but in tents you shall dwell all of your days so that you may live many days on the face of ground where you are sojourning there. *Jeremiah 35:7*

(55) וַיֹּאמֶר אֵלַי הֲרָאִיתָ בֶן־אָדָם הֲנָקֵל לְבֵית יְהוּדָה מֵעֲשׂוֹת אֶת־הַתּוֹעֵבוֹת אֲשֶׁר עָשׂוּ־פֹה כִּי־מָלְאוּ אֶת־הָאָרֶץ חָמָס וַיָּשֻׁבוּ לְהַכְעִיסֵנִי וְהִנָּם שֹׁלְחִים אֶת־הַזְּמוֹרָה אֶל־אַפָּם׃

And he said to me, "Have you seen, son of man? Is it light (too small a thing) for the house of Judah to do the abominations that they do here, that they fill the land [with] violence? And they return to make me discontent (angry), and behold they are stretching out the branch to their nose."

Ezekiel 8:17

(56) בְּצֵאת עִזְבוֹנַ֙יִךְ֙ מִיַּמִּ֔ים הִשְׂבַּ֖עַתְּ עַמִּ֣ים רַבִּ֑ים בְּרֹ֤ב הוֹנַ֙יִךְ֙ וּמַעֲרָבַ֔יִךְ הֶעֱשַׁ֖רְתְּ מַלְכֵי־אָֽרֶץ׃

When your wares (merchandise) came out from the seas, you satisfied many peoples. With abundance of your wealth and your goods, you enriched the kings of the earth.

Ezekiel 27:33

(57) כֹּה־אָמַר֩ אֲדֹנָ֨י יְהוִ֜ה בָּרִאשׁ֗וֹן בְּאֶחָ֤ד לַחֹ֙דֶשׁ֙ תִּקַּ֤ח פַּר־בֶּן־בָּקָר֙ תָּמִ֔ים וְחִטֵּאתָ֖ אֶת־הַמִּקְדָּֽשׁ׃

Thus says the Lord YHWH: "In the first [month], on the first [day] of the month, you shall take a young bull, a son of the herd complete (without blemish), and you shall cleanse from sin the sanctuary."

Ezekiel 45:18

(58) וַיְהִ֣י ׀ כִּזְרֹ֣חַ הַשֶּׁ֗מֶשׁ וַיְמַ֨ן אֱלֹהִ֜ים ר֤וּחַ קָדִים֙ חֲרִישִׁ֔ית וַתַּ֥ךְ הַשֶּׁ֛מֶשׁ עַל־רֹ֥אשׁ יוֹנָ֖ה וַיִּתְעַלָּ֑ף וַיִּשְׁאַ֤ל אֶת־נַפְשׁוֹ֙ לָמ֔וּת וַיֹּ֕אמֶר ט֥וֹב מוֹתִ֖י מֵחַיָּֽי׃

And it came about, as the sun arose, that God appointed a scorching east wind, and the sun struck upon the head of Jonah, and he became faint. And he asked his soul to die, and he said, "Better my death than my life."

Jonah 4:8

(59) בְּטֶ֙רֶם֙ לֶ֣דֶת חֹ֔ק כְּמֹ֖ץ עָ֣בַר י֑וֹם בְּטֶ֣רֶם ׀ לֹא־יָב֣וֹא עֲלֵיכֶ֗ם חֲרוֹן֙ אַף־יְהוָ֔ה בְּטֶ֙רֶם֙ לֹא־יָב֣וֹא עֲלֵיכֶ֔ם י֖וֹם אַף־יְהוָֽה׃

Before the statute gives birth (comes into effect), like chaff the day passes by. Before it will not[2] come upon you the burning anger of YHWH, before it will not come upon you the day of the anger of YHWH.

Zephaniah 2:2

---

2. This construction has a double negative that makes the clause more emphatic though in the wooden English translation it is difficult to capture. See GKC, §152y for the explanation.

(60) יְהִי שְׁמוֹ לְעוֹלָם לִפְנֵי־שֶׁמֶשׁ יִנּוֹן שְׁמוֹ וְיִתְבָּרְכוּ בוֹ כָּל־גּוֹיִם יְאַשְּׁרוּהוּ:

May his name exist forever. Before (as long as) the sun [exists], may his name sprout forth, and may they (the peoples) be blessed in him; may all the nations consider him fortunate. *Psalm 72:17*

(61) אוֹדְךָ עַל כִּי נוֹרָאוֹת נִפְלֵיתִי נִפְלָאִים מַעֲשֶׂיךָ וְנַפְשִׁי יֹדַעַת מְאֹד:

I will praise you because fearfully and miraculously I was [created]. Miraculous are your deeds, and my soul knows [it] very well. *Psalm 139:14*

(62) שָׁמְעוּ כִּי נֶאֱנָחָה אָנִי אֵין מְנַחֵם לִי כָּל־אֹיְבַי שָׁמְעוּ רָעָתִי שָׂשׂוּ כִּי אַתָּה עָשִׂיתָ הֵבֵאתָ יוֹם־קָרָאתָ וְיִהְיוּ כָמוֹנִי:

They heard that I myself was groaning; [but] there does not exist one who comforts me. All of my enemies have heard of my misfortune; they rejoice that you have done [it]. You have brought the day you proclaimed and [now] let them be like me. *Lamentations 1:21*

(63) וַיֹּאמֶר אֵלַי אַל־תִּירָא דָנִיֵּאל כִּי מִן־הַיּוֹם הָרִאשׁוֹן אֲשֶׁר נָתַתָּ אֶת־לִבְּךָ לְהָבִין וּלְהִתְעַנּוֹת לִפְנֵי אֱלֹהֶיךָ נִשְׁמְעוּ דְבָרֶיךָ וַאֲנִי־בָאתִי בִּדְבָרֶיךָ:

Then he said to me, "Do not be afraid, Daniel, because from the first day that you gave your heart to understand and to be bowed low (humbled) before your God, your words have been heard, and I myself have come on [account of] your words." *Daniel 10:12*

(64) וַיְהִי כְּשָׁמְעִי אֶת־הַדְּבָרִים הָאֵלֶּה יָשַׁבְתִּי וָאֶבְכֶּה וָאֶתְאַבְּלָה יָמִים וָאֱהִי צָם וּמִתְפַּלֵּל לִפְנֵי אֱלֹהֵי הַשָּׁמָיִם:

And it came about as I heard these words [that] I sat down, and I wept, and I mourned [for] days. And I was [as] one who fasts and prays before the God of the heavens. *Nehemiah 1:4*

(65) וַתָּעַד בָּהֶם לַהֲשִׁיבָם אֶל־תּוֹרָתֶךָ וְהֵמָּה הֵזִידוּ וְלֹא־שָׁמְעוּ לְמִצְוֹתֶיךָ וּבְמִשְׁפָּטֶיךָ חָטְאוּ־בָם אֲשֶׁר־יַעֲשֶׂה אָדָם וְחָיָה בָהֶם וַיִּתְּנוּ כָתֵף סוֹרֶרֶת וְעָרְפָּם הִקְשׁוּ וְלֹא שָׁמֵעוּ:

And you testified against (warned) them to return them back to your law, but they behaved presumptuously, and they did not listen to your commandments, and against your judgments they sinned, which a man will do [them] and will live by them, but they gave a stubborn shoulder, and their neck they stiffened and did not hear (obey). *Nehemiah 9:29*

(66) וָאֹמְרָה אֱלֹהַי בֹּשְׁתִּי וְנִכְלַמְתִּי לְהָרִים אֱלֹהַי פָּנַי אֵלֶיךָ כִּי עֲוֹנֹתֵינוּ רָבוּ לְמַעְלָה רֹּאשׁ וְאַשְׁמָתֵנוּ גָדְלָה עַד לַשָּׁמָיִם:

And I said, "O my God, I am ashamed, and I feel humiliated to lift, my God, my face to you because our iniquities have become many to the height of [our] head, and our guilt has become great to the heavens." *Ezra 9:6*

(67) וַיֵּלְכוּ וַיַּגִּידוּ לְדָוִיד עַל־הָאֲנָשִׁים וַיִּשְׁלַח לִקְרָאתָם כִּי־הָיוּ הָאֲנָשִׁים נִכְלָמִים מְאֹד וַיֹּאמֶר הַמֶּלֶךְ שְׁבוּ בִירֵחוֹ עַד אֲשֶׁר־יְצַמַּח זְקַנְכֶם וְשַׁבְתֶּם:

And they went, and they reported to David about the men. Then, he sent to meet them because the men were greatly ashamed, and the king said, "Dwell in Jericho until when your beards sprout and (then) return." *1 Chronicles 19:5*

(68) וַיְהִי כִּרְאוֹת שָׂרֵי הָרֶכֶב אֶת־יְהוֹשָׁפָט וְהֵמָּה אָמְרוּ מֶלֶךְ יִשְׂרָאֵל הוּא וַיָּסֹבּוּ עָלָיו לְהִלָּחֵם וַיִּזְעַק יְהוֹשָׁפָט וַיהוָה עֲזָרוֹ וַיְסִיתֵם אֱלֹהִים מִמֶּנּוּ:

And it came about as the officials of the chariots saw Jehoshaphat that they said, "He [is] the king of Israel." And then they turned against him to fight. And Jehoshaphat cried out, and YHWH helped him, and God drew them away from him. *2 Chronicles 18:31*

(69) וַתֵּרֶא וְהִנֵּה הַמֶּלֶךְ עוֹמֵד עַל־עַמּוּדוֹ בַּמָּבוֹא וְהַשָּׂרִים וְהַחֲצֹצְרוֹת עַל־הַמֶּלֶךְ וְכָל־עַם הָאָרֶץ שָׂמֵחַ וְתוֹקֵעַ בַּחֲצֹצְרוֹת וְהַמְשׁוֹרְרִים בִּכְלֵי הַשִּׁיר וּמוֹדִיעִים לְהַלֵּל וַתִּקְרַע עֲתַלְיָהוּ אֶת־בְּגָדֶיהָ וַתֹּאמֶר קֶשֶׁר קָשֶׁר:

And she looked and behold the king was standing beside his pillar at the entrance, and the officials and the trumpeters [were] beside the king, and all the people of the land [were] joyful and blowing with trumpets, and the singers with the instruments of song [were] making known (leading or giving signal) to praise. And Athaliah tore her garments, and she said, "Conspiracy! Conspiracy!" *2 Chronicles 23:13*

(70) וַיְהִ֣י ׀ בְּדַבְּר֣וֹ אֵלָ֗יו וַיֹּ֤אמֶר לוֹ֙ הַלְיוֹעֵ֤ץ לַמֶּ֙לֶךְ֙ נְתַנּ֔וּךָ חֲדַל־לְךָ֖ לָ֣מָּה יַכּ֑וּךָ וַיֶּחְדַּ֣ל הַנָּבִ֗יא וַיֹּ֙אמֶר֙ יָדַ֗עְתִּי כִּֽי־יָעַ֤ץ אֱלֹהִים֙ לְהַשְׁחִיתֶ֔ךָ כִּֽי־עָשִׂ֣יתָ זֹּ֔את וְלֹ֥א שָׁמַ֖עְתָּ לַעֲצָתִֽי׃

And it came about as he was speaking to him, that he said to him, "An advisor to the king have we made you? You stop! Why should they strike you down?" So, the prophet stopped, and he said, "I know that God advises (plans) to destroy you because you have done this [thing], and you have not listened to my advice." *2 Chronicles 25:16*

Scripture Index

Old Testament
Genesis
1:2. 70
1:5. 122
1:20. 89
1:29. 67
2:2. 109
2:6. 106
2:9. 115
2:19. 125
2:22. 109
3:3. 60
3:10. 119
3:14. . . . . 92, 106
3:16. . . . . 109, 110
3:22. 117
4:1. 50
4:2. 45
4:7. . . . . 55, 133
4:14. 70
4:26 36
5:22. 53
6:6. 33
6:21. 67
7:2. 66
8:8. 111
8:10. 50
8:10, 12 50
8:11. . . . . 50, 93
8:12. 50
8:21. 45
9:3. 26
9:9. 87
9:23. 79
10:18. . . . . 30, 85
11:4. 109
11:5. 111
11:9. 96
11:10. 50
11:27. 45
12:3. 97
12:7. . . . . 60, 109
12:9. 64
12:13 55
12:15. 66
13:6. 50
13:9. 55
13:10. 71
13:14. 110
13:16. 109
14:21. 67
14:23 . . . . 36, 66
14:24 66
15:5. 54
15:7. . . . . 132, 133
15:14. 37
16:9. 110
16:10. 110
17:11. 99
17:17. 44
17:20. . . . . 15, 71
17:26. 85
18:4. 66
18:5. 66
18:15. 71
18:17. 112
19:9. 64
19:11. 63
19:14. 71
19:16. 101
19:35. 83
20:6 64
21:6. 117
21:7. 55
21:12. 117
21:24 116
22:3. 79
22:12, 16 33
22:16. 119
22:17. 110
24:3 120
24:14. . . . . 63, 134
24:31 106
24:45 126
24:48 67
24:50 54
24:54 79
24:56 116
24:60 71
26:29 120
27:4, 7. 40
27:12. 98
27:25. 40
27:26 134
27:34. 117
27:43. 117
29:2. 109
29:5. 119
29:7. 110
29:10. 97
29:19. 68
30:8. 54

149

30:32 35	3:19. 53	23:29 96
31:6. 119	4:4. 118	23:33 36
31:13. 119	5:1. 97	25:20 92
31:28. 64	5:14. 106	26:28 117
31:35. 33	6:6. 113	26:29 109
33:3. 64	7:10. 79	26:30 106
33:7. 60	7:15. 38	27:17. 33
34:9. 66	7:27. 117	27:20. 111
34:15 85	8:1. 109	28:11. 102
34:16. 67	8:12. 63	28:43 64
34:21 60	8:13. 62	29:1. 67
34:22 85	8:17. 117	29:27 88
35:1. . . . . 49, 120	8:22. 117	30:2 117
35:7. 106	8:25. 38	30:20 64
36:7. 53	9:14. 25	32:6. 135
37:7. . . . . 93, 95, 96, 97	9:17. 101	33:7. 66
39:1. 46	9:23. 53	33:16. 106
39:15. 134	9:34. 34	33:19. . . . . 36, 95
40:15 7	10:15. 45	34:3. 109
41:1. 33	10:24 135	34:8. 96
41:18. 112	10:26 66	36:5. 112
41:32. 85	12:4. . . . . 92, 96, 97	38:27 52
41:40 60	12:5. 66	39:6, 13 102
42:1. 109	12:15. 12	39:13. 102
42:33 67	12:27 64	40:25 109
43:18. 88	12:34 92	40:35 53
43:32 34	12:39 101	
44:33 51	14:3. 84	*Leviticus*
45:5. 134	14:5. 119	1:9. 73
45:11. 89	14:15. 73	2:6. . . . . 92, 98
46:31 40	15:15. 84	2:14. 113
48:5. 45	15:16. 93	5:3. 38
49:4. 101	15:21. 110	6:2. . . . . 46, 109, 135
49:10. 101	16:24 73	7:2. . . . . 70, 72
	16:33. 67	7:30. 125
Exodus	17:5. 34	8:8. 79
1:10. 125	17:9. 24	8:11. 63
1:16. 106	18:18. 60	12:2. . . . . 116, 135
2:4. 49	18:23 54	13:14. . . . . 33, 135
2:12. 62	19:13. . . . . 37, 44	14:41. 116
2:13. 60	20:7. 60	15:29. 66
2:15. 34	21:22 33	19:20 36
2:16. 125	21:29 36	20:24 50
2:19. 134	21:30 88	25:16. 108
3:3. 73	21:35. 60	25:21. 105
3:5. 65	23:13 115	25:22 119

Scripture Index • 151

25:30	73
26:25	67
26:31	101
26:34	102, 105
26:35	102
26:39	99
26:43	102
27:29	36

Numbers

4:19	64
5:7	135
5:19	110
6:26	79
9:6	53
12:6	44
13:30	54
14:16	54
14:18	110
14:29	60
14:35	93, 136
15:28	92, 98
16:30	123
17:11	67
17:25	109
20:11	109
21:4	98
21:23	136
22:6	36, 54
22:13-16	53
22:15	25
22:23	62
22:34	136
22:38	54
23:8	97
24:11	120, 136
25:4	116
30:4	60
30:9	118
32:38	102
34:18	64
36:7	97

Deuteronomy

2:1	97
2:35	96
3:7	93, 96
4:35	50
4:40	42
5:23	120
5:31	34
6:4	118
7:2	36
8:19	106
9:21	96
9:28	54
12:20	40
13:9	136
15:5	117
16:9	101
16:15	97
17:4	55
17:16	111
19:14	87
20:7	66
20:8	99
21:2	96
21:18	98
21:18, 20	91
21:23	137
22:24, 27	72
23:22	73
24:1	125
24:4	137
24:5	115
24:16	88
28:38	35
28:57	126, 127
29:18	71
30:4	61
31:6	33
31:14	125
31:20	137
32:38	79
32:39	125
33:3	92
33:11	71, 73

Joshua

3:9	64
3:10	45
4:16	110
5:9	93, 96
6:7	93, 98
6:15	92
6:26	137
7:9	99
7:12	54
8:1	138
8:8	138
9:24	63
10:26	113
14:11	118
18:4	79
19:49	64

Judges

3:10	97
3:24	101
7:4	45
7:5	94
8:3	54
8:9	60
8:21	117
9:32	34
9:43	138
11:9	87
11:35	138
13:8	79
13:14	109
14:7	55
14:13	54
16:3	39
16:24	36
19:6	54
20:4	11
20:38	110
20:39	60

Ruth

1:9	121, 125
1:14	121
2:11	63
2:14	64
2:16	98

1 Samuel

| 2:10 | 99 |

3:2. 101	19:43 126	**1 Chronicles**
3:11. 97	20:18. 72	11:17. 109
3:12. 101	21:17. 141	12:2. 56
3:21. 33	22:14. 73	19:5. 147
4:3. 66	23:1. 88	21:10. 24
4:11, 22 66	24:12 . . . . 24, 73	
4:13. 79	24:13 141	**2 Chronicles**
4:15. 53	24:22 109	14:10. 26
4:19. 49		18:14. 116
5:9. 101	***1 Kings***	18:16. 85
7:2. 99	1:11. 119	18:31. 147
8:3. 62	2:46 85	23:13 147
9:26 138	6:6. 71	25:16. 148
10:6. 121	6:35. 44	29:19. 116
10:13. 121	7:15. . . . . 94, 97	32:13. 54
13:8. 50	7:23. 46	36:21 102
14:13. . . . . 89, 139	10:18. 102	
14:16. 85	11:38. 141	***Ezra***
15:12. 139	14:10. 98	1:3. 109
16:11. 97	16:31. 100	9:6. 147
17:39. 60	17:10. 67	
21:15. 117	17:11. 67	***Nehemiah***
22:17. 139	19:16. 117	1:4. 146
24:5. 54	20:14. 38	9:29. 147
24:9. 139	20:23 35	10:32. 60
25:23 50	20:27 89	
26:25 54	21:7. 54	***Esther***
28:15. 140	21:19. 93	2:9. 113
	22:35 36	4:13. 109
2 Samuel		6:1. 96
1:24. 110	***2 Kings***	6:13. 101
3:35. 140	1:10. 51	9:31. 88
6:21. 111	3:18. 100	
6:22 100	4:1. 141	***Job***
10:11. 37	4:24 64	3:26. 106
12:18. 140	4:41. 52	4:20 102
12:19 71	5:7. 142	11:20 121
13:2. 111	5:8. 79	15:7. 89
13:17. 64	8:29. 142	16:22 53
13:28 140	9:33. 62	17:5. 121
14:13. 61	9:37. 105	20:22 97
14:18. 72	10:25. 142	23:15. 73
14:24 97	15:16. 116	24:24 102
18:22 . . . . 126, 140	19:26 92	28:2. 66
19:3. 36	25:24 54	28:10. 25
19:8. 95		31:1. 89

32:19. 116	139:14. 146	14:31. . . . . 72, 86
32:20 75	141:4. 62	16:4. 61
34:15 75		16:12. 54
	Proverbs	17:6. 112
Psalms	3:6. 44	17:10. 60
4:7. 121	4:5, 27 62	19:7. 42
5:10. 85	4:25. 56	19:14. 111
13:5. 54	5:3. 60	22:2. 112
18:39. 54	7:11 112	22:7. 83
19:14. 60	8:2. 60	22:17. 142
22:9. 98	8:25. 114	23:4. 89
22:15 100	17:4. 101	23:10. 33
26:4. 35	17:10. 59	23:12 127
27:9. 62	17:14. 115	23:16. 93
31:10. 98	22:28 87	24:3 99
32:1. 121	23:1. 83	24:19 . . . . 89, 98
34:14. 64	23:3. 109	25:10. 85
35:14. 95	23:10. 87	26:10. 76
35:25. 118	24:25 45	28:22 37
36:13 72	26:18. 101	28:27 102
37:23. 89	27:8. 98	29:22 75
38:3. 58		30:1. 64
38:9. 84	*Ecclesiastes*	30:25 64
40:13 54	6:8-9. 53	30:30 25
42:10. 40	7:18 39	31:4. 143
45:16. 81	7:19. 94	32:9. 82
48:12 82		32:11. 98
51:10. 82	*Song of Solomon*	34:4. 64
51:12. 125	1:3. 88	35:4. 120
58:9. 53	1:7. 112	35:5. 119
68:10. 112	2:14. 116	37:26. 143
72:17. . . . . 71, 146	3:11. 110	40:3 110
73:9. 53	7:9. 40	40:31 37
74:15. 42		41:2. 97
75:11. 89	*Isaiah*	42:11 75
79:8. 95	1:23. 98	42:22 . . . . 38, 143
91:10. 109	3:16. 92	44:3 51
104:3 53	6:12. 96	44:7. 125
104:35 97	8:6. 92	47:9. 81
107:9. 98	8:9. 98	47:12. 54
109:23 53	9:10. 89	49:24, 25 66
113:2 71	9:16. 101	50:5. . . . . 84, 85
114:5. 97	10:31. 92	51:6. 143
119:71 106	12:6. 98	54:1. 98
132:1. . . . . 7, 111	13:7. . . . . 94, 109	66:11 . . . . 55, 143
139:13 98	14:10. 106	

Jeremiah
2:23 144
4:31 116
5:3 67
6:22 85
7:8 45
7:20 61
8:14 97
9:4 110
9:17 121
17:9 47
19:3 97
20:9 144
20:11 54
21:12 144
21:13 59
22:10 110
23:14 144
23:26, 32 61
25:29 110
26:9 121
28:6 121
31:21 83
31:29 97
35:7 144
40:10 83
42:18 60
46:5 .... 93, 102
46:7 72
48:2 97
49:14 25
50:20 125
50:24 106
50:34 83
51:50 53
51:53 10

Lamentations
1:12 101
1:21 146
2:10 97
4:8 60

5:5 64

Ezekiel
1:12 93
4:1 93
4:7 121
8:17 145
11:17 85
13:11 60
13:18 109
15:3 66
16:4 119
16:6 89
16:55 81
17:23 26
18:4, 20 126
18:9 53
21:12 100
21:18 72
23:49 125
24:3 52
24:8 64
24:23 100
26:2 100
27:33 .... 119, 145
31:3 101
32:18 98
33:6 66
36:4 35
36:9 35
41:7 100
41:24 102
42:19 92
45:18 145

Daniel
1:12 110
10:12 146

Hosea
4:18 110
10:1 98

10:15 110

Joel
4:3 96

Amos
4:1 98

Jonah
4:8 145

Micah
1:7 102
4:14 62
6:14 87

Nahum
1:14 .... 95, 96
2:8 106
2:11 100

Zephaniah
2:2 .... 50, 145
3:7 66

Zechariah
3:5 79
5:7 61
5:11 .... 64, 88
8:14 96
11:17 97
13:4 121
14:12 100

Malachi
1:2 39
3:5 63
3:21 96

New Testament
Romans
11:33 128

Subject Index

/a/ sounds/a-class
    Canaanite shift and, 39
    guttural preferences for, 21, 24–25,
        66–67, 70, 114, 115–17, 127
    in *hiphil*, 55
    preformative vowels as, 29–30, 44, 45,
        46, 76, 81, 85, 101, 127
    qal, 81
    variation of, 59
assimilation, 26–27, 58, 59–64

biconsonantal roots, 5
binyanim, xxix

Canaanite shift, 39–40, 111
cohortative conjugation, xxix, 4
comparative Semitics, methods of, xxiv
compressed form, 77–80
conjugations, terminology for, xxix. See also *specific conjugations*
contractions
    avoiding writing of two identical
        consecutive, 29
    common, 29
    diphthong and triphthong, 27, 75, 103,
        108, 121
    explanation of, 28
    I-ו/י verbs and, 43, 44–46
    hophal, 46, 88
    original shell in, 15
    parsing of, 46
    in perfect conjugation, 103, 105
    III-א verbs and, 126, 127
    III-ה verbs (III-י verbs) and, 103–5, 106
    transliteration of, 27
    unraveling, 46, 55, 57

dagesh forte (doubling *dagesh*)
    assimilating as, 27
    I-guttural verbs and, 32, 33–34
    I-ו/י verbs and, 44
    geminate verbs and, 29, 91, 92–93,
        94–95
    gutturals and, 21, 22–23
    indications of, 5
    niphal, 85
    נתן and, 67, 68
    of *piel* participle, 12
    II-guttural verbs and, 70, 71–72
    II-י/ו (Biconsonantal) verbs and, 76
derived stems chart, 5–7
diphthong contractions, 27, 28
diqduq, xxii
dissimilation, 39, 40–41
dotted circles, 5

epenthetic vowel, 37
exercises for weak verb morphology
    introduction to, 131–33
    overview of, 133–47

final consonant, doubling of, 94
finite verbal forms, 115–16
firm consonant, defined, 59
I-א ōPV, xxxii, 38–41
I-gutturals. See also gutturals
    dagesh forte (doubling *dagesh*) and, 32,
        33–34

155

introduction to, 32
overview of, 24, 41
shewas and, 32, 34–38
silent *shewa* and, 37–38
strong forms of, 32–33
vowel dissimilation of, 35
as weak verb type, 20

I-נ verbs
assimilates of, 58, 59–64
dropping in, 58, 64–65
hiphil, 61–63
hophal, 63–64
introduction to, 58
niphal, 60–61
overview of, 69
qal, 59–60
silent *shewa* in, 58, 61, 64

I-ו/י verbs
contractions and, 43, 44–46
dropping out in, 47–50, 57
general principles of, 43–44
hiphil, 45, 55–56
hophal, 46
introduction to, 42–44
jussives of, 50–51
mixed forms, 56–57
niphal, 44–45
original, 44–56
overview of, 57
parsing and, 46
qal imperfect and, 55
silent *shewa* and, 43, 47, 57
vav-consecutives and, 50–51

F.O.C.U.S. acronym, 31

geminate verbs
collapsed form of, 91, 92–93, 94
dagesh forte and, 29, 91, 92–93, 94–95
defined, xxxii, 29
doubling of, 92–93
general characteristics of, 92–95
gutturals in, 21, 94–95
helping vowels in, 95
hiphil, 101
hithpael, 100–101
hithpoel, 100–101

hophal, 102
introduction to, 91
niphal, 99–100
overview of, 102
piel, 100–101
poal, 100–101
poel, 100–101
pual, 100–101
qal, 96–99
representative paradigm of, 99
specific characteristics of, 95–102
strong forms of, 91
syllabic sufformatives in, 95
thematic vowel shifts in, 94
grammarians, influences to, xxii
gutturals
/a/ sounds and, 21, 24–25, 66–67, 70, 114, 115–17, 127
א quiesces and, 25–26
characteristics of, 21–26, 114
composite *shewas* and, 21, 23–24
dagesh forte (doubling *dagesh*) and, 21, 22–23
at end of word, 25
I, 24 (*See also* I-gutturals)
furtive *patah* and, 25
hatef shewas and, 21, 23–24
II, 24 (*See also* II-gutturals)
segolate patterns with, 118
silent *shewa* and, 25–26
III, 24–25, 26 (*See also* III-gutturals)

half-doubling, defined, 71
hatef patah, 36
hatef segol, 35
hatef shewas, 21, 23–24, 35–36
heavy disjunctive accent, 25
Hebrew language, historical background of, xxi–xxiii, xxvii
helping vowels, 95
hiphil
cohortative 1cs, 55
contractions and, 45
as derived stem, xxix
derived stems chart for, 5–7
doubly weak, 62

Subject Index • 157

I-ו/י verbs and, 55–56
I-נ verbs and, 61–63
as geminate verb, 101
hireq yod and, 9, 115
imperative 2fp, 8, 62, 87
imperative 2fs, 62, 63, 87, 116
imperative 2mp, 62, 87, 110, 116
imperative 2ms, 62, 63, 87, 109, 110, 115–16
imperative 3fp, 8
imperative 3ms, 63
imperfect 1cp, 62, 87
imperfect 1cs, 36, 45, 62, 87, 109, 120
imperfect 2fp, 8, 9, 62, 87, 125
imperfect 2fs, 62, 87, 127
imperfect 2mp, 12, 52, 62, 87
imperfect 2ms, 6–7, 36, 55, 62, 87, 108
imperfect 3cp/3mp, 62, 87
imperfect 3fp, 8, 9, 62, 87, 125
imperfect 3fs, 45, 62, 87, 116
imperfect 3mp, 56, 62, 109
imperfect 3ms, 9, 15, 62, 87, 101, 115, 116, 120
imperfect shell of, 12, 15
infinitive absolute, 55, 62, 101, 110
infinitive construct, 62, 101, 111
jussive 3ms, 73, 109
jussives, 107
participle fp, 62, 87
participle fs, 62, 87, 126
participle mp, 56, 62, 63, 87, 112
participle ms, 62, 87, 117
perfect 1cp, 62, 87, 101
perfect 1cs, 38, 62, 87
perfect 2fp, 62, 87
perfect 2fs, 62, 87, 119
perfect 2mp, 62, 87
perfect 2ms, 42, 62, 87
perfect 3cp, 8, 63, 101
perfect 3cp/3mp, 62, 87
perfect 3fp, 62
perfect 3fs, 8, 55, 62, 87
perfect 3ms, 8, 25, 53, 56, 62, 73, 87, 106, 116
preformative vowel in, 30
representative paradigm of, 62, 87

as II-ו/י (Biconsonantal) verb, 86–87
shewa and, 35, 36
strong verb thematic vowel symbols in, 7, 8–9
thematic vowel in, 87
III-א effect and, 124
tsere, nuances for, 11
vav-consecutives 3ms, 109
hireq
  as preformative vowels, 28, 29–30, 55, 76, 101
  virtual doubling and, 23
hireq yod
  contracting with, 55
  example of, 88, 101
  hiphil and, 9, 87, 115, 116
  retainment of, 42, 104, 124
  silent *shewa* and, 28
  strong verb thematic vowel symbols in, 8, 9, 13
  III-ה verbs (III-י verbs) and, 104, 106, 127
  vocalic sufformative/ending and, xxx
hishtaphel perfect 2ms, 106
hithpael
  as derived stem, xxix
  derived stems chart for, 5–7
  I-guttural verbs and, 32
  as geminate verb, 100–101
  gutturals and, 22
  imperative 2fs, 110
  imperfect 1cs, 44
  imperfect 2mp, 109
  imperfect 3fs, 116
  imperfect 3mp, 71, 72
  imperfect 3ms, 33, 53
  infinitive construct, 111, 121
  jussive 2ms, 109
  nuances for, 11
  participle mp, 71
  participle ms, 117
  perfect 2fs, 106
  perfect 2ms, 121
  perfect 3ms, 71, 115
  as II-ו/י (Biconsonantal) verb, 88–90
  strong verb thematic vowel symbols in, 7

158 • Weak Verb Morphology

III-א effect and, 124
vav-consecutives 3ms, 109
hithpalpel infinitive construct, 101
hithpoel, 100–101
hithpolel, 88–90
holem vav
   example of, 82, 111, 112, 127
   in geminate verbs, 95
   infinitive absolute, 83–84
   for *niphal*, 84, 85
   parsing from, 86
   for performative vowel, 15–16
   as thematic vowel, 99, 100, 125
hophal
   contractions and, 46
   as derived stem, xxix
   derived stems chart for, 5–7
   I-נ verbs and, 63–64
   as geminate verb, 102
   imperfect 1cp, 63
   imperfect 1cs, 63
   imperfect 2fp, 63
   imperfect 2fs, 63
   imperfect 2mp, 63
   imperfect 2ms, 63
   imperfect 3cp/3mp, 63
   imperfect 3fp, 63
   imperfect 3fs, 46, 63, 66, 88
   imperfect 3mp, 88, 93, 102
   imperfect 3ms, 36, 63, 88, 102
   infinitive absolute, 63
   participle fp, 63, 102
   participle fs, 63
   participle mp, 63, 88
   participle ms, 36, 46, 63, 102
   perfect 1cp, 63
   perfect 1cs, 63
   perfect 2fp, 63
   perfect 2fs, 63, 119
   perfect 2mp, 63
   perfect 2ms, 63, 106
   perfect 3cp, 38, 102, 114
   perfect 3cp/3mp, 63
   perfect 3fp, 63
   perfect 3fs, 63
   perfect 3ms, 36, 46, 63, 64, 88

qibbuts and, 63
representative paradigm of, 63
as II-י/ו (Biconsonantal) verbs, 88
shewa and, 36
strong verb thematic vowel symbols in, 7
huphal, 46

i-class
   of II-י/ו (Biconsonantal) verbs, 80, 82, 83, 84
   of preformative vowel, 99
   qal, 80, 81, 82, 83, 84
   thematic vowel as, 75
imperative conjugation. *See also specific cases*
   dagesh forte and, 33
   in derived stem chart, 6
   method for building, 12
   in *qal* paradigms, 4
   strong verb thematic vowel symbols in, 7
   in III-ה verbs (III-י verbs), 105, 109–10
imperfect conjugation. *See also specific cases*
   in derived stem chart, 6
   in *qal* paradigms, 4
   strong verb thematic vowel symbols in, 7
   in III-ה verbs (III-י verbs), 105, 107–9
infinitive absolute conjugation, in III-ה verbs (III-י verbs), 105, 110. *See also specific cases*
infinitive conjugation. *See also specific cases*
   dagesh forte and, 33
   in derived stem chart, 6
   strong verb thematic vowel symbols in, 7, 9
infinitive construct conjugation. *See also specific cases*
   overview of, 49–50
   in III-ה verbs (III-י verbs), 105, 111

J.I.I.V.E. (Jussive; Imperative 2ms; Infinitive absolute; *Vav*-Consecutive all get an E *[tsere]* thematic vowel), 9, 115
jussive conjugation, xxix, 4, 50–51, 79–80

Karaite grammarians, xxi–xxii

linguistic leveling, defined, xxv

long vowels, defined, 43
lower case letters, in Hebrew vowels, 8

mappiq, 101, 114
maqqef, 67
Masoretic Text, xxii, xxv
matres lectionis, 43
mixed morphology, 42–43
mnemonics, xxii–xxiii
monophthongization, 28
morphology, xx, xxiii, xxiv–xxvi, xxvii–xxviii

Neogrammarian Hypothesis, xxiv
Neogrammarian method to biblical Hebrew, xxiv
niphal
   contractions and, 44–45
   dagesh forte and, 33, 85
   as derived stem, xxix
   derived stems chart for, 5–7
   of I-נ verbs, 60–61
   as geminate verb, 99–100
   gutturals and, 22
   imperative, 85–86
   imperative 2fp, 86
   imperative 2fs, 86, 110
   imperative 2mp, 86
   imperative 2ms, 86
   imperfect, 85–86
   imperfect 1cp, 86
   imperfect 1cs, 73, 86, 116
   imperfect 2fp, 86
   imperfect 2fs, 86
   imperfect 2mp, 86
   imperfect 2ms, 86
   imperfect 3fp, 86, 119, 125
   imperfect 3fs, 86
   imperfect 3mp, 36, 86, 99
   imperfect 3ms, 33, 36, 44, 56, 58, 73, 85, 86, 94, 99, 109, 115, 116
   infinitive, 85–86
   infinitive 1cs, 86
   infinitive 3fs, 86
   infinitive 3ms, 86
   infinitive absolute, 110

   infinitive construct, 85, 111, 121
   jussive 3ms, 109
   parsing, 12–13
   participle, 44–45, 85
   participle fp, 35, 61
   participle fs, 11, 61, 85, 112, 126
   participle mp, 35, 45, 61, 85
   participle ms, 36, 61, 85
   participle t-form, 36
   perfect, 44–45, 59, 84, 85
   perfect 1cp, 26, 61, 84, 106
   perfect 1cs, 36, 53, 61, 84, 85, 119
   perfect 2fp, 61, 84
   perfect 2fs, 61, 84
   perfect 2mp, 35, 61, 84, 85, 99
   perfect 2ms, 61, 84, 121
   perfect 3cp, 30, 61, 85, 99, 106
   perfect 3fs, 61, 85
   perfect 3ms, 30, 36, 38, 45, 61, 85
   preformative vowel in, 30, 59
   as II-י/ו (Biconsonantal) verb, 84–86
   shewa and, 35, 36
   silent *shewa* and, 44, 86
   strong verb thematic vowel symbols in, 7
   syllabic sufformatives for, 84
   thematic vowel for, 84
   III-א effect and, 124
   vav-consecutives 3ms, 109
nonfinite verbs, 116–17
nonstative verbs, 7
nun, 26–27

o-class
   to *pataḥ*, 24
   qal, 59, 80, 81, 82, 83, 84
   of II-י/ו (Biconsonantal) verbs, 80, 82, 83, 84
   shifting to, 38
   thematic vowel, 75
   verbs, 64
operative pedagogical principle, 3

palpel, imperfect 3ms, 89
parsing
   conjugations for, 66, 92
   databases, 98, 113

exercises for, 133–47
final forms for, 36, 52, 57, 76, 86
of I-ו/י verbs, 46, 55, 57
F.O.C.U.S. acronym for, 31
function of, 76
of geminate verb, 92–93, 100, 102
helping vowel in, 81
identifying root for, 28
as matching standard verb paradigm, 64
shells for, 5, 15, 91
in strong verb methodology, 12–13
syntactical context for, 73
thematic vowel for, 76, 84
of III-ה verbs (III-י verbs), 105, 106–7
yod and, 54
participle conjugation. *See also specific cases*
Ā in, 10
active, 112
in derived stem chart, 6
dropping in, 27
method for building, 11
passive, 91, 113
qal, 4–5, 77–80
strong verb thematic vowel symbols in, 7, 9–10
t-form, 118
in III-ה verbs (III-י verbs), 105, 111–13
pataḥ
I-guttural verbs and, 35
furtive, 25 (*See also pataḥ*)
gutturals and, 21
ḥatef, 36
in *hiphil*, 87
in *niphal*, 99
in participles, 10
preformative vowel as shifting to, 30, 101
qal and, 81, 125
qamets and, 10, 125
recognizing, 12–13
reconstruction with, 14
II-guttural verbs and, 24, 70
shewa and, 36
t-form participles and, 118
thematic vowel symbols and, 8, 9
III-guttural verbs and, 25, 115–16
tsere as becoming, 115

pausal forms, 25, 40
perfect conjugation. *See also specific cases*
in derived stem chart, 6
dropping in, 27
in *qal* paradigms, 4
strong verb thematic vowel symbols in, 7
in III-ה verbs (III-י verbs), 105–7
person, gender, and number (PGN), xxix, 4–5
phonology, xxiv
piel
as derived stem, xxix
derived stems chart for, 5–7
I-guttural verbs and, 32
as geminate verb, 100–101
gutturals and, 22
imperative 2mp, 110
imperative 2ms, 109, 110
imperfect 1cp, 120
imperfect 2fs, 72, 109
imperfect 2ms, 73, 109, 120
imperfect 3fp, 125
imperfect 3fs, 10–11, 31, 71
imperfect 3mp, 71, 72
imperfect 3ms, 33, 44, 53, 58
infinitive absolute, 110
infinitive construct, 64, 71, 88, 92, 111, 117
jussive 3fs, 109
participle ms, 53, 71, 112, 117
perfect 1cp, 118, 119
perfect 1cs, 71, 106
perfect 2fp, 118, 119
perfect 2mp, 106, 118, 119
perfect 2ms, 101
perfect 3cp, 88
perfect 3ms, 25, 88, 115, 116, 118
as II-י/ו (Biconsonantal) verb, 88–90
strong verb thematic vowel symbols in, 7, 9
III-א effect and, 124
vav-consecutives 3ms, 109
pilpel perfect 1cs, 89
poal, 100–101
poel, 100–101
polal, 88–90

Subject Index • 161

polel, 88–90
polpal, perfect 3cp, 89
prefixes, terminology for, xxxi–xxxii
preformative vowels
    a-class, 47, 76
    contraction and, 47
    example to changes to, 38
    hiphil, 87, 101
    hireq, 76
    holem, 39
    as i-class, 99
    patah/hatef patah pattern in, 36
    qamets hatef, 36
    qibbuts and, 63
    as shifting to A-class vowels, 29–30
    silent *shewa* and, 37
    terminology for, xxx
    tsere, 47
proto-Hebrew, system of, 14
pual
    as derived stem, xxix
    derived stems chart for, 5–7
    I-guttural verbs and, 32
    as geminate verb, 100–101
    gutturals and, 22
    imperfect 3fs, 109
    infinitive construct, 111
    participle mp, 33
    participle ms, 44, 71
    perfect 1cs, 106
    perfect 2ms, 106
    perfect 3fs, 106
    as II-י/ו (Biconsonantal) verb, 88–90
    III-א effect and, 124

qal
    a-class of, 81
    assimilation and, 59–60
    Canaanite shift and, 39–40
    cohortative 1cp, 4
    cohortative 1cs, 4
    defined, xxix
    I-guttural verbs and, 32
    I-נ verbs and, 59–60, 64
    as geminate verb, 96–99
    i-class of, 80, 81, 82, 83, 84

imperative, 48–49, 66, 67, 73, 80–84
imperative 1cs, 125
imperative 2fp, 4, 48, 65, 82, 98, 99, 110, 125
imperative 2fs, 4, 32, 33, 48, 65, 67, 69, 72, 82, 93, 98, 99, 125
imperative 2mp, 4, 32, 33, 48, 53, 65, 67, 69, 82, 93, 98, 99, 125
imperative 2ms, 4, 7, 23, 24, 34, 48, 52, 53, 56, 65, 67, 69, 73–74, 82, 98, 99, 110, 117, 118, 121, 125
imperative as taking *patah* thematic vowel, 125
imperative/infinitive construct by vowel class, 65
imperfect, 30, 38, 47–48, 55, 59–60, 73, 80–84
imperfect 1cp, 4, 35, 54, 60, 66, 81, 97, 99, 109, 117
imperfect 1cs, 4, 35, 39–40, 51, 53, 54, 60, 66, 81, 96, 97, 98, 99
imperfect 2fp, 4, 48, 60, 81, 99, 107, 109, 125
imperfect 2fs, 4, 30, 48, 54, 60, 66, 81, 97, 99, 107, 125
imperfect 2mp, 4, 48, 54, 55, 60, 66, 81, 92, 96, 97, 99, 107, 125
imperfect 2ms, 4, 48, 54, 60, 66, 73, 81, 97, 98, 99, 107, 117
imperfect 3cp/3mp, 99
imperfect 3fp, 4, 26, 60, 81, 93, 95, 96, 97, 99, 107, 109, 121, 125
imperfect 3fs, 4, 28, 50, 53, 55, 60, 62, 66, 81, 94, 97, 99, 125
imperfect 3mp, 4, 29, 37, 60, 62, 66, 72, 75, 81, 93, 97, 107, 125
imperfect 3ms, 4, 15, 30, 35, 37, 38, 42, 47, 50, 53, 54, 55, 56, 58, 60, 62, 66, 73, 75, 81, 94, 96, 97, 98, 99, 107, 117, 123, 125
imperfect as taking *patah* thematic vowel, 125
infinitive absolute, 33, 64, 83–84, 92, 98, 99, 110, 117
infinitive construct, 25, 34, 49–50, 52, 53, 56, 65, 67, 68, 69, 73–74, 80–84, 92, 98, 99, 111, 117, 118, 120

jussives, 79–80, 107
jussive 2fp, 4
jussive 2fs, 4
jussive 2mp, 4
jussive 2ms, 4, 62
jussive 3fp, 4
jussive 3fs, 4, 51
jussive 3mp, 4
jussive 3ms, 4, 51, 97, 109
נתן and, 67–69
o-class of, 59, 80, 81, 82, 83, 84
paradigms, 4–5, 13
participle, 4–5, 77–80
participle fp, 4, 78, 98, 99, 112
participle fs, 4, 78, 79, 92, 98, 99, 112, 126
participle mp, 4, 78, 92, 98, 99, 112
participle ms, 4, 25, 33, 78, 91, 92, 98, 99, 112, 117
participle t-form, 4
passive fp, 4
passive fs, 4
passive mp, 4
passive ms, 4
passive participle fp, 91–92, 112, 113
passive participle fs, 112, 113
passive participle mp, 112, 113
passive participle ms, 25, 92, 112, 113, 117, 121
pausal forms of, 98
perfect, 77–80
perfect 1cp, 4, 26, 69, 78, 93, 95, 96, 99
perfect 1cs, 4, 26, 54, 69, 78, 93, 95, 96, 99, 103, 104, 119, 122
perfect 2fp, 4, 78, 99, 106
perfect 2fs, 4, 69, 78, 99, 119
perfect 2mp, 4, 58, 78, 96, 99, 119
perfect 2ms, 4, 33, 54, 69, 78, 93, 95, 96, 99, 104, 106, 119
perfect 3cp, 13, 15, 53, 78, 92, 93, 96, 104
perfect 3cp/3mp, 99
perfect 3fp, 99
perfect 3fs, 4, 15, 53, 72, 78, 79, 92, 95, 96, 99
perfect 3mp, 4

perfect 3ms, 4, 26, 53, 58, 78, 80, 92, 96, 99, 120, 122
perfect standard verbs of, 124
preformative vowels in, 29–30
as II-guttural verb, 24, 70
II-י/ו (Biconsonantal) verbs and, 76–84
shewa and, 34
silent *shewa* and, 66
standard forms of, 98
stative verbs in, 96, 124
strong verb thematic vowel symbols in, 7, 8
t-forms of, 98
thematic vowels and, 73
III-א effect and, 124
u-class of, 80, 81, 82, 83, 84
vav-consecutives, 79–80, 97, 107
vav-consecutives 3fs, 109
vav-consecutives 3ms, 109
qamets, 10, 14, 30, 81, 125
qamets ḥatuf, 36
qibbuts, 88, 102
quiescent א, 25–26, 122–23, 126

Rabbanite grammarians, xxi–xxii, xxiii
roots/root consonants
    dotted circles for, 5
    terminology for, xxviii–xxix

II-gutturals. *See also* gutturals
    composite *shewa* in, 72–73
    dagesh forte rejection and, 70, 71–72
    introduction to, 70–71
    minor implications of, 73–74
    overview of, 24, 74
II-י/ו (Biconsonantal) verbs
    dagesh forte and, 76
    hiphil, 86–87
    hithpael, 88–90
    hithpolel, 88–90
    hophal, 88
    i-class of, 80, 82, 83, 84
    introduction to, 75–76
    niphal, 84–86
    o-class of, 80, 82, 83, 84
    overview of, 90

Subject Index • 163

parsing of, 76
piel, 88–90
polal, 88–90
polel, 88–90
pual, 88–90
qal, 76–84
strong forms of, 75
u-class of, 80, 82, 83, 84
II-ע verbs, 51–54
segol, 35, 125, 126
segol yod, 95
segolate patterns, 118
sharp syllable, defined, 63
shell, 12–13, 15
shewas. See also silent *shewa*
    composite, xxxi, 34–38, 72–73
    fight, 28, 37, 64
    I-guttural verbs and, 32, 34–38
    I-ו/י verbs and, 43
    gutturals and, 21, 23–24
    ḥatef, 21, 23–24, 35–36
    medial, 120
    II-guttural verbs and, 72–73
    simple vocal, 34
    III-guttural verbs and, 118–20
    vocal, 48, 49, 58
shureq sufformative, 13, 88, 102
shureq thematic vowel, 91
silent *shewa*
    I-guttural verbs and, 34–38
    I-ו/י verbs and, 43, 47, 57
    I-נ verbs and, 58, 61, 64
    gutturals and, 25–26
    niphal and, 44, 86
    nun with, 26–27
    III-guttural verbs and, 118–19
    III-א verbs and, 122–23, 126
Siloam Tunnel inscription, 105
stative verb, 7
stems, terminology for, xxix
Strong Verb Equation, 30–31
strong verb methodology
    approach to, 3
    conclusion to, 15–16
    derived stems chart in, 5–7
    examples of, 11–12

introduction to, 3
meaning of thematic vowel symbols in, 7–10
method for building Hebrew verbs in, 10–11
parsing in, 12–15
qal paradigms in, 4–5
vowel adjustment rules in, 13–15
strong verbs, 3, 19
suffixes, terminology for, xxxi–xxxii
sufformatives, terminology for, xxx
syllabic sufformative/ending, 84, 95, 104, xxxi

tense, aspect, and mood (TAM), xxix
Textbook Plus, 132
t-form participle, 61, 118, 126
thematic vowel. *See also specific cases*
    classes of, 76
    defined, 5
    dissimiliation of, 40–41
    in geminate verbs, 94, 100
    in *hiphil*, 87
    i-class, 75
    for *niphal*, 84
    qal imperfect and imperative and, 73
    shureq, 91
    symbols for, 7–10
III-א verbs
    2/3fp forms as taking *segol* thematic vowel, 125
    introduction to, 121–22
    miscellaneous issues regarding, 124–26
    overview of, 127–28
    silent *shewa* and, 122–23, 126
    t-form participles and, 126
    tsere thematic vowels in perfect conjugation, 123–24
III-gutturals. *See also* gutturals
    a-class vowels and, 115–17
    heavy pronomial suffixes of, 120
    infinitive and participle (nonfinite verbs) and, 116–17
    introduction to, 114
    miscellanous issues regarding, 117–20
    overview of, 24–25, 120
    pataḥ and, 25, 115–16

perfect, imperfect, imperative (finite verbs) and, 115–16
perfect 2fs forms of, 119
in *qal* imperfect and imperative, 117–18
quiescent א in, 26
segolate patterns with, 118
shewas and, 118–20
III-ה verbs (III-י verbs)
   basic endings of, 105
   dropping, 104
   general principles of, 103–4
   imperative conjugation and, 109–10
   imperfect conjugation and, 107–9
   infinitive absolute in, 110
   infinitive construct in, 111
   introduction to, 103
   parsing of, 105, 106–7
   participles in, 111–13
   perfect conjugation and, 105–7
   specific principles of, 105–13
Tiberian Masoretic vocalization, xxv
triconsonantal root, 5, xxiii
triphthong contractions, 27, 28
tsere
   as becoming *pataḥ*, 115
   as expected thematic vowel, 25
   in finite verbal forms, 115–16
   in imperative forms, 49
   lengthening to, 28
   performative vowel, 34
   shift to, 47
   strong verb thematic vowel symbols in, 9
   in t-form participles, 126
   as thematic vowel, 100, 101
   III-א verbs and, 123–24

u-class
   of II-י/ו (Biconsonantal) verbs, 80, 82, 83, 84

qal, 80, 81, 82, 83, 84
upper case letters, in Hebrew vowels, 8

vav-consecutives, xxix, 27–29, 50–51, 79–80
verb morphology, themes of, xix
verbal adjustment rule, 15
verbal forms, terminology for, xxviii–xxxii
verbal irregularities, 19
verbs, xix, 10–11. *See also specific types*
virtual doubling, defined, 23, 70
virtually strengthening, defined, 71
vocalic sufformative/ending, terminology for, xxx–xxxi
voiceless guttural stop, 25
vowel adjustment rules, 13–15
vowel assimilation, 47
vowel contractions, 43
vowel markers, 43
vowels, 95, 122. *See also specific types*

weak verbs. *See also specific types*
   characteristics of, xix
   consistency of, xx, xxii, xxiv
   defined, 22
   exceptional forms of, xx
   general characteristics of, 21–30
   gutturals as, 21–26
   introduction to, xix, 19, 131–33
   as irregular, 19, 20
   methodologies regarding, xxvii–xxviii
   statistics regarding, xix
   Strong Verb Equation and, 30–31
   types of, xxxii, 19–21
   vavs in, 27–29
   yods in, 27–29

yods, 27–29, 54–55, 95. See also *ḥireq yod*

zaqef qaton, 117

Author Index

Anderson, Francis, 91

Betts, T. J., xxvii
Blau, Joshua, xxiv–xxv, 21, 26, 27, 28, 33, 35, 38, 39, 47, 49, 51, 52, 58, 59, 65, 67, 68, 75, 77, 84, 86, 87, 89, 91, 92, 93, 94, 95, 96, 99, 100, 101, 102, 103, 104, 105, 106, 108, 111, 115, 116, 118, 119, 120, 121, 122, 125
Bruck, Ammon, 28

Callaham, Scott, xxx
Choi, Kyoungwon, xxvii, 3, 11, 14, 22, 28, 37, 41, 42, 56, 65, 66, 72, 93, 123, 124, 126
Crawford, Timothy G., xxii

Edzard, Lutz, 108

Faraj, ʾAbū al-Faraj Hārūn ibn, xxii
Fassberg, Steven, xxx, 26, 39, 116
Fuller, Russell T., xxvii, 3, 11, 14, 22, 28, 37, 41, 42, 56, 65, 66, 72, 93, 123, 124, 126

Gaon, Ḥay, xxiii
Gaon, Saʿadya, xxiii
Gesenius, Wilhelm, xxix, 15, 21, 22, 23, 48, 49, 52, 59, 66, 68, 71, 72, 76, 84, 87, 88, 93, 102, 104, 119, 121

Hardy, H. H., II, 79
Harrod, Joe, 131
Ḥayyūj, Yehuda ben David, xxiii
Hornkohl, Aaron, xxv
Huehnergard, John, 39

Janāḥ, Jonah ibn, xxiii
Jerusalmi, Isaac, 72
Joosten, Jan, 79
Josberger, Rebekah L., 14, 22, 30, 42
Joüon-Muraoka, xxix, 21, 22, 34, 42, 49, 51, 63, 68, 71, 85, 91, 103, 111, 119, 123, 126, 127

Kelley, Page H., xxii
Khan, Geoffrey, xxi, xxii, 21
Kutz, Karl V., 14, 22, 30, 42

Labraṭ, Dunash ben, xxiii

Maman, Aharon, xxiii
McAffee, Matthew, 79
Mynatt, Daniel S., xxii

Nūḥ, ʾAbū Yaʿqūb Yūsuf ibn, xxi

Pratico, Gary D., 22, 82, 131

Qimḥi (Radaq), David, xxiii, 39, 40, 44, 53, 64, 65, 67, 76, 77, 84, 87, 88, 96, 101, 103, 105, 108, 111, 112, 121
Quarysh, Yehuda ben, xxiii

Reymond, Eric, xxv, 19, 27, 33, 37, 38, 47, 49, 50, 51, 58, 64, 65, 68, 75, 78, 79, 80, 81, 84, 89, 91, 92, 93, 94, 96, 100, 101, 103, 104, 105, 108, 111, 116, 121, 122
Ross, Allen, 22

Saruq, Menaḥem ben, xxiii

Shivtiel, Avihai, 11
Shulman, Ahouva, xxx
Suchard, Benjamin, xxiv, 38, 45, 46, 49, 58, 68, 75, 78, 84, 93, 95, 99, 104, 105, 108, 121

Van Pelt, Miles V., 22, 82, 131
Vidro, Nadia, xxii

Zewi, Tamar, xxviii

textbook*plus*

Equipping Instructors and Students with
FREE RESOURCES for Core Zondervan Textbooks

Available Resources for **Weak Verb Morphology**

Study Resources

- Extended Exercises
- Extended Exercises Without English Translations
- Answer Key

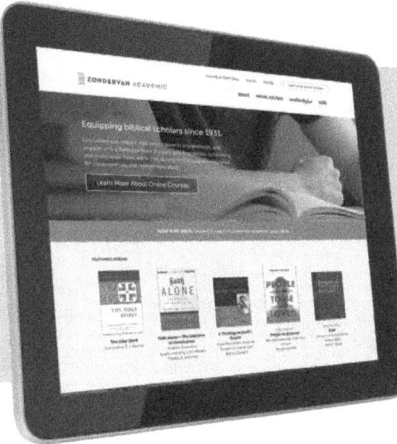

*How To Access Resources

- Go to www.ZondervanAcademic.com
- Click "Sign Up" button and complete registration process
- Find books using search field or browse using discipline categories
- Click "Teaching Resources" or "Study Resources" tab once you get to book page to access resources

www.ZondervanAcademic.com